D1627075

THE COOKBOOK
OF THE
UNITED NATIONS

compiled and edited by Barbara Kraus

REVISED AND UPDATED EDITION

SIMON AND SCHUSTER / NEW YORK

Contents

Recipes in this updated and revised edition of *The Cookbook of the United Nations* come from every one of the 126 countries represented in the organization.

FOREWORD	7	Cuba	58
Afghanistan	9	Cyprus	60
Albania	12	Czechoslovakia	62
Algeria	14	Dahomey	66
Argentina	15	Denmark	67
Australia	17	Dominican Republic	69
Austria	20	Ecuador	73
Barbados	23	El Salvador	73
Belgium	24	Equatorial Guinea	75
Bolivia	29	Ethiopia	76
Botswana	31	Finland	77
Brazil	32	France	79
Bulgaria	33	Gabon	84
Burma	35	Gambia	85
Burundi	37	Ghana	86
Byelorussian Soviet		Greece	88
Socialist Republic	37	Guatemala	91
Cambodia	39	Guinea	93
Cameroon	40	Guyana	94
Canada	41	Haiti	95
Central African		Honduras	98
Republic	43	Hungary	100
Ceylon	44	Iceland	103
Chad	46	India	105
Chile	48	Indonesia	110
China	49	Iran	111
Colombia	52	Iraq	113
Congo (Democratic		Ireland	115
Republic of)	54	Israel	117
Congo, Republic of		Italy	120
the (Brazzaville)	55	Ivory Coast	123
Costa Rica	56	Jamaica	124

Japan	125	Somalia	194
Jordan	128	South Africa	195
Kenya	130	Southern Yemen	197
Kuwait	131	Spain	198
Laos	132	Sudan	201
Lebanon	134	Swaziland	202
Lesotho	136	Sweden	203
Liberia	137	Syria	206
Libya	139	Tanzania (United	
Luxembourg	140	Republic of)	208
Madagascar	143	Thailand	210
Malawi	144	Togo	211
Malaysia	145	Trinidad and	
Maldive Islands	148	Tobago	212
Mali	149	Tunisia	213
Malta	151	Turkey	215
Mauritania	152	Uganda	217
Mauritius	153	Ukrainian Soviet	
Mexico	154	Socialist Republic	218
Mongolia	157	USSR (Union of	
Morocco	158	Soviet Socialist	
Nepal	160	Republics)	221
Netherlands	161	United Arab	
New Zealand	163	Republic	225
Nicaragua	164	United Kingdom of	
Niger	165	Great Britain and	
Nigeria	166	Northern Ireland	228
Norway	169	United States	232
Pakistan	172	Upper Volta	237
Panama	174	Uruguay	238
Paraguay	175	Venezuela	239
Peru	177	Yemen	241
Philippines	180	Yugoslavia	242
Poland	183	Zambia	244
Portugal	185		
Romania	187	Large-scale buffet	
Rwanda	188	menus and recipes	
Saudi Arabia	189	to serve 50 persons	246
Senegal	190		
Sierra Leone	192	ACKNOWLEDGMENTS	263
Singapore	193	INDEX	266

Foreword

Since ancient times, sharing a meal has been a traditional and happy way of sharing friendship. The United Nations is founded on the principles of sharing and of coming together for the purpose of improving human understanding. A very simple way for each of us to participate in this ideal is to prepare and serve the dishes of other countries in our own homes.

Increased communication among the people of the world, ranging from travel to movies to television, has spurred a tremendous interest in international cuisine.

Restaurants all over the world have helped to introduce us to new culinary delights. In New York and Paris and Tokyo—and scores of other large cities—one can dine out on the specialties of a different country night after night. In homes throughout America the interest in foreign dishes and their preparation is growing constantly.

The recipes included in this book have come from all over the world via the people who represent their countries in the UN. All 126 member nations of the UN are represented in this book. The diplomats and their families have a special interest in introducing others to their country's best cooking, for entertaining is a large part of diplomacy.

Since a good many of the following recipes were given to me in the city where the UN is located, the contributor has taken into consideration the availability of the ingredients, and very few recipes require ingredients that are difficult to obtain. The recipes are meant to be fun to cook and are not exorbitant; they provide, as well, an inexpensive way to travel the world and enjoy new taste sensations.

Barbara Kraus

AFGHANISTAN

Afghanistan, admitted to the UN on November 19, 1946, is a land of high mountains and extremely fertile valleys, located in Central Asia, surrounded by the USSR, China, India, Pakistan and Iran. Almost its whole population, mostly Moslem, lives in rural areas. The Afghanistan cuisine includes pelaus (composed of lamb or chicken, spices and rice), luscious melons of many varieties, nuts and grapes, the latter three being heavily exported.

Afghan Pelau

LAMB AND RICE

6 lamb shanks (see Note)	½ cup butter
1 medium onion, diced	1 teaspoon ground cumin
1½ teaspoons salt	1¾ cups long-grain rice

Place lamb, ½ the diced onion and ¾ teaspoon salt in a 3-quart saucepan; cover with water. Cover; simmer until lamb is tender, about 1½ hours. Lift lamb from the broth; fry in hot butter until brown. Remove lamb. Brown remaining half of onion in butter in which lamb was browned. Add onion with butter, cumin, and rice to 3½ to 4 cups of broth in which lamb was cooked; cover and cook until broth has been absorbed, about 20 minutes.

Place lamb in oiled baking pan, about 10" x 14"; cover with rice. Bake for 30 minutes in a preheated 450°F. oven. Serve as main dish for dinner. Yield: 6–8 servings.

Note: A stewing chicken, cut up, may be substituted for the lamb shanks.

Kabuli Pelau

CHICKEN AND RICE

1 4-pound stewing chicken,
  cut up
2 large onions, sliced
2 teaspoons salt
8 cups hot water
1 cup long-grain rice
1 cup thinly sliced onions

2 tablespoons butter
1 teaspoon ground cardamom
  seeds
1 teaspoon ground cumin
3 carrots, sliced and cooked
½ cup seedless raisins

Place chicken, the 2 sliced onions, salt, and hot water in a 3-quart saucepan. Simmer for 2½ to 3 hours; chicken should be tender, yet firm. Remove and cool chicken; save broth. Remove meat from bones; use only large pieces for this dish. Cook rice according to directions on package. When done, keep covered until used.

Sauté the cup of onions in hot butter; when very soft, remove from heat; add cardamom and cumin to onion and mash to form a paste. Add 2½ cups of the reserved chicken broth; simmer for 5 minutes; taste for seasonings.

Combine cooked rice, broth-onion sauce and chicken; put in buttered 2-quart casserole. Place carrots on top of mixture and sprinkle raisins on top of carrots. Cover. Cook in a preheated 325°F. oven for 35 to 45 minutes. Add more broth or water if dish is dry. When done, mix carrots and raisins lightly with chicken and rice. Broth not used in main dish can be served as soup course. Yield: 6–8 servings.

Ashaks

LEEK RAVIOLI

Ashaks:
3 cups flour
1½ teaspoons salt
1 cup water

Filling:
20 tender leek stalks
2 tablespoons melted butter
½ teaspoon salt
⅛ teaspoon black pepper

Rapidly boiling water

Sour Cream Mixture:
1 pint sour cream

½ clove crushed garlic
(or to taste)
½ teaspoon salt

Meat Sauce:
2 cups chopped onions
½ cup melted butter
1 pound ground beef
1 teaspoon salt
½ teaspoon black pepper
2 tablespoons tomato sauce
1 cup water
2 tablespoons chopped mint

Combine flour and salt in a mixing bowl; add ½ cup water and mix with a fork. Add remaining water, 2 tablespoons at a time until the dough is of right consistency to roll. Turn out on floured board and knead lightly. Cover and allow to stand for 15 minutes. Divide dough into quarters. Roll out each quarter very thin; cut into circles with a 3-inch cookie cutter.

To make filling: Clean leeks and remove any discolored leaves. Chop entire leek very fine. Add melted butter, salt and pepper.

Put 2 teaspoons of leek filling on lower half of each circle. Moisten edges of top half with water and place on lower; seal edges with tines of a fork. Place on a lightly floured plate, at least 1 inch apart to prevent their sticking together. Drop filled circles (*ashaks*) into a large pot, ¾ filled with rapidly boiling water. Boil for 5 minutes from time the water returns to boiling. Remove *ashaks* from water with slotted spoon.

To make sour cream mixture: Combine sour cream, garlic and salt. Place *ashaks* on a platter over which a thin layer of sour cream mixture has been spread; cover *ashaks* with remaining sour cream mixture.

To make meat sauce: Cook onions in butter until lightly browned; add remaining ingredients except the water and mint. Cook over low heat until meat loses its pinkish color. Add water and cook slowly until water evaporates. Spoon meat sauce over the top of the *ashaks* and sprinkle with chopped mint. Yield: 6–8 servings.

ALBANIA

The people of Albania called their country "Eagle's Land," most appropriately, as more than two thirds of the country is mountainous. Agriculture employs most of the manpower. Fruits, wines and tobacco are raised for export, and there is large home consumption of chicken, lamb and yogurt. The history of Albania includes domination by Romans and Ottomans, resulting in a population primarily Moslem, with a large Christian minority. Their Mediterranean cuisine is heavily in debt to the Turks and the Italians. Albania joined the UN on December 14, 1955.

Pule Me Harr

CHICKEN WITH WALNUT SAUCE

1 3½–5-pound stewing chicken
1 teaspoon salt
½ teaspoon black pepper
3 cups water

1 pound (2 cups) shelled walnuts
4 tablespoons butter
2 tablespoons flour
½–1 clove garlic, minced

Season chicken with salt and pepper. Place in large baking dish; add water; cover and cook in a preheated 325°F. oven for 2 hours or until chicken is tender. When chicken is done, remove and cut into serving pieces. Save broth.

Crush walnuts in a blender or with a rolling pin. Melt butter in a 12-inch skillet over low heat; stir in flour, continuing to stir until flour is brown. Add the crushed walnuts, garlic and chicken broth gradually to the browned mixture. Blend the ingredients. Add chicken to the sauce, coating each piece with the sauce. Continue cooking over low heat until sauce is thick. Remove from heat; cover and let stand 5 to 10 minutes before serving. Yield: 6 servings.

Pule Me Drop

SWEET STUFFING FOR CHICKEN

2 cups soft bread crumbs	½ cup chopped mixed nuts
½ cup butter	¼ cup sugar
¼ cup currants	1 tablespoon chicken broth
¼ cup raisins	

Brown bread crumbs in butter. Add rest of ingredients and mix well, tossing lightly. Stuff neck and body cavity of prepared roasting chicken. Yield: enough stuffing for a 3–4-pound chicken.

Kos Me Krastabec

YOGURT AND CUCUMBER SALAD

2 medium cucumbers	2 tablespoons salad oil
½ teaspoon salt	1 pint yogurt
¼ teaspoon white pepper	Paprika
1 or 2 cloves garlic, minced	

Peel cucumbers; cut into ½-inch cubes; sprinkle with salt, pepper and garlic. Stir oil and yogurt into cucumber mixture. Cover; refrigerate until very cold. Serve in individual salad bowls; garnish with a dash of paprika. Yield: 6 servings.

E Matur

PASTRY WITH ALMONDS

1 cup butter, melted	2 cups sifted flour
1 cup water	Blanched almonds
1 cup sugar	

Combine butter, water and sugar; bring to boil. Boil for 2 minutes. Add flour all at once; beat over low heat until mixture leaves sides of pan and forms compact ball. Cook 1 minute longer, stirring constantly. Spread the mixture in a greased 8-inch square pan. Cut into diamonds with a sharp knife. Place a blanched almond in the center of each diamond. Bake in a preheated 400°F. oven for 15 minutes; reduce heat to 300°F. and bake 20 minutes longer or until done. The product is a cross between pastry and cake. Yield: 6 servings.

Note: The Albanian recipe uses no additional flavoring, but a few drops of almond extract may be added before spreading mixture in baking pan.

ALGERIA

Algeria became independent of France in 1962 and joined the UN shortly thereafter, on October 8. Although the country has an area of almost a million square miles, most of the Algerians live and earn their livelihoods in a narrow northern zone among the massive Atlas Mountains. Mint is a popular flavoring throughout the Arab world, and it is particularly tasty when combined with meat in the hors d'oeuvre recipe that follows.

Kefta

MEATBALLS

2 slices dry bread
½ cup milk
1 pound ground beef or lamb
½ cup finely chopped onion
½ teaspoon dried dill weed
½ cup chopped fresh parsley
  or ¼ cup dried parsley

½ teaspoon dried mint leaves
1 egg, slightly beaten
¾ teaspoon salt
¼ teaspoon black pepper
Oil or fat for deep-fat frying

Soak bread in milk until soft; squeeze out excess milk. To the bread, add all ingredients listed except fat for frying. Mix ingredients very thoroughly; if too thick to shape easily, add milk in which the bread was soaked. Form mixture into 1-inch balls. Fry a few at a time in deep fat at 370°F. until balls are golden brown. Remove from fat, drain and serve. Yield: 18–24 appetizers.

Note: For recipe to serve 50, see LARGE-SCALE BUFFET MENUS section, page 251.

Chakchouka

MIXED VEGETABLES WITH EGGS

4 large onions, sliced	1 small hot pepper, chopped
3 tablespoons oil	1 tablespoon vinegar
4 large tomatoes, peeled and sliced	1½ teaspoons salt
	6 eggs
3 large sweet green peppers, chopped	1 green pepper, grilled, skinned, and cut in thin strips

Sauté onions in oil in a 10-inch frying pan until golden brown; add all of the ingredients except the eggs and pepper strips. Simmer until the vegetables are reduced to a pulp—about 45 minutes.

Make 6 indentations in the vegetables and carefully break an egg into each one. Cover the frying pan and cook over low heat until eggs are well set, about 10 minutes. Or beat eggs with 6 tablespoons of milk, pour over the vegetables, cover, and cook until set. Garnish each serving with the strips of green pepper. Yield: 6 servings.

ARGENTINA

Argentina is as long as the United States is wide. It is the second-largest country in Latin America in area, and second also in population. The ancestry of nine out of ten Argentinians is European, most often Spanish or Italian. The Argentinian cuisine reflects this as well as the fact that the country is the world's largest producer of corn and wheat. Livestock raising is on a par with farming, and meat is served at almost every meal and between meals—as a steak, or thinly sliced, stuffed and rolled up, or chopped and encased in a corn dough. Argentina's membership in the UN commenced on October 24, 1945.

Niños Envueltos

MEAT ROLLS

2 pounds sirloin or top round steak, cut ½ inch thick

Marinade:
¾ cup white wine or cider vinegar
2 tablespoons chopped green pepper
1 teaspoon salt
1 teaspoon dry mustard
1 teaspoon sugar
½ clove garlic, minced

Stuffing:
6 slices stale bread, cubed
¾ cup milk
2 eggs, beaten slightly
1 tablespoon chopped parsley
½ teaspoon salt
½ teaspoon black pepper

1 tablespoon butter, melted
3 tablespoons fat

Sauce:
1 clove garlic, minced
1 medium onion, finely chopped
3 tablespoons olive oil
1 1-pound can tomatoes
1 tablespoon chopped parsley
3 tablespoons chopped green pepper
½ teaspoon salt
½ teaspoon black pepper
½ cup white wine

3 medium potatoes, cut in quarters
1 10-ounce package frozen peas

Pound steak with mallet until meat is thin. Cut in 6 equal strips.

To make marinade: Combine all marinade ingredients, simmer for 10 minutes and cool. Pour cooled marinade over meat and let stand 2 to 3 hours. Remove meat from marinade.

To make stuffing: Soak bread cubes in milk until soft. Squeeze out excess milk. Combine bread with remaining stuffing ingredients and mix well.

Place an equal portion of stuffing on each of the 6 strips. Roll tightly and secure with string. Brown rolls lightly in fat and place side by side in shallow casserole or baking dish with a cover.

To make sauce: Cook garlic and onion in oil until yellow. Add other sauce ingredients and simmer for 20 minutes.

Pour sauce over meat rolls, cover, and bake in a preheated 325°F. oven. Add potatoes after the meat has cooked for 1 hour; add peas 15 minutes later, and continue cooking for 15 minutes. Yield: 6 servings.

Humita Mendocina

CORN SUPREME

1 clove garlic, minced
1 large onion, finely chopped
2 tablespoons olive oil
1 small green pepper, chopped
1 teaspoon salt
1 bay leaf
¼ teaspoon black pepper
¼ teaspoon ground cinnamon
1½ teaspoons paprika
1 ripe tomato, chopped

12 ears of fresh corn, grated, or
   4 cups frozen or vacuum-
   packed whole kernel corn
½ cup milk

Optional:
1 large pumpkin
2 cups milk
2 tablespoons butter
1 tablespoon sugar
Bread crumbs
Butter

Cook garlic and onion in oil in saucepan until tender. Add green pepper and cook 2 more minutes. Add salt, bay leaf, black pepper, cinnamon and paprika and mix well. Cook 1 minute. Add tomato and simmer 10 minutes. Add corn and milk. Cook very slowly, stirring frequently, for 15 minutes or until the corn is tender. Serve hot or cold.

To prepare Corn Supreme served in a pumpkin: Wash pumpkin and cut off top; remove seeds and membranes. Pour milk, butter and sugar into pumpkin and bake in preheated 300°F. oven for 1½ hours or until pumpkin meat is tender. Pour off milk and fill with Corn Supreme. Sprinkle open top with bread crumbs and dot with butter. Bake in a preheated 325°F. oven 30 minutes, until top is golden brown. Serve Corn Supreme along with a scooped-out portion of pumpkin meat. Yield: 8 servings.

AUSTRALIA

Australia is in itself a continent with so many different climates that many dishes eaten in the north would be quite unlike those eaten in Tasmania, an island off the southern mainland. Basically, however, Australian cook-ing is like the country cooking of England, a heritage handed on from the first settlers. The nearness of the sea and the abundant grazing acreage encourage the preparation of delicious fish and meat dishes which are eaten to the accompaniment of the excellent wines of the country. Australia joined the UN on November 1, 1945.

Bread and Cheese Soup

4 medium onions, sliced
2 cups thickly sliced celery
  with leaves
1 teaspoon black peppercorns
1 bay leaf
6 tablespoons butter
6 cups boiling water

1 teaspoon salt
6 thin slices of bread
½ pound Cheddar cheese,
  grated
¾ cup dry white wine,
  preferably Australian

Add onions, celery, peppercorns and bay leaf to 5 tablespoons of the butter, melted, in a 2½- to 3-quart saucepan. Stir mixture. Simmer for 5 minutes, stirring once or twice. Add boiling salted water; cover saucepan and simmer for 1 hour. Cool for 1 hour. Strain liquid from vegetables. With remaining butter, grease a 2- to 2½-quart casserole or ovenware dish. Cover bottom with slices of bread and sprinkle with a generous layer of cheese. Repeat until dish is about ¾ full. Pour cooled vegetable broth over layers of bread and cheese; cover and cook in a preheated 375°F. oven for 1 hour. Serve from casserole, adding 1 to 2 tablespoons of dry white wine to each serving. Yield: 6 servings.

Baked Fillets of Whiting

Oil
½ cup grated cheese
1½ pounds fillet of whiting or
  similar fish
½ teaspoon salt
¼ teaspoon black pepper

4 tablespoons chopped
  shallots or green onions
½ pound fresh mushrooms or
  1 4½-ounce can, drained
6 tablespoons white wine
1½ teaspoons lemon juice
1 tablespoon chopped parsley

Oil shallow baking dish; sprinkle with grated cheese. Place fish fillets on cheese; add salt, pepper and shallots or onions. Top with mushrooms. Pour wine over fillets. Bake in a preheated 450°F.

oven for 15 minutes. Sprinkle with lemon juice and parsley before serving. Yield: 6 servings.

Veal and Ham Pie

1 pound veal, raw or cooked, sliced thin
¼ pound ham or Canadian bacon, sliced thin
¼ teaspoon black pepper
1 teaspoon salt
2 tablespoons chopped parsley

2–3 medium potatoes, peeled and sliced
¾ cup stock
2 tablespoons butter
Pastry dough for a single-crust pie

Cover the bottom of a 2-quart casserole with ⅓ of the meat. Sprinkle ⅓ of the pepper, salt, and parsley over meat. Add ⅓ of the sliced potatoes. Continue layers until all is used, with sliced potatoes on top. Add stock. Dot with pieces of butter. Cover casserole with pastry dough and bake in a preheated 350°F. oven for 1½ hours. Serve hot. Yield: 5–6 servings.

Pocket Steak

3 pounds round or sirloin beef, 1½ inches thick
2 dozen small oysters, drained
2 tablespoons bread crumbs
1½ tablespoons butter
⅛ teaspoon black pepper
¼ teaspoon salt
2 tablespoons chopped onion

1 tablespoon lemon juice
3 tablespoons flour mixed with ½ teaspoon salt and ¼ teaspoon black pepper
¼ cup fat
1 cup oyster liquor
1 cup bouillon

Make a pocket in the beef by slicing horizontally almost through the meat. Combine oysters, crumbs, butter, the ⅛ teaspoon pepper and ¼ teaspoon salt, onion, and lemon juice. Stuff mixture into the beef pocket, distributing it evenly. Secure pocket with metal skewers or close by sewing with a large needle and coarse thread.

Rub the surface of the meat with the flour mixture; brown the meat on both sides in hot fat in a heavy frying pan. Remove the meat. Add the oyster liquor and bouillon to the frying pan; bring to a boil. Return meat to the frying pan; reduce the heat and simmer, covered, for 1 hour or until meat is tender. Place meat on serving platter and remove skewers or thread. Strain remaining pan liquid over meat and serve hot. Yield: 6 servings.

Lamingstons

CHOCOLATE FROSTED SQUARES

⅔ cup butter	¼ teaspoon baking soda
1 cup sugar	⅛ teaspoon salt
1 teaspoon vanilla extract	½ cup milk
2 eggs	Chocolate Frosting (below)
2 cups sifted flour	1 cup or 7-ounce package
¾ teaspoon cream of tartar	grated coconut

Cream butter, sugar and vanilla. Add one egg at a time and beat well. Combine dry ingredients and sift; add to the creamed mixture alternately with the milk. Turn mixture into an oiled 10" x 10" cake pan lined with oiled wax paper. Bake in a preheated 350°F. oven 35 to 40 minutes. Cool for 10 minutes; turn out on cake rack. When cold, cut in 2-inch squares and cover with chocolate frosting, then roll in grated coconut. Yield: 25 squares.

Chocolate Frosting

1 pound confectioners' sugar	6–8 tablespoons boiling water
3 tablespoons cocoa	

Combine sugar, cocoa and boiling water and beat until smooth. (For a frosting with more body and additional flavor, beat 2 tablespoons of soft butter into the frosting.) Yield: enough frosting to cover 25 2" cake squares.

AUSTRIA

Bordered by Germany, Italy, and Hungary, Austria was once the center of the Holy Roman Empire. Its cuisine has been influenced by all these countries, and Vienna has remained one of the cultural and intellectual capitals

*of the world. German-speaking and 90 percent Roman
Catholic, Austrians have great vitality and gaiety. These
qualities are reflected in their love of rich food, occa-
sions to eat it occurring almost every three hours.
Austria has been a member of the UN since December
14, 1955.*

Gefüllter Kalbsbraten

VEAL ROLLS

7 veal cube steaks or veal scaloppine	2 anchovies
	½ teaspoon salt
1 medium onion	¼ teaspoon black pepper
2 slices lean bacon, half cooked	6 hard-cooked eggs
2 tablespoons capers	3 tablespoons butter

Grind together one of the veal steaks, onion, bacon, capers and
anchovies; mix well. Sprinkle salt and pepper over the remaining
steaks; spread the ground mixture on steaks. Roll each steak
around 1 hard-cooked egg, and secure roll with string. Pan-fry
in butter until brown and well done, about 20 minutes. Serve hot
as rolls or serve cold cut in slices. Yield: 6 servings.

Kaiserschmarren

THE EMPEROR'S OMELET

4 eggs	½ cup flour
5 tablespoons sugar	½ teaspoon baking powder
½ cup milk	¼ cup raisins, optional
½ teaspoon salt	3 tablespoons butter, melted

Beat eggs, 4 tablespoons of the sugar, the milk and the salt together. Add flour, baking powder and raisins, if used. Cover bottom and sides of an 8″ x 8″ baking pan with the butter. Pour egg
mixture into pan; bake 10 to 12 minutes in a preheated 400°F.
oven. To serve, break omelet into irregular pieces and sprinkle
with remaining sugar. Serve for breakfast or as a dessert. Yield:
6 servings.

Linzer Torte

RASPBERRY TART

1½ cups flour	½ cup butter
½ cup sugar	1 egg
½ teaspoon baking powder	½ cup unblanched almonds,
½ teaspoon salt	chopped
½ teaspoon cinnamon	2 cups raspberry jam
½ cup sugar	

Sift flour, sugar, baking powder, salt and cinnamon together. Add sugar and cut in butter. Add egg and almonds. Blend with a pastry blender or fork. Reserve ½ cup of dough for topping and chill. Press remaining dough evenly into bottom and sides of an 8-inch pie pan. Do not cover rim of pie pan.

Fill pastry-lined pie pan with raspberry jam. Roll out chilled dough on floured pastry cloth to ⅛-inch thickness. Cut into ½-inch strips with a pastry wheel. Arrange over filling in a crisscross pattern. Cover the ends of the lattice with another strip, circling the pie, but not covering rim of pan. Press to seal. Bake in a preheated 375°F. oven 30 to 35 minutes. Yield: 6 servings.

Tyrolese Soup

SPLIT PEA SOUP

½ cup split peas	¼ cup diced celery
4 cups water	1 large potato, diced
1 teaspoon salt	1 large onion, sliced
2 tablespoons butter or bacon	1 tablespoon chopped parsley
fat	1 tablespoon flour

Cook peas, water and salt until peas are soft; sieve peas and return to water. In separate pan, melt fat; add celery, potato, onion, and parsley; cook until vegetables are tender. Stir flour into fat and vegetable mixture. Combine the 2 mixtures; simmer for 15 minutes. Yield: 6 servings.

BARBADOS

Barbados, the most eastern of the West Indies, is a tightly populated, proud little island. It has magnificent beaches which lure tourists. Much of the fertile acreage is rich in sugar cane; as a result, molasses and rum are the chief exports. After three hundred years of British control, Barbados became independent in 1966 and a member of the UN the same year, on December 9.

Peas and Rice

1 coconut
4 cups water
2 cups rice
1 10-ounce package frozen
  peas

1 or 2 slices salt pork, cubed
Salt
Black pepper
1 large tomato, sliced

Remove shell from coconut. Grate coconut or whirl in blender with 1 cup water. Combine in a saucepan with total of 4 cups water, bring to quick boil, allow to stand for 40 minutes, then strain through cheesecloth to extract liquid. (If desired, 4 ounces packaged coconut can be substituted for the fresh.) Cook rice according to package directions, using the coconut liquid instead of the water and adding more water if necessary. After 12 minutes, add peas.

Sauté cubed salt pork; add pork and its fat to the rice and peas and cook till these are done, about 8 minutes. Salt and pepper to taste. Garnish with sliced raw tomato. Yield: 8 servings.

West Indian Banana Pudding

4 bananas, peeled
2 eggs
½ cup sugar
6 slices of bread, made into
    soft bread crumbs
½ teaspoon vanilla extract
1 cup milk
4 tablespoons melted butter

1 tablespoon chopped candied
    peel
Pinch of cinnamon
Juice of 2 limes

Rum Sauce:
1 cup sugar
1 cup water
½ cup dark rum

Mash the bananas. Beat the eggs into the mashed bananas. Add the remaining ingredients and beat until you have a mixture the consistency of a soufflé. Pour the mixture into a baking dish and bake in a preheated 350°F. oven for 1 hour.

To make rum sauce: Dissolve sugar in hot water; add rum. Serve pudding from the baking dish with rum sauce. Yield: 8 servings.

BELGIUM

Belgium is primarily an industrial nation with agriculture playing a secondary role. It is a land divided linguistically, and to some extent culturally, between the Flemish in the north (about 55 percent of the population speak Flemish) and the French-speaking Walloons in the south. The excellence of Belgium's national dishes is well recognized, as is her contribution of the luscious endive to international tables. On December 27, 1945, the UN admitted Belgium to membership.

Pâté à la Flamande

FLEMISH LIVER PÂTÉ

⅓ pound sliced bacon, cut in
    1-inch pieces
¾ pound pork liver
1 bay leaf
½ teaspoon dried thyme
2 tablespoons chopped onion

½ clove garlic, minced
1½ teaspoons brandy
¼ teaspoon salt
⅛ teaspoon black pepper
2 slices fat pork, ¼ inch thick

Place bacon, liver, bay leaf, thyme, onion and garlic in heavy skillet and cook over low heat for 1 hour. Do not drain. Remove bay leaf. Grind this mixture twice through the finest blade of food chopper or blend to a smooth paste in electric blender. Mixture should be free of lumps; strain it if necessary. Add brandy, salt and pepper to paste. Put paste in a small oblong porcelain or ovenware pâté casserole. Cover top of pâté with sliced fat pork; cover casserole with foil and casserole top. Place casserole in pan of water and bake in a preheated 450°F. oven for about 50 minutes. Cool and store in refrigerator. Serve as appetizer with crisp crackers or toast rounds. Yield: about ¾ pound.

Soufflé de Poisson

FISH SOUFFLÉ

¾ cup mushrooms, diced	⅛ teaspoon celery salt
2 tablespoons butter	⅛ teaspoon onion salt
¼ cup butter	¼ teaspoon paprika
¼ cup flour	¼ teaspoon monosodium
1 cup milk	glutamate, optional
3 egg yolks, slightly beaten	½ pound fillet of haddock (or
1 teaspoon salt	similar fish), cooked, flaked
Dash of nutmeg	and diced
Dash of Cayenne pepper	5 egg whites
⅛ teaspoon powdered mace	

Sauté mushrooms in the 2 tablespoons of butter over moderate heat for 5 minutes. Melt the ¼ cup of butter in a saucepan; blend in flour; add milk slowly. Cook, stirring constantly until thickened and smooth. Stir a small portion of the cream sauce into the beaten egg yolks; return to cream sauce. Add seasonings, mushrooms and fish; remove from heat to cool slightly.

Beat egg whites stiff but not dry. Fold into fish mixture. Turn into a greased 2-quart casserole. Set in a pan containing 1 inch of cold water and bake in a preheated 350°F. oven until firm and brown, about 1 hour. Serve immediately. Yield: 6 servings.

Jambon et Endive au Gratin

HAM AND ENDIVE WITH CHEESE

12 stalks endive	1 cup milk
½ teaspoon salt	¼ pound Swiss cheese, grated
1 cup water	1 egg, beaten
12 small slices cooked ham	⅛ teaspoon nutmeg
4 tablespoons flour	¼ teaspoon salt
6 tablespoons butter, melted	Few grains of black pepper
Light cream	1 cup bread crumbs

Simmer endive in salted water for 10 minutes. Drain; save liquid. Roll each endive stalk in slice of ham; place in a flat baking dish with folded edge of ham underneath.

Combine flour and 3 tablespoons of the melted butter in frying pan. Add sufficient cream to endive liquid to make 1 cup; add this and the milk to flour-and-butter mixture; stir and cook over low heat. Put aside ⅓ cup of cheese. Add remaining cheese, egg, nutmeg, salt and pepper to mixture. Stir until cheese is melted.

Pour sauce over ham-and-endive rolls. Combine bread crumbs and remaining melted butter and cheese; sprinkle over sauce. Bake in a preheated 400°F. oven for 30 minutes. Yield: 6 servings.

Vlaams Rundvlees en Bier Casserole

FLEMISH BEEF AND BEER CASSEROLE

2½ pounds beef—boned neck, top shoulder or thin flank	12 ounces beer
¼ pound smoked ham hock, cut in ½-inch cubes	½ teaspoon black pepper
	2 teaspoons sugar
½ cup lard or vegetable fat	½ teaspoon mixed herbs (marjoram, thyme and rosemary)
2 teaspoons salt	
1 pound onions, sliced thin	1 clove garlic, minced
2 tablespoons flour	2 tablespoons vinegar

Cut the beef into strips about 2 inches long, 1 inch thick and 1 inch wide. Brown beef and ham hock in hot fat in large skillet. Remove meat from fat and sprinkle with 1 teaspoon of salt; reserve. Brown onions in same fat; remove from fat and place in a separate dish. Drain off remaining fat except for 2 tablespoons.

Stir flour into the fat in the pan and make a light-brown roux. Gradually add the beer and stir continuously until the mixture boils. Add the remaining teaspoon of salt, pepper, sugar, herbs and garlic to the sauce.

Arrange alternate layers of meat and onions in a 2-quart casserole; cover with the sauce. Cover the casserole. Cook in a preheated 300°F. oven for 2½ hours. If it begins to dry out, more beer may be added. Just before serving, add the vinegar. Serve from the casserole with plain boiled potatoes. Yield: 8–10 servings.

Filets de Sole Ostendaise

SOLE WITH SEAFOOD AND MUSHROOM SAUCE

1 4½-ounce can mushrooms
1 tablespoon minced onion
2 tablespoons butter
1 tablespoon minced parsley
1 teaspoon salt
12 oysters, shucked
1 teaspoon lemon juice
1 cup fresh clams with juice or
   1 6-ounce can whole clams
Water
12 small sole fillets

Sauce:
4 tablespoons flour
3 tablespoons melted butter
Liquid from fillets
3 egg yolks
1 cup cream
¼ cup sherry

Parsley
12 shrimp, cooked and
   deveined

Reserve mushroom juice. Simmer mushrooms and onion in butter; add parsley and salt. Cook oysters in their juice with lemon juice. Heat clams in their juice. Place fillets in frying pan or skillet. Combine clam, oyster, and mushroom juices; add water to make 2 cups and pour over fillets. Simmer for 12 minutes. Remove fillets to serving dish; place clams, oysters, and mushrooms around fillets. Keep warm while making sauce.

To make sauce: Combine flour and melted butter and cook until brown; add fillet liquid. Cook over low heat, stirring constantly until thick. Combine egg yolks and cream; add to first mixture and heat but do not boil; add sherry.

Pour sauce over fillets. Garnish with parsley and shrimp. Yield: 6 servings.

Gâteau Wallon

APPLE PIE

¼ cup soft butter
¼ cup sugar
½ teaspoon salt
1 cup flour
1 egg, well beaten
2 cups thick applesauce, sweetened

1 cup confectioners' sugar
Grated rind of 1 lemon
¼ teaspoon lemon juice
1 egg white
¼ cup chopped almonds

Cream butter, sugar, and salt; add flour and blend well. Add egg and mix. Refrigerate for 2 to 3 hours. Divide dough in half; roll ⅛ inch thick and to fit a 6" x 8" baking pan or dish. Line pan with dough; add a layer of applesauce about ¾ inch thick. Cover with other half of dough, also rolled thin.

Combine confectioners' sugar, lemon rind and juice, and enough of the egg white to make a thick paste. Spread over crust and sprinkle with almonds. Bake in a preheated 400°F. oven for 30 minutes. Yield: 6 servings.

Tarte Liégeoise

BAKED RICE DESSERT

1 cup rice
3 cups milk
½ teaspoon salt
¼ to ½ cup sugar, optional

12 coconut macaroons
⅔ cup rum
1 uncooked piecrust
Confectioners' sugar, optional

Cook the rice, milk and salt in a double boiler until rice is tender and practically all the milk is absorbed. Add the sugar, if used. Soak the macaroons in the rum until the rum is absorbed. Spread the soaked macaroons over the piecrust. Spread the cooked rice over the macaroons. Bake in a preheated 300°F. oven for 25 to 30 minutes until golden, and sprinkle with confectioners' sugar, if desired. Yield: 8 servings.

BOLIVIA

Bolivia is one of two countries in South America without a seacoast. The principal cities are located on plateaus, although much of the country consists of low plains. La Paz, at 12,000 feet, is the highest capital in the world. Over half the population is Indian, descended from the Incas, whose advanced civilization centered in the Andean region. The remainder is European or mestizo (of mixed Indian and European heritage). The Bolivians use more hot pepper in their cooking than do most Latin Americans. On November 14, 1945, Bolivia became a member of the UN.

Empanadas de Carne

INDIVIDUAL MEAT PIES

Dough:
4 tablespoons vegetable
    shortening
1½ cups flour
1 tablespoon oil
2 eggs, beaten
2½ tablespoons water

Filling:
1 small onion, chopped
½ clove garlic, minced
½ cup green pepper, diced
½ cup red pepper, diced

3 tablespoons fat
½ pound chopped beef
¼ cup raisins
½ cup beef stock
½ teaspoon salt
Few grains black pepper
½ teaspoon chili powder
2 tablespoons flour
2 tablespoons water

2–3 cups oil for deep-fat
    frying

Blend the fat and flour in mixing bowl; add the oil and half the beaten eggs. Mix well and gradually add water until dough has a smooth consistency. Cover the dough and refrigerate for an hour. Roll on floured board to approximately $\frac{1}{16}$ inch in thickness. Cut into 4-inch circles.

To make filling: Sauté the onion, garlic, green and red peppers in the hot fat; add the meat and brown lightly, stirring constantly.

Stir in the raisins and stock. Simmer until the mixture is done, about 20 minutes. Add salt, pepper and chili powder. Make a paste of the flour and water; add half to meat mixture, stirring constantly. Add additional paste, if needed to make thick mixture. Cool the mixture.

Place 1 heaping tablespoon of meat mixture in the center of each circle; fold the dough to form a half circle. Press the edges together firmly. Brush each circle with remainder of beaten eggs. Fry in deep fat at 375°F. until brown. Serve as appetizers. Yield: 12 *empanadas*.

Lla-Uchitas

CHEESE TIDBITS

Dough:
½ envelope dry yeast
½ cup warm water
2 tablespoons butter or shortening
½ tablespoon salt
1 teaspoon sugar
1½ cups flour

Filling:
12 ounces creamed cottage cheese
1 teaspoon salt
4 tablespoons flour
¼ teaspoon Cayenne pepper or 2 teaspoons paprika
1 egg white, slightly beaten

Dissolve yeast in water and add butter or shortening, salt and sugar. Work in flour. Knead until dough springs to touch and will not stick to board. Divide dough into balls 1 inch in diameter. Flatten them with a rolling pin so that they form circles 4 inches in diameter.

To make filling: Combine cheese, salt, flour and Cayenne or paprika and mix until creamy. Put a teaspoonful of filling on half of each circle of dough. Fold over and press edges together very firmly. Brush all over with egg white to seal. Put the *lla-uchitas* on a greased cookie tin. When they begin to rise, coat them with more of the egg white. Allow them to rise until light to touch (about 45 minutes to 1 hour in a warm room); brush top again with egg white. Place in a preheated 450°F. oven and bake until brown, about 8 minutes. Yield: 16 *lla-uchitas*.

Note: Other seasoning, such as chopped chives, may be used for flavor. A sharp cheese might also be used for filling.

Escabeche de Pollo

PICKLED CHICKEN

1 3½-pound chicken, cut up
2 large onions, quartered
3 carrots, cut in sticks
½ green pepper, sliced
½ cup oil
1 cup wine vinegar
¼ cup water
Salt
Black pepper
1 bay leaf
Few grains of allspice

Simmer all ingredients in a covered pot until chicken is tender, about 1 hour. Chill. Serve cold. This is a good main course for a buffet or picnic. Yield: 4–6 servings.

BOTSWANA

Botswana, the former British protectorate of Bechuana-land, became independent in 1966, and a UN member on October 17 of that year. A large country, it has a dry region receiving less than 9 inches of rain a year, and a fertile eastern area, where 80 percent of the people live in villages. Almost all speak Bantu, and most of the people are engaged in the raising of livestock.

Boshebo

CASHEW NUT SAUCE

3 tablespoons flour
½ tablespoon butter, melted
½–1 cup unsalted cashew nuts, finely chopped
1 cup beef stock or bouillon
Pinch of sugar
Salt
Black pepper

Brown flour in melted butter; add nuts. Gradually add beef stock; add sugar. Boil for 5 minutes. Skim. Season with salt and pepper. Serve with fish, rice or yams. Yield: 6 servings.

BRAZIL

Brazil, which is larger than the continental United States, covers half the area and contains half the population of South America. The capital, Brasilia, is located in the central west of the country. Designed to link the heavily populated coast with the underdeveloped interior, it is a model of modern architectural and urban planning. The cuisine of Brazil is quite different from the rest of South America, reflecting its three main stocks: Indian, Portuguese, and African Negro. As is appropriate to the country's large sugar and coffee production, Brazilians serve and drink a great deal of coffee. Brazil was admitted to the UN on October 24, 1945.

Chocolate Gelado

ICED CHOCOLATE

2 squares unsweetened
  chocolate
4 tablespoons sugar
1 cup strong, hot coffee

4 cups milk
Ice cream, optional
Sweetened whipped cream,
  optional

Cut up or shred chocolate and melt in double boiler. Add sugar. Pour in hot coffee gradually, stirring all the while. Scald milk and combine it with chocolate-coffee mixture. Cook for 10 minutes or until it is smooth. Remove from stove. Chill thoroughly. If desired, before serving add a scoop of ice cream or ice cubes and top with whipped cream. Yield: 6–8 servings.

Creme de Abacate

AVOCADO WHIP

1 avocado
Juice of 1 lime

2 tablespoons sugar
½ pint vanilla ice cream

Remove peel and pit from avocado. Press through a sieve. Add lime juice and sugar. Combine avocado mixture and ice cream and beat with rotary beater until smooth. Place in freezing tray and chill but do not freeze. Yield: 3–4 servings.

Torta de Banana

BANANA TART

4 large bananas, peeled	½ teaspoon nutmeg
½ cup sugar	1 8-inch baked pie shell or
⅛ teaspoon salt	4–6 individual pastry shells
1 tablespoon butter	Whipped cream
¼ cup white wine or juice of 1 lime	

Press bananas through sieve. Put pulp into saucepan with sugar, salt, and butter. Stir and cook until mixture starts to boil. Remove from fire and cool. (If firmer mixture is desired, 1 teaspoon softened plain gelatin may be added at this point.) When cool, whip in the wine or lime juice and nutmeg. Pour into baked pie shell or individual shells. Top with whipped cream. Yield: 4–6 servings.

BULGARIA

Bulgaria is a popular tourist attraction with its rapidly increasing beach resorts on the Black Sea, its extraordinary ancient mosques and Byzantine churches, and its very warm, hospitable people. It is the largest producer of attar of roses, which is used as a base for perfumes. Bulgaria entered the UN December 14, 1955.

Soupa sus Topchetas

MEATBALL SOUP

3 chicken bouillon cubes	¼ teaspoon black pepper
3 beef bouillon cubes	1 teaspoon chopped parsley
6 cups boiling water	or ½ teaspoon dried
3 tablespoons rice	1 small onion, chopped
1 pound ground lean beef	¼ cup yogurt
4 eggs	Chopped parsley for garnish
1 teaspoon salt	

Add bouillon cubes to boiling water. When dissolved add rice; cover and simmer until rice is tender, about 14 minutes. Strain rice from bouillon. Combine rice, ground beef, 2 eggs, salt, pepper, parsley and onion. Make into small balls about the size of a walnut and drop into boiling bouillon—add water, if necessary, to make 4 cups. Simmer gently for 15 minutes.

Beat 2 eggs; combine slowly with small amount of soup until 2 cups of soup have been added. Stir egg-and-soup mixture into remaining soup; add yogurt. Serve meatballs in soup; garnish with chopped parsley. Yield: 6 servings.

Musaka

BAKED HASH WITH YOGURT TOPPING

1 onion, diced	1 6-ounce can tomato sauce
2 tablespoons fat	2 pounds potatoes, peeled
2 pounds ground lean beef	and diced
1¼ teaspoons salt	1 cup hot water
¼ teaspoon black pepper	1½ cups yogurt
Few grains of Cayenne pepper	3 eggs, beaten
1 tablespoon chopped parsley	2 tablespoons flour

Sauté onion in hot fat until brown; add the meat, 1 teaspoon of salt, the 2 peppers, parsley and tomato sauce. Simmer for about 15 minutes, stirring occasionally. Add potatoes and hot water to meat mixture; simmer for 10 minutes. Turn mixture into baking pan, about 10″ x 14″. Bake for 30 minutes, or until browned, in a preheated 375°F. oven.

Combine yogurt, eggs, flour and remaining salt. Spread evenly over browned meat. Return to oven to brown for about 10 minutes. Yield: 6–8 servings.

Kebat

PRIEST STEW

2 pounds boneless beef, cut in 1-inch cubes	1 bay leaf
	1 cup red wine
2 tablespoons fat	Hot water
2 onions, diced	2 tomatoes, diced
1 tablespoon flour	1 pound small white onions, peeled
1 tablespoon paprika	
1 teaspoon salt	1 clove garlic
¼ teaspoon black pepper	Chopped parsley

Brown beef in fat in large frying pan; add onions and cook until yellow. Combine flour and paprika and add to meat. Stir in well and cook for 2 minutes. Add salt, pepper, bay leaf and wine to meat mixture. Cover and simmer gently for 1 hour or until meat is tender. Add hot water as needed. Add tomatoes, onions and garlic. Cover; cook over low heat until onions are done. Remove bay leaf and garlic. Garnish with parsley. Yield: 6 servings.

BURMA

Burma is a gloriously exotic land, rich in natural resources, including teak forests and deposits of silver, gold, jade, amber and rubies. The Burmese people adorn themselves in vivid fabrics. The majority are devout Buddhists, and the golden pagodas of that religion dot the landscape. As in India, curries are very popular, especially when combined with shrimp in some form or other. The UN voted Burma into membership on April 19, 1948 and, after the tragic death of Dag Hammarskjöld, elected Burma's distinguished statesman U Thant the third UN Secretary General.

Kyet-U-Hin

EGG CURRY

3 cups minced onions
3 cloves garlic, minced
½ teaspoon ground ginger
4 tablespoons oil
1 teaspoon salt
½ teaspoon turmeric
1 teaspoon paprika

1 cup tomato purée
1 cup water
1 tablespoon shrimp sauce or
   fish soy sauce (see Note
   below)
6 hard-cooked eggs, cut in
   halves lengthwise

Cook onions, garlic and ginger in oil over low heat until onions are soft but not browned. Stir in salt, turmeric and paprika. Gradually add tomato purée mixed with water; bring to boiling point and add shrimp sauce and egg halves. Cook over low heat until sauce and oil appear to separate and egg whites are tinged with color of sauce. Serve over hot rice. Yield: 6 servings.

Note: Shrimp sauce (which has the consistency of a paste) and fish soy sauce are available at Asiatic import shops. Both are of strong flavor.

Pa-Zun Hin

SHRIMP CURRY

12 medium shrimp, shelled
   and deveined
1 tablespoon shrimp sauce or
   fish soy sauce (see above
   Note)
½ teaspoon turmeric
1 teaspoon paprika

3 cups minced onions
3 cloves garlic, minced
½ teaspoon ground ginger
4 tablespoons oil
1 cup tomato purée
1 cup water

Combine shrimp, shrimp sauce, turmeric and paprika and marinate for 1 hour. Cook minced onions, garlic and ginger in oil for about 2 minutes. Add shrimp mixture to onion mixture; stir occasionally to cook shrimp evenly. When shrimp are almost done, about 3 minutes, add tomato purée mixed with water. Cook over low heat until sauce and oil appear to separate. Serve over hot rice. Yield: 6 servings.

BURUNDI

Burundi, formerly part of the Belgian colony of Ruanda-Urundi, is a small, densely populated highland country in Central Africa. Two tribal groups, the Hutu and the Tusi (or Watusi), are dominant, with the former mostly engaged in farming and the Tusi traditionally herdsmen. Despite being only 15 percent of the population, the statuesque Watusi long dominated the Hutu. Coffee is the main export. On September 18, 1962, Burundi joined the UN.

Ibiharage

FRIED BEANS

2 cups dry white beans	1 clove garlic, minced
Boiling water	2 teaspoons salt
½ cup cooking oil	Dried hot red pepper to taste
3 large onions, sliced	

Wash beans and remove any foreign matter. Put beans in large saucepan and cover with 4–6 cups boiling water. Boil 2 minutes; remove from heat and let soak 1 hour or more. Return to stove and simmer until tender, about 1½ hours. Heat oil to smoking point in a 12-inch saucepan; add onions and garlic to hot oil and cook until onions are transparent and soft. Drain cooked beans and add to onions; cook for 5 minutes. Add salt and hot pepper. Mix well. Yield: 8–10 servings.

BYELORUSSIAN SOVIET SOCIALIST REPUBLIC

Byelorussian Soviet Socialist Republic, a constituent state within the USSR, was admitted to the UN on October 24, 1945. Byelorussia's capital is Minsk, located on a branch of the Berezina River, about 47 miles southwest of Moscow and 150 miles east of the Polish

*border. Trucks, tractors and radios are produced there.
Food, as in all parts of the Soviet Union, is often cooked
or served with sour cream, a favorite dating from the
days before refrigerators.*

Machanka

PORK AND SAUSAGE WITH SOUR CREAM

1 pound boneless pork
   shoulder, cut in ½-inch
   cubes
¾ pound bulk pork sausage
1 tablespoon fat
1 large onion, diced

2 cups water
4 tablespoons minced parsley
1 tablespoon flour mixed with
   ¼ cup cold water
¾ cup sour cream

Brown pork and sausage in fat in frying pan. Add onion and cook
for 3 minutes, stirring constantly. Add water and stir to combine
ingredients and to loosen any meat sticking to bottom of pan.
Add parsley. Add flour paste to meat, stirring constantly until
well mixed. Cover. Simmer for 15 minutes, stirring occasionally.
Add more water if necessary to prevent mixture from sticking
to pan. When done, add sour cream; heat but do not boil. Serve
with potato pancakes or noodles. Yield: 6 servings.

Rebra Kuritsy

CHICKEN BREAST FILLETS

3 chicken breasts with wings
   attached
1 teaspoon salt
½ teaspoon black pepper

Stuffing:
½ pound chicken livers
½ cup finely chopped onion
1½ tablespoons butter, melted
Salt
Black pepper

2–3 tablespoons sour cream
2 eggs
4 tablespoons water
·1½–2 cups finely rolled dry
   bread crumbs
½ cup butter, melted
2 cups water
2 tablespoons flour mixed
   with 2 tablespoons cold
   water

To prepare breasts for stuffing: Split down center, remove breast-
bone and cut breasts into halves. Remove tips of wings. Make

a 2- to 3-inch slit in each fillet above the rib bones on the under-wing side of breast. Sprinkle with salt and pepper.

To make stuffing: Cook liver and onion in the 1½ tablespoons butter over low heat 10–15 minutes. When done, chop or mash liver and onion until fine and blended. Place in small bowl; add salt and pepper to taste and sour cream to give consistency similar to chicken stuffing.

Place equal portions of stuffing in slit of each fillet. Stuff in well and secure slit if necessary with toothpick or small skewer. Beat eggs slightly in shallow dish and stir in water. Put bread crumbs in a second shallow dish. Dip fillets first in egg mixture, then into crumbs. Dip each fillet again in both egg mixture and bread crumbs, coating well each time.

Cook fillets in ½ cup butter in large frying pan until brown, about 5 minutes on each side. When brown, add water. Cover; simmer gently for 30 minutes or until meat is tender. Add more water, if needed. Remove chicken to serving platter and thicken remaining liquid with paste of flour and water, using only enough to thicken sauce. Blend and simmer 3 minutes. Serve sauce over chicken or separately. Yield: 6 servings.

CAMBODIA

Cambodia's history reaches back to the first century A.D., *when the kingdom of Funan was established. It was overthrown in the sixth century and succeeded by an empire centered on a plain at Angkor. The magnificent ruins of the palaces, monuments and the temple of Angkor Wat have only recently been rediscovered and are in the process of being restored. Cambodia's membership in the UN commenced on December 14, 1955.*

Cary au Jus deCoco

CHICKEN IN SPICY COCONUT SAUCE

4 small onions, peeled and cut into eighths

1 teaspoon finely chopped garlic

1 tablespoon butter

2 tablespoons curry powder

1 tablespoon chili powder

2 teaspoons salt

3 cups Coconut Milk (see Note, also page 23)

2 2-pound fryers, quartered

4 large potatoes, peeled and cubed

½ cup shelled, skinned and chopped roasted peanuts

Cook onions and garlic in butter until onions are soft and yellow. Stir in curry and chili powders, add salt and mix well. Add 2 cups of the coconut milk, the chicken and potatoes. Cover tightly and simmer 20 to 30 minutes or until chicken is tender. Add remaining cup of coconut milk and peanuts. Simmer for 10 minutes and serve. Yield: 6 servings.

Note: To make coconut milk, combine 4 ounces packaged coconut with 1 quart milk; let stand in refrigerator overnight. Drain off milk, squeezing or mashing coconut against strainer to get full flavor. Discard coconut.

CAMEROON

The Republic of Cameroon is truly a child of the UN (admitted on September 20, 1960) having been formed by the federation of two former UN trust territories, one French-administered, the other under British control. The official language is French, although Bantu-speaking people inhabit parts of the south, where forests are home for the celebrated Pygmies. Coffee and cacao are important exports.

Nfiang Koss

FISH STEW WITH RICE

2 slices onion

⅓ cup oil

3 tablespoons tomato paste

2½ pounds fish fillets, such as swordfish or halibut, cut in large pieces

1 quart water

2 teaspoons salt

2 carrots, sliced

½ pound cabbage, shredded

2 small sweet potatoes, cut in 1-inch cubes

½ 10-ounce package frozen, sliced okra

3 cups cooked rice

Cook onion in hot oil in a 4-quart saucepan until yellow but not brown; add tomato paste and fish. Cover; cook over low heat ½ hour. Add water, salt and vegetables to fish mixture; cook gently for about ½ hour.

Place a serving of rice in the center of each soup bowl or plate; ladle stew over rice, serving some of the fish, vegetables and broth in each portion. Yield: 6 servings.

CANADA

Canada is a land of two distinct cultures, English and French. The English heritage is most prevalent, but Scots, Italians, Ukrainians, Americans and native Indians have all contributed to what can be called Canadian cuisine. The tourtière *recipe that follows is one version of a famous regional dish, served particularly at the French-Canadian celebration called "Le Reveillon" which is held after midnight mass on Christmas Eve. Canada became a member of the UN on November 9, 1945.*

Tourtière de la Gaspesie

THREE MEATS PIE

1 3½-pound stewing chicken,
  cut up
6 cups water
½ pound ground fresh pork
½ pound ground beef
¼ cup chopped onion

2 cloves garlic, minced
2 teaspoons salt
½ teaspoon black pepper
Dough for 2 9-inch piecrusts
¼ cup flour

Simmer chicken pieces in 4 cups water 2–3 hours or until tender. Remove chicken; save broth.

Simmer pork, beef, onion, and half the garlic in 1½ cups water 15–20 minutes. Drain, set aside, and save broth.

Remove chicken from bone; grind and combine with pork and beef mixture, salt, pepper and remaining garlic, and ¼ cup of the chicken broth. Place in an uncooked-pastry-lined 9-inch pie plate; spread evenly; cover with top crust; make slits in crust. Bake 40–45 minutes, or until crust is golden brown, in a preheated 400°F. oven.

To make accompanying sauce: Combine flour and remaining ½ cup water. Combine chicken and meat broths. Add flour mixture to 2½ cups of the combined chicken and meat broth and simmer 5 minutes. Yield: 8 servings.

Butter Tarts

Pastry:
2 cups flour
1 teaspoon salt
¾ cup vegetable shortening
5 tablespoons ice water

Tart Filling:
2 eggs, slightly beaten
2 cups brown sugar
2 tablespoons vinegar

1 tablespoon vanilla
½ cup melted butter
1⅓ cups currants, mixed, if
  desired, with any
  combination of raisins,
  chopped dates, figs, or nuts

½ cup heavy cream, whipped
  with sugar

To make pastry: Sift flour and salt; blend fat into flour until mixture particles are the size of small peas. Add water; mix with a fork. Knead dough slightly to form smooth ball. Roll dough out and cut to fit tart pans, 3 to 4 inches in size.

To make tart filling: Combine eggs, sugar, vinegar and vanilla; stir in butter, fruits and nuts (various combinations may be used).

Fill tart shells ½ to ⅔ full. Bake for 10 minutes in a preheated 450°F. oven; reduce heat to 325°F. and cook for 20 to 25 minutes. Top each tart with whipped cream. Yield: 6–8 tarts.

Blueberry Crisp Pudding

4 cups fresh blueberries	⅓ cup brown sugar, firmly
⅓ cup sugar	packed
2 teaspoons lemon juice	⅓ cup sifted flour
4 tablespoons butter	¾ cup quick-cooking oats
	Plain or whipped cream

Place blueberries in a 1½-quart baking dish. Sprinkle with sugar and lemon juice. Cream butter; gradually add brown sugar. Blend in flour and oats with fork. Spread topping over blueberries. Bake in a preheated 375°F. oven 35 to 40 minutes. Serve with plain or whipped cream. Yield: 6 servings.

CENTRAL AFRICAN REPUBLIC

The Central African Republic is sparsely populated, mostly by farmers. Only recently has the exploration of diamond mines begun. The country lies on a plateau, some 21,000 feet above sea level, which produces an ideal climate, with temperatures ranging from 70° to 80°F. Formerly a member of the Federation of French Equatorial Africa, the Republic became fully independent in 1960 and joined the UN on September 20 of that year.

Epinards à l'Africaine

AFRICAN SPINACH

2 onions, chopped
2 tablespoons oil
2 tomatoes, thinly sliced
1 green pepper, seeded and chopped

2 10-ounce packages chopped frozen spinach, thawed
1 teaspoon salt
⅛ teaspoon black pepper
½ cup peanut butter

Sauté onions in oil until tender; add tomatoes and green pepper and cook for 1 minute. Add spinach, salt, and pepper; cover and simmer for 5 minutes. Add peanut butter to spinach mixture; combine well and cook for 10 minutes over low heat. Stir occasionally to prevent sticking. Serve hot. Yield: 6 servings.

CEYLON

Ceylon has been called "the Isle of Spices," and Ceylonese recipes use many of the island's native spices, such as coriander, cinnamon, chili, turmeric and ginger. In addition to spices, tea, rubber and coconut are important crops. Over a period of four centuries the island was governed by the Portuguese, the Dutch and the British, but in 1948 Ceylon achieved independent status in the British Commonwealth of Nations. It was elected to the UN on December 14, 1955.

Mulligatawny Soup

4-pound stewing chicken, cut up
2 teaspoons salt
6 cups cold water
½ teaspoon coriander seeds
1 teaspoon cumin seeds
½ teaspoon powdered ginger
1 bay leaf
1 stick cinnamon

10 peppercorns
1 clove garlic, minced
1 cup canned tomatoes
1 medium onion, chopped
2 teaspoons fat
2 tablespoons lemon juice
1 cup light cream or Coconut Milk (pages 23 and 40)

Stew chicken in salted water in large covered saucepan. After 30 minutes, add seasonings, tomatoes and half of the onion. Continue cooking over low heat until chicken is tender, 2 to 3 hours. Add water, if necessary. Remove chicken and strain stock. Brown remaining half of onion in fat. Add chicken cut into bite-size pieces, skin and bones removed, browned onion, lemon juice and cream to strained stock. Reheat, but do not boil mixture. Yield: 4–6 servings.

Mus Curriya

VEAL CURRY

2-pound piece boneless veal shoulder (or lamb, or pork shoulder, or beef chuck)	⅛ teaspoon turmeric
	2 slices green ginger, chopped, or ½ teaspoon ground ginger
1 medium onion, thinly sliced	
3 cloves garlic, minced	2-inch piece cinnamon stick
2 teaspoons salt	¼ cup vinegar
2 teaspoons chili powder	2 cups water
2 teaspoons ground coriander	1 cup milk
1 teaspoon ground cumin	¼ cup oil

Place meat in large saucepan or Dutch oven. Add onion, garlic, salt, chili powder, coriander, cumin, turmeric, ginger, cinnamon, vinegar and water. Stir to blend spices. Cover. Simmer 1 hour. Uncover. Simmer ½ hour or until meat is tender. Add milk and simmer 15 minutes. Remove meat. Pour sauce into a bowl and keep hot.

Pour oil into heavy saucepan and fry meat until lightly browned. Serve sauce with sliced meat. Yield: 6–8 servings.

Aba Curriya

DEVILED FISH

1 large onion, chopped	2 teaspoons sugar
1 tablespoon oil	1 cup light cream or Coconut
1 tablespoon dry mustard	Milk (pages 23 and 40)
2 teaspoons chili powder	2 tablespoons vinegar
1 bay leaf	1 pound fish fillets or canned
1 teaspoon salt	salmon or tuna fish
1 tablespoon Worcestershire sauce	

Cook onion in oil until yellow. Add seasonings and sugar and mix well. Add cream or coconut milk and stir until sauce is smooth. Stir in vinegar slowly and keep on very low heat.

If fresh fish is used, boil for 5 minutes in salted water and drain; if frozen fillets are used, follow directions on package; if canned fish is used, drain off oil. Add fish in large pieces to sauce and heat. Yield: 4–6 servings.

Note: For recipe to serve 50, see LARGE-SCALE BUFFET MENUS section, page 259.

Vata Cappan

COCONUT CUSTARD

3 eggs	1½ cups milk
2 tablespoons sugar	1 teaspoon vanilla extract
¼ teaspoon salt	1 cup grated coconut

Beat the eggs slightly. Add the sugar, salt, milk and vanilla. Stir to dissolve sugar. Add coconut and stir. Pour mixture in oiled casserole and bake in a preheated 350°F. oven about 35–40 minutes or until knife blade inserted in center of the custard comes out clean. Serve hot or cold. Yield: 4 servings.

CHAD

Chad was for many centuries an important crossroads in Africa. From about 200 B.C. to A.D. 1000, the inhabitants maintained close ties with the Nile valley, with which they shared a fairly similar culture. Christianity flourished in central Chad about A.D. *300, but later nomads of Sudan overran the areas. Today the people of Chad are Christian, Islamic, or traditional religionists. They grow cotton, millet and peanuts, and export mostly to their former rulers, the French. December 14, 1955 marked the entrance of Chad into the UN.*

Viande à la Sauce Okra

MEAT WITH OKRA SAUCE

2 pounds cubed beef or lamb
2 tablespoons fat
1 medium onion, chopped
1 teaspoon salt
1 6-ounce can tomato paste
Water
8 fresh okra pods or ½ of 10-ounce package frozen whole okra

Brown meat in fat. Add onion and cook until yellow. Add salt and tomato paste diluted with an equal amount of water. Cover; simmer about 1½ hours or until meat is tender, adding water as needed. Add okra 30 minutes before end of cooking period. Serve with boiled rice. Yield: 6 servings.

Salade de Patates Douces

SWEET POTATO SALAD

4 large sweet potatoes
½ medium onion, chopped
3 tablespoons lemon juice
½ cup peanut oil
1 teaspoon salt
½ teaspoon pepper
2–3 medium tomatoes, sliced

Boil sweet potatoes in their skins until tender. Peel and slice. Add onion, sprinkle with lemon juice; add oil, salt and pepper. Chill for several hours. Garnish with tomatoes. Yield: 10 servings.

CHILE

Chile is only 100 miles wide, but the distance from its northern to its southern tip is 2,650 miles, more than that from New York to Los Angeles. The cuisine is varied and rich, aided by the long seacoast yielding seafood unlike anything ever tasted outside that area. Grapevines were brought into Chile by missionaries in the sixteenth century, and from those beginnings over 30,000 vineyards have developed, well regulated by the government to encourage the high quality of Chile's white and red wines. Chile joined the UN on October 24, 1945.

Gallina en Escabeche

CHICKEN MOLD

¼ cup olive oil
3 pounds chicken breasts, boned, skinned, and quartered (reserve bones)
2 medium onions, sliced, rings separated
3 large carrots, sliced
3 tablespoons chopped pimiento
12 black peppercorns
1 teaspoon salt
1 cup dry white wine

Dressing:
½ cup liquid from cooked chicken
½ cup olive oil
¼ cup vinegar
1 teaspoon tomato juice
¼ teaspoon salt
Few grains of Cayenne pepper

Fresh greens
Black olives

Pour the oil in a heavy saucepan or Dutch oven which has a tightly fitting lid. Arrange a layer of breast quarters symmetrically in the oil, using ⅓ of the chicken. Place a layer of ⅓ of the onion rings, carrot slices, pimiento, peppercorns and salt over the chicken. Repeat, making second and third set of layers. Place the chicken bones over the top layer; add the wine. Cover the pot tightly and simmer gently for 3 hours. When done, remove the bones; cool the chicken in the uncovered pot. When cool, remove ½ cup liquid to use for salad dressing. Replace cover and refrigerate chicken overnight.

To make dressing: Combine all ingredients and keep in refrigerator.

Unmold chicken and serve with the dressing. Garnish with greens and olives. Yield: 6 servings.

Porotos Exquisitos

DELICIOUS PEAS

3 cups boiling water

1½ teaspoons salt

½ pound dried whole green peas

¼ cup butter

4 tablespoons flour

2 tablespoons chopped sweet chili pepper

1½ cups milk

Pour water with 1 teaspoon of the salt over the peas in a large heavy saucepan; boil 2 minutes, remove from heat and soak 2 hours. Boil slowly 1 hour or more until tender. Add water if necessary.

Melt butter in a large frying pan. Add flour, remaining salt and chili pepper, stirring constantly. Add the milk and stir steadily over direct heat until the sauce boils. Add peas to sauce and continue cooking until mixture is the consistency of a thick white sauce. It could be served in small patty shells. Yield: 6 servings.

CHINA

The cuisine of China is among the most varied in the world. There are five important schools of Chinese cooking. Of those, the dishes of Peking, Shanghai, and Yang Chow are the most elegant, those of Szechuan the most highly spiced, and those of Canton the most familiar to the Western world. The Cantonese are great travelers and have taken their way of cooking everywhere. The Republic of China became a member of the UN on October 24, 1945. It retained its UN membership after its seat of government was moved to Taiwan in 1949, when the Communists won control of the mainland.

Chi Tang

CHICKEN SOUP

1 4–5-pound stewing chicken, halved
1 teaspoon salt
6 cups water
1 large onion, finely chopped
¾ cup finely cubed pork, cooked
2 pounds shrimp, cooked and deveined
2 cups fresh mushrooms, sautéed in 2 tablespoons butter

¼ pound transparent Chinese noodles (cellophane noodles)
1 teaspoon soy sauce
½ pound scallions, finely cut
2 cloves garlic, minced
2 tablespoons oil
½ teaspoon powdered coriander

Simmer chicken in salted water with onion until chicken is tender, 2 to 3 hours. Remove chicken from broth; skin and bone chicken; cool and cut into long thin slivers. Return chicken to broth; add pork, shrimp and mushrooms; boil for 5 minutes; add noodles and soy sauce and simmer for 5 minutes more. Sauté scallions and garlic in oil with coriander for 5 minutes; add to soup. Serve hot. Yield: 8 servings.

Note: Transparent Chinese noodles are found in Chinese food shops, where they are known as *sai fun.*

Chêng Yü Ju Szŭ

STEAMED FISH

2 pounds fillet of sole, or whole flounder or sea bass
2 teaspoons sugar
1 teaspoon salt
3 tablespoons soy sauce
2 teaspoons sherry
6 dried Chinese mushrooms, soaked in cold water for 30 minutes and sliced thinly

1 piece fresh ginger, about 1½ inches, sliced thinly
6 scallions or green onions, cut in ½-inch pieces
4 slices bacon, cut in 1-inch pieces
1 cup water

Rub cleaned fish with sugar and salt; add soy sauce and sherry; let fish marinate for 5 minutes. Reserve marinade.

Place fish on heatproof serving platter which will fit on a rack in a covered roasting pan, Dutch oven or similar ovenware having a tight-fitting lid. Cover fish with mushrooms, ginger, scallions or onions, and bacon; add reserved marinade. Place platter on rack in the pan for steaming; add water to pan holding platter. Cover; steam for 35 minutes. Serve as main dish with rice. Yield: 4 servings.

Shih Chen Chao Fan

10-INGREDIENT RICE DISH

8 tablespoons vegetable oil

2 pounds loin of pork, cut into 1-inch strips, ¼ inch thick

2 green onions, chopped

1 tablespoon soy sauce

2 teaspoons salt

½ teaspoon black pepper

¼ teaspoon monosodium glutamate, optional

2 10-ounce packages frozen mixed vegetables, thawed and drained

8 eggs, beaten

1 pound rice, cooked

Heat half the oil to sizzling in large skillet. Add meat and brown slightly. Add green onions, soy sauce, salt, pepper, monosodium glutamate, if used, and vegetables. Cook on medium heat for 5 minutes.

In another frying pan, heat the remaining oil. When it sizzles, add eggs and stir until cooked. When eggs are done, add to meat mixture, to which cooked rice has been added. Cook 2 or 3 minutes until all is thoroughly heated. Yield: 8 servings.

Ma Ti Chi K'uai

CHICKEN WITH WATER CHESTNUTS

1 3-pound fryer

1 teaspoon salt

Water

6–8 dried Chinese mushrooms

Cold water

2 ½-inch slices fresh ginger

4 tablespoons vegetable oil

⅓ cup soy sauce

1 tablespoon sugar

1 tablespoon sherry

2 5-ounce cans water chestnuts, drained

2 cups chicken broth

Simmer chicken in salted water to cover until tender but firm (about 20 minutes). Remove chicken from broth and cool, reserving broth; remove from bones and cut into 2-inch pieces. Soak mushrooms in cold water for ½ hour. Fry ginger in hot oil in heavy 12-inch frying pan; add chicken and thinly sliced mushrooms; sauté for 5 minutes. Add soy sauce, sugar, sherry, water chestnuts and broth. Simmer about 15 minutes uncovered; remove ginger slices before serving. Yield: 6–8 servings.

Yang Ts'ung Niu Ju

BEEF AND ONIONS

1½ pounds flank, boneless round, or sirloin steak

Marinade:
¼ cup cornstarch
1 teaspoon sugar
3 tablespoons soy sauce or Chinese oyster sauce

2 teaspoons sherry

5 tablespoons vegetable oil
2 large onions, sliced
½ cup chicken broth or bouillon

Slice beef across the grain into thin strips, about ½ inch wide and 3 inches long.

Combine marinade ingredients and blend well. Place beef strips in marinade; turn gently until all pieces are coated. Let marinate for about 5 minutes. Remove meat and discard marinade.

Heat oil in large frying pan and sauté beef for about 2 minutes, stirring constantly. Remove and reserve meat. Cook onion in remaining oil (add more oil, if necessary) until onions are limp, or about 2 minutes. Return beef and add broth to onions and simmer uncovered for about 3 minutes. Yield: 6 servings.

COLOMBIA

Colombia is famous world-wide for its coffee, but it is also an important producer of bananas, sugar cane, tobacco, cotton and cacao. It is unique among South American nations in that it has coastline both on the Caribbean Sea and the Pacific Ocean. Few people real-

*ize that Colombia is the world's most important source
of emeralds. Restaurants in the capital city of Bogotá
have a renowned international cuisine. Colombia has
been a member of the UN since November 5, 1945.*

Aguacate Picante

SPICED AVOCADO

2 medium onions

1 clove garlic

2 large green peppers, seeds
and stems removed

2 small hot red peppers (or
several dashes of Cayenne
pepper, to taste)

¼ cup olive oil

¼ cup tomato sauce

½ cup vinegar

1 teaspoon salt

3–4 large avocados, peeled
and diced

½ pound bacon, fried and
chopped

Grind onions, garlic and peppers. Cook in hot oil until onions are
golden yellow; add the tomato sauce, vinegar and salt. Simmer
mixture for 20 to 30 minutes; cool slightly and gently stir in the
avocados and bacon. Serve as a vegetable. Yield: 8 servings.

Sopa de Habas

LIMA BEAN SOUP

½ pound meaty beef bones or
short ribs

1 medium onion, chopped

1 large carrot, chopped

2 tablespoons chopped parsley

1½ cups canned tomatoes

Water

1 12-ounce package frozen
green baby lima beans

⅓ cup cornstarch

⅓ cup milk

2 teaspoons salt

⅛ teaspoon black pepper

Place beef bones, onion, carrot, parsley and tomatoes in deep soup
kettle with water to cover. Cover kettle. Bring contents to a boil;
reduce heat and simmer until the meat is tender, about 2 hours.
Remove meat from bones and return to soup. Add the lima beans.
Simmer for about 20 minutes or until beans are barely tender.
Combine cornstarch and milk; add a small amount of hot liquid
from soup to cornstarch-milk mixture and blend well. Add this,

with salt and pepper, to soup. Simmer 10 to 15 minutes to blend flavors. Yield: 6–8 servings.

Papas Chorriadas

POTATOES WITH CHEESE SAUCE

6 medium potatoes, pared
Salt
Water

Sauce:
2 tablespoons butter
1 tablespoon flour
1 teaspoon salt

1 large onion, sliced
1 large tomato, sliced
1½ cups milk
¼ pound Gruyère cheese, grated
1 tablespoon heavy cream

Boil potatoes in salted water (2 teaspoons of salt for 1 quart of water) until tender. Drain off water and keep potatoes warm.

To make sauce: Melt butter in 8-inch frying pan. Add flour and salt and blend; add onion and tomato. Stir and cook for 3 minutes. Add milk, stirring constantly. Cook over low heat until sauce boils. Add cheese and cream. Stir until cheese melts.

Pour sauce over hot potatoes. Yield: 6 servings.

CONGO (DEMOCRATIC REPUBLIC OF)

The Democratic Republic of Congo, also known as Congo (Kinshasa) after its capital city, is famous for Chicken à la Moambé, a delicious chicken dish cooked with the equivalent of our peanut butter. Politically the country's struggle for independence from Belgium and subsequent civil wars have involved all members of the United Nations, of which it became a member on September 20, 1960. Congo (Kinshasa) is very rich in minerals, including copper, cobalt, zinc, gold and diamonds.

Chicken à la Moambé

FRIED CHICKEN WITH PEANUT BUTTER SAUCE

1 3-pound fryer, cut up	1½ teaspoons salt
½ cup oil	½ teaspoon black pepper
1 6-ounce can tomato paste	¼ cup peanut butter
2 6-ounce cans water	

Brown chicken pieces in hot oil in a 12-inch frying pan. When chicken is browned, drain oil from pan and discard. Combine tomato paste and water; pour over chicken. Loosen chicken from pan and simmer for 10 minutes. Add salt, pepper and peanut butter; simmer for additional 20 minutes. Yield: 6 servings.

CONGO, REPUBLIC OF THE (BRAZZAVILLE)

The Republic of the Congo (Brazzaville), a member of the UN since September 20, 1960, is a land of treeless plains, woodland, grassy plateaus, swamps and forests. The economy of the country centers around the growing of bananas, manioc, peanuts, rice, tropical fruits and corn, as well as timber. Formerly French Equatorial Africa, the country borders on the Atlantic Ocean, and the cuisine makes frequent use of the fish found there.

Mokila N'Gombe

OXTAIL STEW

5 pounds oxtails, ready for use	1 teaspoon salt
Meat tenderizer	Water
1 cup diced onions	1 10-ounce package frozen,
2 tablespoons oil	sliced okra
1 6-ounce can tomato paste	2 tablespoons chopped parsley
1 tablespoon paprika	

Wash oxtails and dry. Use meat tenderizer on oxtails according to directions on package. Cook onions in oil in large frying pan until yellow. Add tenderized oxtails and brown on one side. Turn oxtail pieces. Spread half the tomato paste and all of the paprika on the browned side. Brown the other side. Add salt and remainder of tomato paste and cover with water. Cover; simmer until ox-tails are tender, about 3 hours. Add okra and cook until tender, or about 10 minutes. Serve with boiled rice and garnish with pars-ley. Yield: 6 servings.

Note: For Americans this dish is more desirable when refriger-ated overnight, then the fat removed and the stew reheated.

Mbisi ye Kalou na Loso

FISH AND COLLARD GREENS

1 cup chopped onion
1 sweet green pepper, sliced, core and seeds removed
3 tablespoons oil
¼ teaspoon black pepper
½ teaspoon paprika

1 12-ounce package frozen collard greens
1 cup water
6–8 tablespoons butter
1½ pounds fish fillets, cut in finger-strips

Cook onion and green pepper in oil in large frying pan for 5 min-utes. Add black pepper, paprika, collard greens and water. Cover and simmer for 5 to 10 minutes. Add butter and fish. Cover and simmer for 20 minutes or until fish is tender and flaky. Serve as main course with yams. Yield: 6 servings.

COSTA RICA

Costa Rica was discovered by Columbus in 1502. Ex-pecting to find gold there, he named it "Rich Coast." Actually, today gold is an important export of the coun-try, along with coffee, bananas, cotton, cattle and lumber. Highly literate—free compulsory education having been established before 1890—the Costa Ricans are also strongly democratic. They held their first free elections in 1889. Costa Rica has been a member of the UN since November 2, 1945.

Mousse de Aguacate

AVOCADO MOUSSE

1 large well-ripened avocado, peeled, pit removed, cut in small pieces
1 small onion, grated
½ teaspoon salt
¼ teaspoon Worcestershire sauce

1 tablespoon gelatin
¾ cup cold water
¼ cup boiling water
¼ cup whipped cream
¼ cup mayonnaise

Blend the avocado, onion, salt and Worcestershire sauce until very smooth. Soften gelatin in ¼ cup of the cold water in a medium-size bowl. Add boiling water and stir until dissolved; stir in remaining ½ cup cold water and cool. When gelatin mixture is the consistency of egg white, gradually fold in whipped cream, mayonnaise and the avocado mixture. Pour into mold rinsed with cold water. Refrigerate until set, preferably 1 day in advance of serving. Serve on slices of tomato placed on lettuce leaves. Yield: 6 servings.

Note: For recipe to serve 50, see LARGE-SCALE BUFFET MENUS section, page 255.

Cacerola de Pollo y Elote

CHICKEN AND CORN

5 eggs, beaten
2 1-pound cans cream-style sweet corn
8 ounces Muenster cheese, finely diced
1 5-pound stewing chicken, boiled
1 cup carrots, diced and cooked
1 1-pound can green beans, drained

1 1-pound can green peas, drained
1½ teaspoons salt
4 ounces pitted green olives, sliced
1 cup chicken stock or broth
4 tablespoons raisins
2 tablespoons butter
1 green pepper, cut in strips
1 red pepper, cut in strips

Combine eggs, corn and cheese in a medium bowl. Remove bones
from chicken and cut meat into small pieces. Combine chicken
with carrots, beans, peas, salt, olives, broth and raisins. Place a
layer of corn mixture in a 3-quart oiled casserole; add a layer of
the chicken mixture; continue alternating layers, ending with layer
of corn mixture. Dot top with butter. Garnish with pepper strips
in flowerlike design. Bake for 40 minutes in a preheated 350°F.
oven. Yield: 8–10 servings.

CUBA

*Cuba, the largest island in the Greater Antilles, joined
the UN on October 24, 1945. The country's consider-
able mineral wealth includes deposits of iron and copper
ore, manganese and nickel. Sugar, tobacco, coffee, vegetables and a great variety of citrus fruits are leading exports. More than half the population lives in the cities,
which include Havana, the capital; Camaguay, the center of the sugar industry; and Santiago, which is a major
port.*

Arroz con Frijoles

CUBAN RICE WITH BLACK BEANS

1¼ cups black beans
1 quart water
1 large onion, minced
2 cloves garlic
1 green pepper
1 bay leaf
1 tablespoon salt

1 teaspoon pepper
2 cloves
1½ cups rice
1½ cups hot water
½ cup olive oil
¼ pound smoked ham,
   minced

Wash beans thoroughly and let them stand overnight in water; use
a 3-quart saucepan with lid, or a Dutch oven. Next day boil in
same water 40 minutes. Add more water if necessary. Beans should
be tender but whole. Add half the onion, garlic and green pepper
and half the bay leaf, salt, pepper, and cloves to the beans. Add
rice and hot water. Cover and cook over low heat until rice is ten-

der and dry, about 40 minutes. Stir once, turning rice from bottom to top. Remove from heat. Add ¼ cup of oil and allow to stand for 5 minutes. In remaining oil, sauté ham. When this is half fried, add remaining onion, garlic, green pepper and seasonings. Sauté until brown. Serve over beans and rice. Yield: 6–8 servings.

Ropa Vieja

RAGGEDY BEEF STEW

2 pounds boneless beef (flank or chuck), cut into 1-inch cubes

3 slices bacon or ½ cup diced ham

1 carrot, peeled and sliced

1 turnip, peeled and sliced

1 leek or 1 green onion, chopped

2 quarts water

1 medium onion, diced

1 clove garlic, minced

3 tablespoons butter

1 green pepper, diced

2 1-pound cans tomatoes

1 bay leaf

2 cloves

1 tablespoon salt

¼ teaspoon black pepper

1 teaspoon paprika

1 cup bread crumbs

3 sweet pimientos, diced

Croutons

Chopped parsley

Place meat in 3-quart saucepan. Add bacon or ham, carrot, turnip, and leek or onion. Add water. Cover and simmer for 3 to 4 hours, or until meat shreds easily. Remove meat from saucepan. Pound it with meat mallet or edge of heavy saucer until meat is a mass of ragged shreds. If necessary, separate fibers with fork, to shred.

Cook onion and garlic in butter in large skillet until yellow. Add green pepper, tomatoes, bay leaf, cloves, salt, pepper and paprika. Simmer for 10 minutes or until green pepper is soft. Add this mixture to the broth in which meat was cooked. Simmer slowly for 5 minutes to blend flavors. Strain mixture and thicken strained liquid with bread crumbs. Add half the pimientos and the shredded meat to thickened stock and simmer slowly for 15 to 30 minutes. Garnish with remaining pimientos, croutons and parsley. Serve hot. Yield: 6 servings.

Picadillo Cubano

CUBAN HASH

1 pound ground beef
¾ pound pork, finely ground
2 teaspoons salt
½ teaspoon black pepper
1 cup dry sherry
2 cloves garlic, minced
1 large onion, chopped
1 medium green pepper,
  chopped
¼ cup capers
½ cup pitted green olives,
  sliced
½ cup olive oil
1 large bay leaf
Dash of cumin, optional
Dash of oregano, optional
1 can tomato paste
½ cup raisins
½ cup blanched almonds

Mix beef and pork thoroughly with the salt and pepper. Add ½ cup sherry and let stand 2 hours. Sauté garlic, onion, green pepper, capers and olives in oil in heavy skillet until onion is light brown. Add meat, bay leaf, cumin, oregano, tomato paste, raisins and almonds. Cook for 1 hour over low heat. Remove from heat, add remaining sherry and let stand 5 minutes. Yield: 6 servings.

CYPRUS

Cyprus is a lovely Mediterranean island with a profusion of fresh fruits, hard goat cheeses, wines, nuts—and lemons, which are served with many dishes. In 1571 the Ottoman Turks conquered the land and held it until 1878, when the British took over. Since 1959, when Cyprus achieved independence, there have been disputes between the majority, Greek Christians, and the minority, Turkish Moslems, regarding communal problems. The UN has been deeply involved in trying to achieve a permanent solution to the recurring crises. On September 20, 1960, Cyprus joined the UN.

Tavá

LAMB AND VEGETABLES

3 pounds lamb shoulder or leg, cut in 1-inch cubes
1 pound rice, uncooked
2 pounds potatoes, sliced
1 pound onions, sliced
2 tablespoons salt

¾ teaspoon black pepper
3 teaspoons powdered cumin
1 pound zucchini, sliced
8 artichoke hearts, cut in halves, optional
2 1-pound cans tomatoes

In a 6-quart ovenproof casserole, place approximately ⅓ of each ingredient in the order listed. Repeat for 2nd and 3rd layers. Fill casserole with water. Cover. Bake in a preheated 350°F. oven for 1½ to 2 hours, or until meat is tender. Add water, if necessary, during cooking. Water should be absorbed when done. Let casserole stand for 20 to 30 minutes before it is served. Yield: 6–8 servings.

Afēlia

PORK AND POTATOES

3 pounds pork, cut in 1-inch cubes
1½ cups dry red wine
¼ cup fat
2 pounds potatoes, peeled and cut in long strips

1 tablespoon salt
1 teaspoon black pepper
1 tablespoon coriander
1 cup water

Place pork and wine in bowl. Cover. Keep in refrigerator for 3 to 4 days, turning meat several times. (If time is limited, refrigerating overnight will give good flavor.)

Remove pork from wine, reserving wine. Brown pork in hot fat in heavy saucepan or Dutch oven; remove meat. Brown potato strips in remaining fat and remove. Return meat and place potatoes on top of meat. Add salt, pepper, coriander and water. Cover; simmer for 1 hour over very low heat. Check to prevent burning and add only a small amount of water, if necessary, during cooking period. When meat is tender, remove from heat and add remainder of wine used for marinating pork. Cover; let stand for 10 minutes. Yield: 6–8 servings.

Plaki

BAKED FISH

6 fish fillets (approximately ½
  pound each)—haddock,
  halibut or cod
2 tablespoons butter
1½ teaspoons lemon juice
1½ cups canned tomatoes
3 medium onions, chopped

½ teaspoon garlic powder
1 teaspoon salt
⅛ teaspoon black pepper
2 teaspoons crushed sage
  leaves
1 cup buttered bread crumbs

Place fish in shallow buttered baking dish, 1 layer deep. Pour
lemon juice over fish. Cook tomatoes and onion until the onion is
tender. Add garlic powder, salt, and pepper; taste and correct seasoning, if necessary. Pour tomato sauce over fish. Sprinkle sage
over sauce; top with bread crumbs. Bake in a preheated 325°F.
oven for 45 to 60 minutes. Yield: 6 servings.

CZECHOSLOVAKIA

*It is from Czechoslovakia that we know the proverb
"The way to a man's heart is through his stomach." The
Czech cuisine reflects its geography and history: main
dishes of game, poultry and meats, particularly pork and
goose, accompanied by the inevitable delicious dumplings, are cooked in styles reminiscent of neighboring
lands. Situated in the heart of Europe, in a countryside
of forests and mountains and studded with castles,
Czechoslovakia is well known for its glorious spas.
United Nations Day is October 24, and Czechoslovakia
joined the UN on that day in 1945.*

Svíčková Pečeně

PICKLED BEEF WITH SOUR CREAM

3 pounds rolled rump or rib roast
3 slices bacon
1 teaspoon salt
¼ cup butter
½ cup diced celery
½ cup diced carrot
2 tablespoons chopped parsley
½ cup diced onion
1 bay leaf

⅛ teaspoon thyme
¼ teaspoon black pepper
¼ cup water
¼ cup vinegar
1 tablespoon sugar

Sour Cream Sauce:
2 tablespoons flour
Juices from meat
1 pint sour cream

Release cord from roast and distribute bacon slices evenly around roast. Retie roast; rub with salt and set aside. Melt butter in casserole. Add celery, carrot, parsley and onion and cook over low heat for 10 minutes. Add bay leaf, thyme and pepper, and place meat on top of vegetable mixture; cover and simmer for 1 hour. Add water, vinegar and sugar. Cover; bake in a preheated 350°F. oven for 1½ hours or until meat is tender. Add water as needed. Remove meat and cut in thin slices.

To make sour cream sauce: Blend flour with juices in pan in which meat was cooked. Simmer for 5 minutes. Add sour cream and heat just below boiling. Strain and serve hot with the beef. Yield: 6 servings.

Kyselé Zelí S Bramborovými Knedlíky

SAUERKRAUT WITH POTATO DUMPLINGS

1 large onion, sliced
6 tablespoons vegetable oil or bacon drippings
3 cups canned sauerkraut with liquid
1 teaspoon caraway seeds
3 tablespoons flour
2 tablespoons sugar
Salt, if needed

Potato Dumplings:
4 cups mashed potatoes, cooled
1 tablespoon salt
½ cup farina or cream of wheat
1 cup flour
1 egg, slightly beaten
Boiling salted water
¼ pound butter, melted

Brown onion in hot fat in 12-inch frying pan or 2-quart saucepan. Add sauerkraut and caraway seeds. Simmer over low heat for 45 minutes. Stir in flour and sugar and salt, if necessary. Simmer for 5 minutes.

To make potato dumplings: Combine potatoes, salt, farina, flour and egg. Knead this dough until it is smooth and pliable. Shape dumplings into balls, using about ½ cup of dough for each. Put dumplings in large kettle of boiling salted water (1 teaspoon of salt for each quart of water) and simmer for 15 minutes. When dumplings are done, separate with a fork; remove to serving dish; pour melted butter over steaming dumplings and serve at once with sauerkraut. This dish is an accompaniment to roast duck, goose or spare ribs. Yield: 6 servings.

Ovocné Knedlíky

FRUIT DUMPLINGS

1½ tablespoons butter	12 fresh plums or prunes or
4 ounces cottage cheese	small apricots and/or peach
1 egg yolk	halves, pitted
½ teaspoon salt	Boiling salted water
¼ cup milk	3 tablespoons melted butter
1¾ cups flour	6 tablespoons sugar

Cream together butter, cottage cheese, egg yolk and salt. Add milk. Add flour, stirring until dough leaves side of bowl and is not sticky to the touch. Cover and set for 30 minutes.

Roll dough on lightly floured board into a rectangle approximately 9″ x 12″ and ¼ inch thick. Cut into 12 3-inch squares. Place a piece of fruit in the center of each square. Wrap dough around fruit into a round ball. Drop dumplings into a 6-quart saucepan of boiling salted water. Cover. Cook dumplings for 8 minutes; remove and drain. Sprinkle with melted butter and sugar. Serve as dessert. Yield: 6 servings.

Milosti

FRIED PASTRIES

2 cups flour	2 teaspoons grape juice or
2 tablespoons butter	other sweet fruit juice
1 egg	2 tablespoons milk
1 egg yolk	Fat for deep-fat frying
2 tablespoons sugar	½ cup sifted confectioners'
1 teaspoon grated lemon rind	sugar

Sift flour into mixing bowl. Cut in butter with 2 knives. Make well in center of flour mixture; add eggs, sugar, lemon rind, juice and milk. Rub together with wooden spoon until well blended. Knead on waxed paper. Wrap in waxed paper and chill about ½ hour. Divide in two and roll out half at a time, keeping remainder cold. Roll very, very thin on floured board. Cut into small triangles or squares. Make slashes in center of each. Fry in deep hot fat (370°F.) until golden brown. Drain. Dredge in confectioners' sugar. Yield: 30–60 pastries, depending on size.

Vanocka

CHRISTMAS BRAID

8 cups sifted flour	2½ cups milk, scalded
½ pound butter	2 envelopes dry yeast
7 egg yolks	1 cup raisins
⅔ cup sugar	½ cup blanched almonds,
2 teaspoons salt	optional
2 teaspoons grated lemon rind	2 tablespoons milk
½ teaspoon mace	

Sift flour and work in butter. Beat together 6 egg yolks, sugar, salt, lemon rind and mace with milk cooled to lukewarm. Soften yeast in liquid mixture. Add liquid mixture to flour. Make a stiff dough. Knead until dough is smooth and elastic. Knead in raisins and almonds. Put in bowl to rise; cover with cloth. When dough doubles its bulk, cut into 4 large and 5 small pieces. Form 4 pieces into rolls, length of cookie sheet, braid together on buttered sheet. Roll 3 small pieces the same length and braid. Lay the second on the first braid and pinch ends together. Roll remaining 2 pieces, twist together and lay on 3-strand braid. Pinch ends. Let rise in warm place until light. Beat remaining egg yolk with the 2 tablespoons milk and spread on *vanocka*. Repeat 3 times while baking, to make a shiny crust. Bake in a preheated 350°F. oven for 10 minutes, then at 300°F. for about 50 minutes. Yield: 24 servings.

DAHOMEY

Dahomey, like many of her African neighbors, has a cuisine that is largely dependent upon palm oil. Formerly a region of French West Africa, Dahomey shows a European influence in many of her dishes, but the use of palm oil, manioc and hot peppers has modified them and created indigenous and interesting recipes. Dahomey is a densely populated agricultural country, with cattle raising and fishing as additional sources of income. After achieving independence on August 1, 1960, Dahomey entered the UN on September 20, 1960.

Boeuf et Crevettes avec une Sauce d'Epinard

BEEF AND SHRIMP IN SPINACH SAUCE

1 pound stew beef, cut in
    1-inch cubes
½ teaspoon salt
¼ teaspoon black pepper
1 clove garlic, cut in half
1 cup diced onions
Water

2 10-ounce packages frozen
    chopped spinach
3 tablespoons oil
4 tomatoes, seeds removed,
    diced
½ pound shrimp, shelled and
    deveined
½ teaspoon powdered thyme

Place meat, salt, pepper, garlic and ½ cup of the diced onions in a 3-quart saucepan. Cover with water; cover saucepan and simmer for 2 hours or until meat is tender. Cook frozen spinach according to package directions; drain well. Heat oil in a 12-inch skillet; cook remaining half of onions and the tomatoes until onions are transparent. Add shrimp and thyme to the onion-and-tomato mixture and simmer for 10 minutes. Add the cooked beef with its liquid and the drained spinach to the shrimp mixture. Simmer for 5 minutes or until sauce is thick, stirring occasionally. Remove garlic. Serve with hot rice. Yield: 6 servings.

Wonders Dessert

1¾ cups flour	Fat for frying
1 teaspoon salt	½ cup sugar
6 tablespoons butter	¼ teaspoon cinnamon or
¼ cup water	mace
1 tablespoon oil	

Combine flour and salt in mixing bowl and cut in the butter until mixture resembles coarse meal. Stir in half the water; add the remaining water and the oil; mix only until dough holds together when pressed. Place dough on floured board and knead gently 8 to 10 times. Roll dough into ¼-inch thickness; cut into strips of various widths and about 2 inches long or into triangles or circles. Fry in 1 inch of fat in heavy frying pan at 375°F., turning once, until delicately browned on both sides and cooked throughout, 8 to 10 minutes. Drain on absorbent paper. Dust with mixture of sugar and spice. Serve warm or cold as dessert or snacks. Yield: 6 servings.

Note: For recipe to serve 50, see LARGE-SCALE BUFFET MENUS section, page 254.

DENMARK

Denmark is the land of open-faced sandwiches. Whereas in Sweden you are offered a smorgasbord of small dishes and bowls of meats, fish, cheeses, pickles, etc., in Denmark these same foods are draped lavishly and carefully in multicombinations on thin slices of dark breads spread with wonderful mustard, horseradish, or other appetite-inducing ingredients. The major exports of Denmark are butter, cheese, fish products and meats, especially pork. The chief markets are Great Britain,

Western Europe and the United States. On October 24, 1945, Denmark entered the UN.

Grønaertesuppe

GREEN PEA SOUP

1 pound green peas, unshelled	2 large carrots, diced
½ teaspoon fresh savory	4 large potatoes, pared and
1 teaspoon whole thyme	diced
1 bay leaf	2 tablespoons butter
¼ teaspoon celery salt	1½ teaspoons salt
1 medium onion, quartered	2 tablespoons minced parsley
7 cups water	Butter

Wash and shell the peas. Put the pea pods, herbs, celery salt and onion in a kettle. Add 4 cups of water. Bring to a boil. Cover and simmer until stock is strong (about 2 hours). Put peas, carrots and potatoes in another kettle. Add remaining 3 cups of water. Cover and cook until vegetables are done, about 15 minutes. Drain liquid from pea pods and add, with the 2 tablespoons of butter, to the vegetables. Add salt. Repeat if necessary. Garnish the soup with parsley and add a little cold butter to the tureen just before serving. Yield: 6 servings.

Note: Tiny flour dumplings may be cooked in the soup.

Rødkaal

RED CABBAGE

2 pounds red cabbage	3 tablespoons red currant jelly
2 tablespoons butter	2 tablespoons vinegar
1 tablespoon sugar	

Remove any wilted outer leaves of cabbage. Cut cabbage in quarters; cut out the core. Rinse with cold water; drain and shred very fine. Melt butter in large saucepan; add sugar, jelly and vinegar. Mix. Add shredded cabbage. Cover tightly; simmer until cabbage is very tender, about 2 hours, stirring occasionally. Serve with pork or pot roast. Yield: 6 servings.

Riz à l'Amande

ALMOND RICE DESSERT WITH CHERRY SAUCE

2 cups milk
¼ cup rice
¼ teaspoon salt
1 teaspoon gelatin
2 tablespoons cold milk
1 tablespoon butter

¼ cup sugar
⅓ cup blanched almonds,
   chopped
1 teaspoon vanilla
1 tablespoon sherry
½ cup heavy cream

Kirsebaersauce

CHERRY SAUCE

1 1-pound can dark, sweet
   cherries, pitted
1 tablespoon cornstarch

1 tablespoon lemon juice or
¼ teaspoon almond extract

Scald milk in 2-quart saucepan. Add rice and salt; cover tightly
and simmer for 1 hour, stirring occasionally. Remove from heat.
Dissolve gelatin in cold milk, add gelatin mixture, butter and sugar
to hot rice-and-milk mixture. When cooled, add almonds, vanilla
and sherry. Beat cream until stiff; fold into rice mixture. Pour into
6 individual serving dishes or 1 large mold. Chill for several hours.
Serve very cold with cherry sauce.

To make cherry sauce: Strain juice from cherries into a saucepan; add other fruit juice or water, if needed, to make 1 cup. Mix
cornstarch with 2 tablespoons of the fruit juice; add to remainder
of juice. Stir the mixture over low heat for 5 minutes. Remove
from heat and add lemon juice or almond extract. When cooled,
add cherries and chill in refrigerator. Store in tightly covered glass
jar, if to be kept several days. (Serve also with vanilla blancmange,
custard or bread pudding.) Yield: 6 servings.

DOMINICAN REPUBLIC

*The Dominican Republic was settled in 1496 and claims
to be the oldest permanent European settlement in the
western hemisphere. Occupying the eastern two thirds of
the island of Hispaniola, this fertile land has had a turbu-*

lent history with many civil wars. It is now on the way to restoring its war-shattered economy, utilizing its very fertile soil and abundant mineral resources. It is a beautiful country, with flowers and tropical trees and birds in abundance. The Republic has been a member of the UN since October 24, 1945.

Pastelitos

LITTLE MEAT PIES

Pastry:
2 egg yolks
4 tablespoons butter, softened
½ cup water
2 cups sifted flour
2 teaspoons salt
½ teaspoon soda

Filling:
1 pound lean pork or boned chicken
2 ounces smoked ham
1 teaspoon salt
¼ teaspoon black pepper
¼ teaspoon oregano

1 clove garlic, minced
1 small onion, chopped
2 teaspoons vinegar
1 bay leaf
2 tablespoons chopped parsley
2 tablespoons oil
2 tablespoons tomato paste
½ cup water
1 teaspoon capers
2 tablespoons raisins
8 ripe olives, chopped
2 hard-cooked eggs, chopped

3 cups oil for deep-fat frying

To make pastry: Blend yolks and butter. Add water and sifted flour, salt and soda alternately to egg and butter mixture. Wrap in waxed paper and place in refrigerator for 1 hour.

To make filling: Grind meats together. Add salt, pepper, oregano, garlic, onion, vinegar, bay leaf, and parsley to ground meats. Add seasoned meat to hot oil in skillet and cook until brown; stir frequently. Add tomato paste and water to meat mixture; stir well. Cover and cook slowly for 25 minutes. Add capers and raisins and cook slowly for 5 minutes more. Add olives and eggs; mix well.

To make pastelitos: Roll ¼ of the pastry dough on a lightly floured board to about ⅛-inch thickness. Cut pastry into 2-inch squares. Place a teaspoon of meat mixture in center of half the pastry squares; moisten edges with water. Cover each with another pastry square; press edges together and seal. Continue until filling and pastry are used. Deep-fat fry in hot oil until *pastelitos* are brown. Serve as appetizers. Yield: 60–70 *pastelitos.*

Sopa de Frijoles

HEARTY BEAN SOUP

1 pound dried pinto or kidney beans

2 quarts boiling water

1 pound salt pork, cut into 6 slices

4 slices bacon, cut into 1-inch pieces

¼ pound bulk or link sausage

3 cloves garlic, minced

1 large onion, chopped

1 teaspoon chili powder

2 drops of Tabasco sauce

2 tablespoons salt

2 tablespoons vinegar

2 tablespoons tomato paste

2 green bananas, sliced

Wash the beans and place in a 4-quart kettle. Add boiling water to beans, cover, and let boil 2 minutes. Remove from heat and let beans soak for 1 hour in same water.

Cook salt pork, bacon and sausage over low heat for 10 minutes. Remove meat from fat and add meat to bean pot. Cook garlic and chopped onion in remaining fat until yellow. Drain and add garlic and onion to beans. Cover kettle and simmer over low heat for 2 hours. Stir occasionally. Add seasonings and sliced bananas to bean mixture and simmer for another hour or until beans are tender and soup is thick. Skim off excess fat and serve hot. Yield: 6–8 servings.

Carne Mechada

STUFFED MEAT

1 4-pound beef tenderloin or round steak
1 cup vinegar
1 tablespoon salt
½ teaspoon black pepper
½ cup finely sliced green olives
¼ cup chopped green pepper
¼ cup capers
½ pound cooked ham, finely diced

1 small onion, sliced
½ cup sliced green pepper
¼ cup chopped parsley
½ tablespoon tomato paste
1 tablespoon vinegar
½ cup oil
½ cup water
¾ cup red wine
Watercress

Trim the fat and gristle from the meat but leave the meat in one piece. Rub with a damp cloth. If a tenderloin is used, make an incision lengthwise through the center of the tenderloin with a long, narrow knife. Be careful not to cut through to the outside. If round steak is used, make incisions over different parts of the meat so that each serving will contain one incision.

Combine the cup of vinegar, the salt and pepper. Pour over the beef and into the incisions. Combine olives, the chopped green pepper, capers and ham. Stuff this mixture into all incisions of the round steak. If tenderloin is used, place the stuffing down the center of the entire length of the meat. Cover the meat with the sliced onion and sliced green pepper, the parsley, tomato paste and 1 tablespoon vinegar. Let stand ½ hour.

Heat oil in a deep skillet. Remove the meat from the vegetable marinade; brown on all sides in hot oil. When meat is well browned, add vegetable marinade and water. If you are using tenderloin, simmer 15 minutes; the tenderloin should be rosy red inside. Round steak should be covered and simmered until the meat is tender, about 1 hour, adding more water if necessary. Just before serving, in either case, add the red wine and let simmer 5 minutes. Adjust seasoning.

Serve on a hot platter, slicing meat so that the stuffing (*mechas*) shows. Garnish with watercress. Pour some of the sauce over the meat and serve the remaining sauce in a sauceboat. Yield: 8–10 servings.

ECUADOR

Ecuador, which originally was the Indian kingdom of Quito, is today a nation of five and one half million people and is the world's largest exporter of bananas. It grows dozens of varieties. The word ecuador *is Spanish for equator, but the temperature varies from moderate on the slopes of the Andes to hot and humid on the seacoast. Ecuador, which became a UN member on December 21, 1945, also is an important exporter of the famous "Panama" hats, so named because they were shipped through the Panama Canal.*

Seviche

PICKLED FISH

1½ pounds thin fillets of bass or any delicate fish	1 chili pepper, minced
¾ cup lemon juice	1 sweet red pepper, chopped
⅓ cup orange juice	1 sweet green pepper, chopped
2 tablespoons tomato ketchup	¼ cup corn kernels
1 medium onion, chopped	½ teaspoon salt

Lay fish fillets on a platter side by side. Cover with ½ cup of the lemon juice. Cover and marinate in refrigerator overnight, thereby "cooking" the fish.

Drain fillets and place on serving platter. Combine all other ingredients into a sauce, including rest of lemon juice; spread over fillets. Serve as an appetizer. Yield: 6–8 servings.

Note: For recipe to serve 50, see LARGE-SCALE BUFFET MENUS section, page 257.

EL SALVADOR

El Salvador once petitioned to be included in the United States, and its constitution is similar to that of the United

States. This country is the smallest and most densely populated of the republics of Central America; its greatest concentration of inhabitants is found on a large, high plateau rich with volcanic soils. Its food echoes that of its Latin American neighbors in the use of cornmeal to encase meat or poultry fillings, but many dishes are evidence that at one time El Salvador was a Spanish colony. She joined the UN on October 24, 1945.

Pastelitos de Picadillo

SALVADORAN TURNOVERS

Dough:
2 cups cornmeal
1 teaspoon salt
2 cups boiling water

Filling:
½ cup chick-peas
½ cup diced cooked potatoes

½ cup green beans, cooked and chopped
½ cup diced lean cooked pork
1 tablespoon chopped onion
4 tablespoons tomato paste
½ teaspoon salt

Fat for frying

To make dough: Combine cornmeal and salt. Add water and stir constantly until you have a stiff dough. Divide into 8 equal portions and cool. Flatten each portion into a thin cake about 5 inches in diameter. If mixture is sticky, add a little cold water.

To make filling: Mix all ingredients together.

Spread two tablespoons of filling evenly on ½ of each cake. Fold the other half of cake over the mixture. Press edges together to seal. Place turnovers in hot shallow fat and fry over low heat until each side is golden brown. Yield: 8 *pastelitos.*

Note: If smaller *pastelitos* are desired, reduce size of cake and amount of mixture used for each.

Robalo a la Española

HADDOCK, SPANISH STYLE

3 pounds haddock fillets
1 teaspoon salt
½ teaspoon black pepper
1 clove garlic, minced
¼ cup lemon juice

3 large onions, sliced
3 medium tomatoes, sliced
2 tablespoons minced parsley
½ cup olive oil

Rub fish with salt, pepper, garlic and lemon juice. Place in oval casserole and allow to stand for 15 minutes. Cover fish with layers of onions, tomatoes and parsley. Add oil and any remaining lemon juice. Cover casserole tightly and bake in a preheated 375°F. oven for 45 minutes, basting occasionally. Cook uncovered another 20 minutes, or until vegetables and fish are tender. Baste often enough to keep moist, adding a little water if necessary. Serve in casserole. Yield: 6 servings.

Gallina en Chicha

CHICKEN IN WINE SAUCE

1 5-pound chicken, cut up
2 large onions, sliced
1 tablespoon salt
Water
2 tablespoons sesame seeds
2 dried sweet red peppers
2 peppercorns
4 small bay leaves
1 small loaf Italian bread soaked in sweet red wine
1 cup cider vinegar

1 teaspoon black pepper
1 cup sweet red wine
1 tablespoon Worcestershire sauce
24 dried prunes, pitted
1 cup small pitted olives
½ cup capers
1 6½-ounce can tomato paste
1 4-ounce can pimientos, cut into strips
1 cup sugar

Place chicken and onions in a skillet. Add salted water to cover bottom of skillet. Cover and simmer slowly about 1 hour. Add water as needed.

Grind into a paste the sesame seeds, red peppers, peppercorns, bay leaves and wine-soaked bread.

When the chicken is soft, add the vinegar, black pepper, wine, Worcestershire sauce, prunes, olives, capers, tomato paste, pimientos, sugar and the sesame-seed paste. Cover and continue to cook slowly for 1 hour. Yield: 6 servings.

EQUATORIAL GUINEA

Composed of islands and land on the coast of West Africa, this newest member of the UN (November 12, 1968) has some of the most magnificent scenery of

*Equatorial Africa—spectacular cataracts, dense under-
growth, and many beautiful lakes filling up the craters of
old volcanoes. It was formerly called Spanish Guinea,
and Spanish is spoken, as well as local dialects and a
form of pidgin English known as "Pickingles," which is a
popular means of expression throughout the coastal zone
of West Africa. Important ingredients in many dishes
are nutmeg, red pepper, bitter herbs and dried shrimp.*

Itókó Dya Betatamu

SHRIMP AND TOMATO STEW

¼ cup peanut oil
1 pound cooked shrimp, very finely chopped
12 large tomatoes, peeled and coarsely chopped
⅛ teaspoon Cayenne pepper

¼ teaspoon salt
½ 10-ounce package frozen okra, cooked and sliced
½ 10-ounce package frozen whole-leaf spinach, cooked
6 hard-cooked eggs, sliced

Heat oil; sauté shrimp and tomatoes with Cayenne and salt for 10
minutes. Add okra and spinach; simmer until thoroughly heated.
Remove from stove. Add sliced eggs and toss lightly before serving. Yield: 6 servings.

ETHIOPIA

*Ethiopia is one of the world's oldest kingdoms. Over the
centuries many religious groups as well as conquering
nations have tried to annex this country. The country is
today predominantly Coptic Christian. Its mountain
masses reach as high as 15,000 feet and there are many
rivers and lakes. Lake Tana, near the center of the Ethiopian highlands, is the source of the Blue Nile. Ethiopian
food is highly seasoned, often served with tala, the local
beer. Ethiopia has been a member of the UN since November 13, 1945. Her capital, Addis Ababa, is the head-
quarters for the Organization of African Unity.*

Doro-Weutt

CHICKEN WITH HOT SAUCE

1 3½-pound fryer, cut up	2 tablespoons chili powder
3 cups boiling water	2 tablespoons tomato paste
Juice of 1 lemon	4 tablespoons red wine
1 teaspoon salt	½ teaspoon ground ginger
6 medium onions, chopped	½ teaspoon black pepper
4 tablespoons fat	6 hard-cooked eggs

Cover chicken with boiling water. Add lemon juice and salt. Cover and simmer for 10 minutes. Remove chicken and drain, reserving broth and keeping it hot. Brown onions in fat. When brown, add 1 cup of the hot chicken broth, chili powder and tomato paste. Blend well and simmer for 5 minutes. Add red wine, ginger, pepper and 1 more cup of hot broth. Place the chicken in this sauce and simmer until chicken is tender, 30 to 40 minutes.

Add hard-cooked eggs about 3 minutes before serving, piercing each egg several times to permit sauce to penetrate egg. Yield: 4–6 servings.

FINLAND

Finland is a nation that has built its society upon Western ideals though its principal European heritage is from the Hungarians and Estonians. The climate is harsh and the land is often unyielding, but the resourceful Finns have an independence and a self-sufficiency which allows them to derive a livelihood from their surroundings. A significant transition is still underway from an agricultural to an industrial society. In Finland, fish of all types are especially abundant (sardines and fresh-water salmon are favorites), and visitors also delight in the country's game birds such as grouse and wild duck. On December 14, 1955, Finland entered the UN.

Sillisalaati

HERRING SALAD

Salad:
1 salt herring
Cold water
1 cup cooked diced beets
1 cup cooked diced carrots
1 cup cooked diced potatoes
1 cup diced apple
½ cucumber, diced

1 tomato, cut in small pieces
2 small onions, diced
Lettuce leaves

Dressing:
1 cup sour cream
¼ cup vinegar
A little beet juice for coloring

Soak salt herring in cold water overnight to partially freshen. Remove skin and bones and cut herring into bits. Add beets, carrots, potatoes, apple, cucumber, tomato and onions to herring. Toss gently. Place on lettuce in large salad bowl or on individual salad plates.

To make dressing: Combine all ingredients but do not mix with salad. Serve dressing separately. Yield: 6 servings as salad, or 12 for smorgasbord.

Kesäkeitto

SUMMER VEGETABLE SOUP

4 small carrots, diced
¾ cup green peas
½ small cauliflower, diced or
    broken in small flowerets
3 small new potatoes, diced
½ cup green beans, sliced
4 radishes, cut in half
Boiling water
2 teaspoons salt
1½ tablespoons sugar

2 cups chopped spinach
1½ tablespoons butter,
    melted
1½ tablespoons flour
1 egg yolk
1 pint milk
¼ cup cream
1 cup shrimp, cooked and
    deveined

Combine all vegetables, except spinach, in a large kettle; cover with boiling water; add salt and sugar and simmer about 45 minutes. Add spinach and simmer for 10 minutes. Combine butter and flour in second kettle; combine egg yolk, milk and cream and stir into butter and flour. Add cooked vegetables and not more than 2 cups of the liquid. Add shrimp and heat. Serve hot immediately. Yield: 6 servings.

FRANCE

In the culinary world France most justly deserves its great reputation for a magnificent, imaginative cuisine, combined with superb wines. French knowledge of techniques and ingredients has contributed to the development of the cuisines of many other nations. Although probably every Frenchman is interested in la bonne table, *the vast majority earn their living in industry. France is well known for her textiles and for many industrial products which have made her one of the world's richest nations. France has been a member of the UN since October 24, 1945.*

Cretons

PORK IN JELLY

3 pounds pork shoulder, ground
2 onions, chopped
1 pig's knuckle or foot
Water
2 teaspoons salt
¼ teaspoon freshly ground black pepper
1 bay leaf
¼ teaspoon thyme
¼ teaspoon basil
8 parsley sprigs
¼ teaspoon ground allspice
Garnishes of pickled beets and sliced egg, or tomatoes and cucumbers

Place ground pork, onion and pig's knuckle or foot in a large pot and cover with cold water. Add all seasonings. Boil for 3 hours. Remove knuckle or foot and bay leaf. Dip a mold in cold water and pour mixture into mold. Refrigerate until jelled. Unmold and serve as an appetizer, sliced and garnished, with or without French bread. Yield: 8–10 servings.

Veau Saumure Angoumois

MARINATED LEG OF VEAL

3–4 pounds leg of veal, boned
    and rolled
1 tablespoon coarse salt
3 medium onions, sliced
2 bay leaves
6 peppercorns
6 juniper berries
½ lemon, sliced
½ teaspoon thyme
½ teaspoon tarragon
½ cup wine vinegar

Ravigote Sauce:
2 tablespoons vinegar
5 tablespoons olive oil
½ onion, finely chopped
1 tablespoon prepared
    mustard
1 hard-cooked egg, chopped
1 teaspoon mixed chopped
    fresh parsley, tarragon and
    chives
¼ teaspoon salt
⅛ teaspoon black pepper

Rub the meat with salt; place in an earthenware bowl or glass casserole. Combine all the remaining ingredients and pour over the meat. Cover the container and let meat marinate in the refrigerator for 4 days, turning the meat every day.

Place meat with the marinade in a saucepan; add cold water to cover meat. Cover pan and simmer gently for 4 hours. Remove meat; place in a bowl and cover with waxed paper. Place a plate and weight on the covered meat and refrigerate for 1 day.

To make ravigote sauce: Mix ingredients in order given. Yield: ¾ cup.

Slice meat thinly and serve with ravigote sauce. Yield: 10 servings.

Boeuf à la Mode Provençale

BEEF IN THE STYLE OF PROVENCE

3 pounds lean round of beef
2 tablespoons oil
3 onions, quartered
3 tomatoes, quartered
½ teaspoon finely chopped
    parsley

½ teaspoon thyme
½ teaspoon salt
¼ teaspoon black pepper
1 orange, quartered
2 bay leaves
1 pound carrots, cut in fingers

Sear meat until well browned in hot oil in a Dutch oven. Place onions and tomatoes around browned meat in the bottom of the pan. Sprinkle the parsley, thyme, salt and pepper over the meat and place orange quarters and bay leaves around it. Cover and cook over low heat for 1½ hours. Add the carrots; continue cooking for 1½ hours or until meat is tender. Remove meat to serving platter. Reduce liquid by boiling, if too thin. Serve vegetables in sauce around the meat or serve sauce separately. Yield: 6–8 servings.

Noisettes d'Agneau et Purée de Marrons

LAMB FILLETS WITH COGNAC SAUCE OVER CHESTNUT PURÉE

Chestnut Purée: (or may be purchased in a can)
2 pounds chestnuts
Water
3 tablespoons butter
2 tablespoons cream

Cognac Sauce:
6 tablespoons butter

1 teaspoon tarragon
2½ tablespoons cognac
6 tablespoons beef bouillon

2 pounds lamb fillets
Flour
Salt
Black pepper
2 tablespoons butter

To make chestnut purée: Remove outer shell from the chestnuts; plunge into boiling water for 5 minutes; drain. Rinse in cold water and then remove the inner skin. Place well-skinned chestnuts in a large pot and cover with water. Allow the chestnuts to simmer for several hours or until very soft, replacing the water when necessary. Drain chestnuts and mash by hand or in a food mill. Add butter and cream and blend thoroughly. Spread over the bottom of a 2-quart casserole dish or other serving dish, and keep warm in a very slow oven (200°F.).

To make cognac sauce: Melt 2 tablespoons of the butter and add the tarragon. Do not allow the butter to color. Add the cognac and bring to simmer. Add the beef bouillon and boil gently for a few minutes. With pot set on the edge of the burner, or over very low heat, add the remaining 4 tablespoons of butter, bit by bit. Stir well and keep warm.

Dip each fillet in flour and gently pound. Salt and pepper the fillets and sauté rapidly in 2 tablespoons of butter. Ten minutes should be sufficient, as the meat should be pink when cut. Arrange the lamb fillets over the chestnut purée in the serving dish. Pour on the cognac sauce and serve immediately. Yield: 6 servings.

Omelette Cardinal

LOBSTER OMELET

9 ounces cooked lobster tails, chopped
4 tablespoons butter
¼ cup cognac
1 cup canned lobster bisque

1 orange
8 anchovy fillets, diced
10 eggs, beaten
1 teaspoon black pepper
1 tablespoon cream

Heat the cooked, chopped lobster in half the butter. Heat cognac; pour over the hot lobster and flame. Heat the lobster bisque in a double boiler; add half to the lobster mixture. Keep hot.

Peel the orange very thin and carefully so as to peel off only the outer rind. Cut peel into very thin julienne strips the length of a matchstick. Reserve. Complete the peeling of the orange and skin and seed each segment of the fruit. Reserve the orange sections.

Add the anchovies to the beaten eggs; add pepper and cream. Melt remaining butter in an omelet pan and cook the omelet over low heat. Just before folding it, fill it with a small amount of the orange-peel julienne strips and a heaping teaspoon of the lobster mixture. Fold and complete the omelet in the classic manner. Slide onto a hot serving dish. Make an incision, lengthwise, down the center of the omelet and fill it with the rest of the lobster mixture. Pour the remaining lobster bisque over one end of the omelet. Arrange the segments of the orange around the omelet and sprinkle the top of the omelet with the rest of the julienne strips of orange rind. Yield: 4–6 servings.

Tourte aux Epinards

SPINACH PIE

3 pounds fresh, cleaned spinach	Salt
	Black pepper
2 eggs, beaten	Puff pastry dough for 2 9-inch
¼ cup heavy cream	pie shells, or 1 10-ounce
1 tablespoon flour	package frozen pastry shells

Cook the spinach in boiling water for 5 minutes. Drain. Chop the spinach; add the eggs, cream, flour, salt and pepper to taste. Mix well.

If you are using the frozen pastry shells, let them defrost in the refrigerator overnight. Roll two thirds of the puff paste into a ball and the remaining third into another ball. Refrigerate for 1 hour. On a floured surface, roll each ball out to less than ¼-inch thickness. With the larger circle of dough, cover the bottom and sides of a buttered 9-inch pan, preferably a false-bottomed straight-sided quiche pan or a metal flan ring set on a baking sheet. Prick sides and bottom of dough with a fork. Fill with the spinach mixture. Cover with the remaining dough; prick the top. Cook in a preheated 350°F. oven for 25 to 30 minutes. Serve as an accompaniment to meat or poultry. Yield: 1 9-inch pie.

Gâteau aux Amandes

ALMOND CAKE

⅓ cup butter	¾ cup flour, or 1½ cups cake
⅓ cup blanched, shredded almonds	flour
	½ teaspoon salt
1 cup confectioners' sugar	⅔ cup ground almonds
4 eggs	1 tablespoon Curaçao
2 egg yolks	3 tablespoons chopped
¾ cup arrowroot flour and	candied fruit or raisins

Press butter evenly over the bottom and sides of a 9- or 10-inch layer-cake pan. Sprinkle shredded almonds on butter; top with ¼ cup of sugar.

Place eggs and egg yolks in bowl resting in hot water; whisk or beat until eggs are blended and light in color. Gradually add the remaining sugar and continue beating until mixture is thick and pale in color.

Sift flour and salt together; add ground almonds to sifted flour. Fold flour mixture, 1 tablespoon at a time, into the egg mixture until well blended. Fold in Curaçao. Pour half of the cake mixture into the prepared cake pan. Sprinkle candied fruit or raisins over the cake and add the remaining half of the cake mixture. Bake in a preheated 350°F. oven for 35 to 40 minutes. Serve cold. Yield: 9–12 servings.

Savarin au Rhum

BABA CAKE

Baba:
4 eggs
½ cup sugar
1¼ cups sifted flour
4 teaspoons baking powder
6 tablespoons butter, melted
½ cup lukewarm milk

Rum Syrup:
½ cup sugar
½ cup water
½ cup rum

Sweetened whipped cream

Beat eggs with sugar until fluffy. Add flour and baking powder sifted together; mix. Add butter and milk. Mix vigorously. Pour into a buttered and floured pudding mold or individual molds. Bake individual molds 25 minutes, a large mold 35 to 40 minutes, in a preheated 325°F. oven.

To make rum syrup: Cook sugar in water until a thin syrup is formed. Remove from heat and add rum.

Remove cake or cakes from oven and unmold. While still hot pour rum syrup over. Cool and serve with whipped cream. Yield: 8 servings.

GABON

Gabon is a richly endowed country on the Atlantic Coast of the former territory of French Equatorial Africa. In addition to concentrated deposits of iron ore and manganese, she also produces uranium, petroleum, natural gas and wood products of great value, exports outreach-

ing imports by about one third. Like most countries of black Africa, Gabon uses nuts in the preparation of many dishes. A few days after Gabon became an independent nation she joined the UN on September 20, 1960.

Poulet au Gnemboue

CHICKEN WITH NUTS

1 cup palm nuts or Macadamia nuts	1 teaspoon salt
1¾ cups water	1 clove garlic, minced
½ teaspoon red pepper	3 scallions or green onions, thinly sliced
¼ teaspoon black pepper	1 2½-pound chicken, cut up

Pulverize nuts with mortar and pestle and mix with the water, or chop nuts in a blender with the water. Pour into a 12-inch skillet or saucepan; stir in the peppers, salt, garlic and scallions or onions. Mix ingredients well. Place pieces of chicken in the nut mixture; cover and cook over very low heat for 1½ hours. Stir often and add water if needed. Yield: 4 servings.

GAMBIA

Gambia, a narrow enclave in the West African nation of Senegal, is a country of only a third of a million population. It is a significant producer of peanuts, which account for 95 percent of the value of its exports. Sorghum and rice are grown for local consumption. A former British colony, Gambia became a UN member on September 21, 1965.

Qchiou Ganar

CHICKEN STEW

1 3½-pound frying chicken, cut up	2 carrots, sliced
¼ cup oil	1 cup shredded cabbage
1 chopped onion	6–8 pods okra, cut in halves
1 tablespoon tomato paste	1 clove garlic and 1 small onion, mashed to a pulp
4 cups water	2 teaspoons salt
2 sweet potatoes, cut in 1-inch cubes	¼ cup peanut butter

Brown chicken in hot oil in heavy saucepan or Dutch oven. Add onion and tomato paste to chicken and mix with fat; add water and bring mixture to a boil. Add vegetables, mashed garlic-and-onion mixture and salt. Cover. Simmer 30 minutes. Remove potatoes, carrots, cabbage and okra; set these aside and keep warm. Mix peanut butter with 1 cup of hot broth; add to chicken and broth and cook 30 minutes. Return vegetables to pot; reheat. Serve stew with hot rice. Yield: 6 servings.

GHANA

Ghana is a country of eight million people and is rich in mineral deposits; in a recent year it produced 2,500,000 carats of diamonds, mostly for industrial use. Gold, manganese and aluminum are among its other major exports. A fascinating attraction to visitors is its ancient castles, which were built by European traders; these same traders coined the name "Gold Coast," as the country was formerly called before it attained its independence. Ghana became a member of the UN on March 8, 1957.

Palaver Stew

SPINACH STEW

2 pounds spinach, cleaned	2 medium onions, thinly sliced
¾ cup water	3 tomatoes, finely chopped
2 pounds meat, chicken, or dried fish	4 small hard-cooked eggs, finely chopped
Salt	2 eggs, beaten
1 green onion, chopped	3 cups cooked beans
Water	Salt
1 cup palm or peanut oil or 4 ounces fat	½ nutmeg, grated or 1 teaspoon powdered nutmeg

Place spinach in saucepan, add water and boil for 10 minutes. Strain spinach and save the liquid. Chop the spinach. Cut meat, chicken or fish into large pieces. Put into a saucepan and sprinkle with a little salt, add chopped onion and water to cover. Simmer gently for 10 minutes.

Heat oil or fat in saucepan; fry sliced onions, tomatoes and chopped eggs for 5 minutes. Add beaten eggs. Cook gently for 5 minutes; add beans, meat, chopped spinach and 1 cup of stock from spinach and meat. Add salt to taste and nutmeg. Stir well. Simmer gently 1 hour or until meat is tender. Yield: 4–6 servings.

"Cook Up"

RICE WITH MEAT

¼ pound smoked bacon, diced in small cubes	2 teaspoons salt
2 teaspoons brown sugar	¼ teaspoon freshly ground black pepper
1 medium onion, chopped	1¾ cups canned tomatoes
1½ cups diced cooked meat or ¾ pound lean ground beef	2¼ cups chicken broth or meat gravy
	2 cups rice

Cook bacon in large skillet or 4-quart saucepan. When lightly browned, remove bacon and leave only 2 tablespoons of fat. Add sugar and heat until the fat bubbles. Add onion, meat, salt and pepper. Stir until onion and meat begin to brown. Add tomatoes, bacon pieces and broth or gravy; bring to a boil. Add rice; lower heat when mixture begins to boil again. Stir, cover and cook slowly for 25 minutes. Turn heat off and allow to stand on the burner an additional 5 minutes. Stir the rice gently with a lifting motion and serve. Yield: 6 servings.

Fante Kotokyim

CRAB SAUCE

1 small onion, finely chopped	½ teaspoon ground ginger
3 fresh tomatoes, peeled and diced	¼ teaspoon white pepper
	½ teaspoon salt
¼ cup butter, melted	½ cup water
1 pound crab or lobster meat	

Cook onion and tomatoes in butter in medium frying pan over low heat for 5 minutes. Add bite-sized pieces of crab or lobster meat, ginger, pepper, salt and water; simmer gently for 15 minutes. Serve hot over dry rice or with baked potatoes. Yield: 4 servings.

Akwadu

BANANA PUDDING

4–5 bananas	2 tablespoons brown sugar
Juice of 1 orange	½ cup grated coconut

Grease an 8-inch pie pan. Peel bananas, cut lengthwise and line pie pan with them. Mix orange juice and sugar; pour over bananas. Sprinkle coconut thickly over bananas. Bake in a preheated 400°F. oven until coconut is brown, about 5 to 8 minutes. Serve hot. Yield: 6 servings.

GREECE

Greece has been producing wines since ancient times to accompany its delicious and now somewhat typical Middle-Eastern cuisine. A distinctive feature of Greek cooking is the imaginative use of lemon juice. The Greeks make good use of the fish that abound in surrounding waters, as they do of lamb, the meat most found in the area. Mixed vegetable dishes are often served as an entrée. The Greek islands and the archaeological sights of the country attract a vast flow of enthusiastic tourists from all over the world. Greece joined the UN on October 25, 1945.

Psari Fourno Spetsiotiko

BAKED FISH—SPETSAI ISLAND

2 pounds red snapper fillets	½ cup white wine
2 teaspoons salt	⅓ cup olive oil
¼ teaspoon pepper	½ cup minced parsley
2 tablespoons lemon juice	2 cloves garlic, crushed
2 cups canned tomatoes, with juice	⅓ cup dry bread crumbs

Cut red snapper fillets into 12 pieces; rub with salt and pepper. Combine all other ingredients except bread crumbs. Pour into a casserole or baking dish. Place fish in sauce. Cover with bread crumbs. Bake uncovered in a preheated 350°F. oven for 1 hour. Yield: 6 servings.

Riganato

LAMB OREGANO

2 pounds boneless leg of lamb	2 tablespoons lemon juice
1½ teaspoons salt	2 cups hot water
⅛ teaspoon freshly ground black pepper	1 teaspoon oregano
1 clove garlic, cut into eighths	1½ pounds small potatoes, peeled
⅓ cup olive oil	

Rub lamb with salt and pepper; insert garlic in slits or pockets made in lamb with sharp knife. Brown lamb in hot oil in Dutch oven or deep skillet with tight-fitting cover. Add lemon juice and 1½ cups hot water; cover and cook over simmering heat for 1 hour. Add oregano and cook for 30 minutes; uncover and allow liquid to evaporate. Brown potatoes separately in a little additional oil, turning often. When potatoes are brown, add to meat; reduce heat; add remaining water. Cover and continue cooking

over low heat for 30 minutes or until potatoes are done. Yield:
6 servings.

Loukoumades

CINNAMON FRITTERS

1 package dry yeast
½ cup lukewarm water
½ cup scalded milk
1 egg, well beaten
2 cups flour
1½ teaspoons baking powder
¼ teaspoon salt

1 quart vegetable oil for
   deep-fat frying
1 teaspoon cinnamon

Syrup:
1 cup sugar
½ cup honey
¾ cup water

Combine yeast and lukewarm water in a mixing bowl; add milk,
which has cooled to lukewarm, and egg. Add flour, sifted with
baking powder and salt, to the yeast mixture. Beat thoroughly
until batter is free of lumps. Cover and let rise in warm, draft-free
place until double in bulk.

Heat oil in deep-fat fryer or heavy saucepan to 350°F. Drop the
batter by teaspoonsful into the hot fat. Brown fritters on both
sides. Remove from fat and drain on absorbent paper. Sprinkle
with cinnamon while hot and serve with hot syrup as a dessert.

To make syrup: Combine sugar, honey and water and boil for
5 minutes.

Yield: 25 fritters.

Karedopeta

WALNUT AND HONEY DESSERT

½ cup butter
1 cup sugar
8 eggs, separated
4 cups finely chopped walnuts
2 teaspoons cinnamon
2 teaspoons baking powder
3 cups sifted flour
¼ cup coarsely chopped
   walnuts

Syrup:
1 cup sugar
½ cup water
1 cup honey
½ teaspoon cinnamon
2 tablespoons dark rum

Beat together the butter and sugar until fluffy. Add egg yolks and beat with rotary or electric beater until very light. Fold in stiffly beaten egg whites. Combine the 4 cups walnuts, cinnamon, baking powder and flour. Fold into butter-sugar-egg mixture until blended. Turn into two buttered 9" x 9" pans. Sprinkle the ¼ cup nuts on top. Bake in a preheated 350°F. oven 45 minutes. Cool in the pans on cake racks about 1 hour.

To make syrup: Boil together sugar and water until the syrup spins a thread (or until a candy thermometer inserted registers 230°F.). Stir in honey, cinnamon and rum.

Cut the baked product into diamond-shaped pieces. Cover with hot syrup and let stand 4 to 24 hours to allow the syrup to permeate. Serve accompanied by forks. Yield: 24 servings.

GUATEMALA

Guatemala, the largest republic in Central America, was part of the great Mayan civilization long before the Spanish conquest of that area in the sixteenth century. It is a mountainous land, about 40 percent of which is forested. Its major food crops include corn, rice, wheat and beans. Popular tourist attractions are its beautiful Mayan ruins and the Indian village of Chichicastenango, with its great church. Guatemala entered the UN November 21, 1945.

Ensalada de Guacamole

AVOCADO SALAD

2 avocados, peeled, pitted and diced
2 hard-cooked eggs, diced
3 small tomatoes, peeled and diced
6 stuffed olives, sliced
1 small onion, minced
1 teaspoon salt
¼ teaspoon black pepper
1 tablespoon vinegar
3 tablespoons oil
Fresh chili pepper or chili powder
Crisp bacon

Mix avocado, eggs, tomatoes, olives and onion. Combine salt, pepper, vinegar and oil and add to avocado mixture. Season to taste with chili pepper or chili powder. Serve on lettuce with crumbled bacon. Yield: 6 servings.

Tamales de Carne

BEEF TAMALES

Sauce:

½ cup chopped canned chili peppers

1 teaspoon chili powder

4 medium tomatoes, chopped

2 teaspoons capers

12 ripe olives, pitted and chopped

¼ teaspoon powdered oregano

¼ teaspoon black pepper

¼ teaspoon garlic salt

2 tablespoons chopped onion

¼ cup seedless raisins

1 pound ground beef, round or chuck

1 cup hominy grits

4 cups boiling water

1 teaspoon salt

2 tablespoons butter

Combine all the ingredients listed under *Sauce*. Simmer for 20 minutes or until sauce is thick and flavors are blended, stirring occasionally.

Divide the meat into 6 equal portions and pat out in rectangles, about 6″ x 8″; place wax paper between each portion and place in refrigerator until ready to use. Cut 6 pieces of parchment paper into 8″ x 10″ rectangles. Pour the grits slowly into the boiling water to which the salt and butter have been added; stir to prevent lumping. Simmer 10 minutes or until thick.

Spread a layer of grits ¼ inch thick on each paper rectangle covering about 6″ x 8″ of its surface. Place a meat patty on top of the layer of grits; add ¼ cup of the sauce to each tamale. With the aid of a spatula, roll the tamale in a rectangle so that the inside portion is completely covered with the grits. Roll the paper around the tamale, folding the ends over and tying securely with string. Place tamales in a large kettle of boiling water and boil for 30 minutes. Remove the tamales; drain and remove paper. Serve hot with red beans and chili. Yield: 6 servings.

Note: Ground leftover meat, pork or chicken may be used in place of beef.

Chiles Rellenos

FRIED STUFFED GREEN PEPPERS

6 large green peppers	⅔ pound ground beef
1 large tomato, chopped	1 quart oil for frying
½ cup minced onion	1 cup cooked rice
1 teaspoon salt	2 eggs
¼ teaspoon black pepper	2 tablespoons milk
Few grains of Cayenne pepper	2 tablespoons flour

Cut tops from peppers; remove seeds and wash well. Save the tops. Place peppers under the broiler for about 5 minutes or long enough to soften slightly. Combine tomato, onion, salt and black and Cayenne pepper and cook until onion is soft. Cook ground beef in a skillet with 2 tablespoons of oil until seared, separating with a fork. Remove beef to paper towelling to absorb excess fat. Heat remaining oil for deep-fat frying in a 2½ to 3-quart saucepan. Combine tomato mixture, ground beef and rice. Fill pepper cups with mixture. Replace pepper tops and tie securely with twine. Combine eggs, milk and flour. Dip the stuffed peppers, one at a time, in the batter. Fat should be heated to 390°F., and a deep-fry pan with basket used. Place 3 peppers at a time in the basket; immerse in hot fat and fry until they are golden brown. Remove; drain and keep in a warm place until all peppers are cooked. Serve with a thin tomato sauce. Yield: 6 servings.

GUINEA

Guinea, a land of about 95,000 square miles on the coast of West Africa, was a former overseas territory of France, and French is still spoken widely, throughout the country. The nation's economy is largely based on agriculture: bananas, coffee, palm products and peanuts are the cash crops. Because of abundant hydroelectric power, the mining and processing of bauxite is of increasing importance. Guinea joined the UN on December 12, 1958.

Kansiyé

GUINEAN GOULASH

1 pound beef or lamb, or a
  small chicken
3 tablespoons oil
1 large onion, chopped
½ teaspoon salt
⅛ teaspoon black pepper
⅛ teaspoon thyme

2 cloves garlic, minced
1 tablespoon minced parsley
1 whole clove, ground
1 6-ounce can tomato sauce
3 cups water
3 tablespoons smooth peanut
  butter

Cut beef or lamb into 1-inch cubes; if chicken is used, cut into
serving pieces. Brown meat in oil in 10-inch frying pan. Add
onion, salt, pepper, thyme, garlic, parsley and clove. Combine
tomato sauce and 2 cups water; add to seasoned meat and mix
well. Dilute peanut butter with remaining water and add to mixture. Cook over medium heat for 1 hour or until meat is tender.
(Small chicken may cook more quickly than beef or lamb; total
amount of water may be reduced to 2½ cups.) Serve hot over
rice. Yield: 4 servings.

GUYANA

*Guyana, a country adjoining Venezuela on the North
Atlantic coast of South America, and formerly the colony of British Guiana, gained independence in 1966.
On September 20 of that year Guyana was admitted to
the UN. In the late sixteenth century, Sir Walter Raleigh
led expeditions into the interior searching for gold. At
a later period the country was occupied by the Dutch.
The people are of diverse backgrounds; the majority
are descendants of East Indian and Negro sugar plantations workers, and the minority groups include Chinese and Portuguese.*

Coo Coo

OKRA AND CORNMEAL MUSH

1 cup okra, sliced	¼ pound cooked corned beef,
2–3 cups water	diced
1 teaspoon salt	1 tablespoon butter
1 cup cornmeal	

Place okra in a saucepan with 1 cup of salted water and boil until soft, 15 to 25 minutes. Mix the cornmeal with 1 cup of water and add to the boiling okra; add corned beef. Cook until thick and smooth. Add more water if mixture seems dry. Butter a mold and pour mixture into it. Bake in a preheated 350°F. oven for ½ hour before serving. Yield: 4 servings.

HAITI

Haiti occupies the western third of an island it shares with the Dominican Republic. Haitians are mainly of African Negro origin. The official language is French as a result of Haiti's former status as a colony of France, although French rule ended in 1804. There is a touch of French also in much of the cooking, but the native beans and rice dish is the backbone of all dinners. Unfortunately, only a third of Haiti's land can be cultivated, and that land is densely populated. Haiti joined the UN on October 24, 1945.

Soupe au Giraumon

VEGETABLE SOUP

1 pound chicken breasts	1 rib celery, sliced
1 1-pound ham hock	1 cup rice
1 cup orange juice	1 onion, sliced and cooked in
2 teaspoons salt	1 tablespoon butter
½ pound summer squash, sliced	3 cloves
	1 tablespoon cider vinegar
2 carrots, sliced	½ pound spaghetti, broken in
1 small head cabbage, shredded	2-inch lengths

Soak chicken and ham hock in orange juice for 1 hour, turning often. Remove chicken and ham; rub in salt. Place in a 5-quart soup kettle; fill with water to within 1 inch of top. Bring to a boil and simmer 2½ to 3 hours; skim top. Add squash, carrots, cabbage, celery and rice; simmer about 25 minutes or until vegetables are tender. Remove meats; strain vegetables from liquid and return liquid to kettle. Add water to liquid to make 3 quarts; bring to a boil; add cooked onion, cloves, vinegar and spaghetti. Boil for about 10 minutes or until spaghetti is done. Taste for seasoning and correct, if necessary. Serve the meat and vegetables separately from the soup or return to the soup after the spaghetti is tender and serve together as a stew. Yield: 6–8 servings.

Plat National

BEANS AND RICE

1 cup dried pinto or kidney beans	1 tablespoon minced parsley
3 cups water	6 tablespoons bacon fat
1¾ teaspoons salt	½ teaspoon black pepper
1 clove garlic, minced	¼ teaspoon ground cloves
1 onion, chopped	1 cup rice

Wash beans. Add water, cover and boil 5 minutes; remove from heat, add salt and let soak 1 hour. Sauté garlic, onion and parsley in bacon fat; add pepper and cloves. Drain the beans, reserving liquid. Sauté beans in fat for 5 minutes. Measure the bean water and add sufficient water to make 5½ cups. Add water to beans and cook for 1 to 1½ hours, or until beans begin to soften. Then add rice to beans and continue cooking until rice is done, about 14 minutes. (If mixture becomes dry before the rice is done, add hot water.) Pour bean-and-rice mixture into a well-oiled 2-quart casserole and bake in a preheated 250°F. oven for 30 minutes. Yield: 8 servings.

Gâteau Pommes de Terre

GOLDEN BEEF-POTATO PIE

1 pound potatoes
3 tablespoons butter
½ cup hot milk
1 tablespoon mayonnaise
1½ cups grated Cheddar
 cheese
1 pound ground beef
1 clove garlic, minced

2 tablespoons lemon juice
1 teaspoon salt
Black pepper to taste
2 teaspoons finely chopped
 parsley
2 tablespoons oil
2 tablespoons tomato paste

Cook potatoes in their skins until tender; peel; mash with 1 table-spoon of the butter. Add milk gradually to make a light, firm purée. Add mayonnaise and 2 tablespoons grated cheese. Season the ground beef with garlic, lemon juice, salt, pepper and parsley. Mix well. Heat oil in a large, heavy skillet; add seasoned beef and sauté for about 5 minutes, stirring frequently. Add tomato paste and remaining butter and continue cooking for 10 minutes, stirring frequently. Remove from heat. In a greased 2-quart casserole, place one layer of mashed potatoes, a layer of the sautéed beef and a layer of the grated cheese. Continue layering, making sure the last layer is grated cheese. Bake in a preheated 350°F. oven for 25 to 30 minutes, until it is heated thoroughly and the cheese is melted. Yield: 6 servings.

Tassau

VEAL CUTLETS

12 veal cutlets, thinly sliced
1 cup warm water
¼ teaspoon garlic powder
⅛ teaspoon thyme
2 tablespoons finely chopped
 parsley

⅛ teaspoon black pepper
1 teaspoon sugar
½ teaspoon salt
½ cup orange juice
½ cup lemonade
4 tablespoons oil

Pound cutlets with mallet. Add cutlets to water. Mix garlic powder, thyme, parsley, pepper, sugar and salt with orange juice; stir this mixture and lemonade into the cutlets-and-water mixture.

Cover; marinate in refrigerator for at least 4 hours. Remove cutlets; drain and brown in hot oil in heavy frying pan. If desired, pour marinade sauce into frying pan, place over low heat (loosening browned bits adhering to pan), reduce till thickened, and serve as a sauce with the cutlets. Yield: 6 servings.

Aubergines en Peau

STUFFED EGGPLANT

1 eggplant, cut in half
  lengthwise
Water
2 tablespoons diced onion
2 teaspoons butter
2 slices stale bread soaked in
  ½ cup milk, squeezed dry

2 tablespoons condensed
  cream of chicken soup
Salt
Black pepper
1 egg, lightly beaten
6 tablespoons grated Cheddar
  cheese
½ cup buttered bread crumbs

Cover eggplant halves with water and boil for 3 minutes. Drain. Remove pulp, leave enough with skin of eggplant to make a firm shell. Dice pulp and cook with onion in hot butter for 5 minutes; add bread, chicken soup and salt and pepper to taste, and continue cooking for 5 minutes more. Remove from heat; stir in egg and 3 tablespoons of the cheese. Fill the eggplant shells with the mixture; sprinkle with remaining cheese and bread crumbs. Place filled shells in greased casserole and bake for 25 minutes in a preheated 350°F. oven. Yield: 4 servings.

HONDURAS

Honduras was reached by Christopher Columbus on his final voyage in 1502. Its capital, Tegucigalpa, was the result of an influx of prospectors when silver was discovered there in 1570. Silver is still a source of its wealth. Two out of three Hondurans are engaged in agriculture, raising bananas, coffee, sugar cane, corn, beans and rice. Honduras is currently in an industrial development program to build roads and to tap the rich hydroelectric power offered by its rivers. On December 17, 1945, Honduras entered the UN.

Pollo Hondureño

HONDURAN CHICKEN

2 cloves garlic, minced
4 tablespoons olive oil or cooking fat
1 3- to 4-pound roasting chicken, cut up
2 tomatoes, peeled and cubed

2 large pimientos, cut in strips
2 tablespoons capers
12 stuffed olives, halved
½ teaspoon salt
¼ teaspoon black pepper
¼ cup tomato juice

Brown the garlic in hot oil. Add the chicken and brown all pieces well, turning as necessary. When well browned, add the tomatoes, pimientos, capers, olives, salt, pepper and tomato juice. Cover and simmer over low heat 1½ hours or until tender. Yield: 6 servings.

Arroz con Pollo

CHICKEN WITH RICE

1 3-pound chicken, quartered
1 teaspoon salt
2 cups water
1 large onion, quartered
1 clove garlic, minced
1 teaspoon caraway seeds
½ cup tomato paste
1 cup rice

2 tablespoons oil
1 cup pitted black olives, sliced
1 cup canned peas
1 carrot, diced
1 cup beer or white wine
2 cups finely shredded cabbage
½ cup capers

Cook chicken in salted water with onion, garlic, caraway seeds and tomato paste until chicken is tender, about 45 minutes. Remove chicken from broth and cool; skin, bone and mince chicken. Fry rice in hot oil in heavy saucepan until golden brown; add chicken, broth, olives, peas and carrot. Add beer or wine to cover mixture; bring to boil and simmer until rice is almost done, about 10 minutes. Add the cabbage and capers; continue simmering for 10 minutes more. Yield: 6–8 servings.

HUNGARY

Hungary (a member of the UN family since December 14, 1955) has been an important influence on her neighbors' cuisines, but none uses the distinctive, mild paprika with so much zest—notably in the famous goulash or gulyás. Other favorite Hungarian culinary ingredients include sour cream, goose fat and goose liver, caraway seeds and poppy seeds. Tokay, the sweet, rich wine of Hungary, is internationally known.

Szekely Gulyás

PORK AND SAUERKRAUT STEW

3 large onions, chopped	2 pounds shoulder of pork
2 tablespoons lard or other fat	1 teaspoon salt
2 cloves garlic, minced	2 pounds sauerkraut
1 teaspoon caraway seeds	Water
1 tablespoon paprika	2 teaspoons flour
1 cup water	1 pint sour cream

Cook onions in fat in Dutch oven or 12-inch frying pan until yellow. Add garlic, caraway seeds, paprika and water; bring to a boil. Add meat and salt. Cover and simmer for 1 hour. Add sauerkraut and enough water to cover. Cook about 45 minutes or until meat is tender; stir occasionally. Blend flour and sour cream; add to the stew and simmer for 5 minutes. Serve with buttered noodles. Yield: 8 servings.

Töltött Kaposzta

STUFFED CABBAGE

1 large head cabbage	1 teaspoon black pepper
Boiling water	1 tablespoon paprika
¾ pound ground pork	1 cup rice
¾ pound ground beef	2½ cups sauerkraut
½ cup finely chopped onion	2½ cups tomato juice
1 egg, beaten	3 cups water
2 tablespoons salt	1 cup sour cream

Core the cabbage and place head down in enough boiling water to cover. Turn off heat. When cabbage has wilted remove from water and peel the leaves off, leaving them whole. Trim heavy vein down to make leaf flat. Combine meat, onion, egg, seasonings and rice. Mix well. In the center of each cabbage leaf place 2 to 3 tablespoons of the mixture. Fold sides in first then roll up. Place in large kettle and spread sauerkraut over the rolls. Add the tomato juice and water. Bring to a boil, then simmer for 1½ hours. Place cabbage rolls on serving dish. Mix a little of the liquid with the sour cream and pour over the cabbage rolls. Yield: 8 servings.

Paprikás Csirke Galuskaval

CHICKEN PAPRIKA WITH DUMPLINGS

½ cup finely chopped onion	*Galuska (Dumplings):*
¼ cup shortening	3 eggs, well beaten
1 tablespoon salt	6½ cups water
1 tablespoon paprika	2½ cups sifted flour
½ teaspoon black pepper	3 teaspoons salt
1 3- to 4-pound roasting chicken, cut up	1 cup sour cream
1½ cups water	

Sauté the onion in the shortening until tender but not browned. Combine the salt, paprika and black pepper and stir into the onions. Add the chicken and fry until all sides are slightly brown. Add water and cover pan. Cook slowly about 1½ hours or until chicken is tender.

To make dumplings: mix eggs, ½ cup water, flour and 2 tea-spoons salt and beat until dough is smooth. Pour remaining water into a 3-quart saucepan, add remaining salt, and bring to a boil. Into this spoon the batter, 1 teaspoonful at a time. Boil 10 minutes; drain.

Remove chicken from skillet and blend the sour cream into the liquid in the skillet. Put dumplings in the sauce and serve hot with the chicken. Yield: 6 servings.

Csokoládé Mignon

CHOCOLATE CAKE SQUARES

¼ cup butter
½ cup sugar
4 eggs, separated
2 squares (2 ounces)
   unsweetened chocolate
1 tablespoon cocoa
¼ cup flour, sifted
2 tablespoons almonds,
   finely ground

Filling:
½ cup apricot or other jam
2 tablespoons rum

Mocha Frosting:
4 tablespoons butter
½ tablespoon cocoa
1¾ cups confectioners' sugar
2 tablespoons strong coffee
½ teaspoon vanilla extract

Cream butter with ¼ cup sugar until fluffy. Add the egg yolks, one by one, beating well after each addition. Melt the chocolate, blend in cocoa and add to egg-and-butter mixture, beating well. Beat the egg whites until stiff and gradually fold the remaining ¼ cup of sugar into them. Fold egg whites into chocolate mixture and blend in flour and almonds. Pour into an oiled and floured 8-inch cake pan or an oblong pan. Bake in a preheated 350°F. oven for 20 to 25 minutes or until done. When done, invert over cake rack and cool.

To make filling: Mix jam and rum. Cut cake into two thin layers, and spread top of bottom layer with filling. Replace top layer. Cut cake in 2-inch squares.

To make mocha frosting: Cream the butter; combine cocoa and sugar. Add mixture of cocoa and sugar gradually to butter, alternating with coffee. Add vanilla and blend until creamy. Spread tops and sides of cake squares with the frosting. Yield: 16 2-inch squares.

ICELAND

Iceland founded the first parliament in the world at Thingveller in A.D. *930. Her people are descendants of the Norwegian Vikings, and their highly reputed physical strength has stood them in good stead in a rugged, barren terrain, less than 1 percent of which is cultivated. Fishing, ship building and other related activities are extremely important to the present economy, which is now well on its way to prosperous industrial development. In 1944 Iceland became an independent nation, joining the UN on November 19, 1946.*

Fiskibudingur

FISH SOUFFLÉ

1 pound fish (cod, haddock or red snapper)	1 teaspoon salt
Water	Few grains freshly ground black pepper
½ cup butter	6 eggs, separated
1 cup sifted flour	1 tablespoon soft butter
1½ cups milk	½ cup bread crumbs

Simmer the fish in a small amount of water until tender. Remove skin and bones. Break into rather thick flakes. Melt the butter in a saucepan; add flour and stir until smooth. Add milk and cook until very thick. Season with salt and pepper. Cool sauce. Add egg yolks and beat well. Combine the fish and sauce and fold the beaten egg whites into the fish mixture. Pour mixture into a buttered 2-quart casserole coated with bread crumbs. Sprinkle remaining bread crumbs over the top and bake in a preheated 375°F. oven for 55 minutes. Yield: 6–8 servings.

Note: 1-inch-thick slices of cold leftover soufflé are sautéed in butter and served for breakfast in Iceland.

Pönnukökur

PANCAKES

½ cup milk   1 cup flour, sifted
2 eggs   Butter, for browning
2–3 tablespoons butter,   Jam
   melted   Whipped cream
2 teaspoons vanilla extract

Add ¼ cup of the milk to the eggs. Stir this mixture, the melted butter, and the vanilla into the flour. Add enough of the remaining milk to make a batter as thick as heavy cream. Cover the bottom of a hot, very lightly buttered 5- or 6-inch skillet with a thin layer of batter by tilting the skillet slightly. Brown pancake lightly on both sides. Spread 1 teaspoon of jam and 1 tablespoon of whipped cream over pancakes. Fold twice and remove to a warm serving plate. Yield: 6 servings.

Potatoes Browned in Sugar

2 pounds white potatoes   ¼ cup butter
   (see Note)   ½ cup sugar
Boiling salted water   Salt, optional

Scrub potatoes. Cover with boiling salted water (2 teaspoons salt to 1 quart of water). Cover and boil gently until tender when tested with steel fork. Drain off the water. Remove skin with a sharp paring knife.

Brown butter in a large preheated frying pan. Add sugar to butter over low heat. Watch mixture closely and when it becomes frothy, add the potatoes at once. Turn repeatedly until the potatoes become light brown and are well coated with butter and sugar mixture. Taste and add salt, if necessary. Yield: 6 servings.

Note: Select potatoes of uniform size for cooking whole so that cooking time will be the same for all. Small new potatoes are preferable for this recipe. If large potatoes are used, cut in ½-inch slices after removing skin.

INDIA

India is famous for her curries. Contrary to the impression of many Westerners, all curries are not fiery hot. In India, the spices for making any curry dish are ground on a stone just before the dish is made, and the variety of spices for each curry differs. Indians do not use the curry powder that they export to the West. If you are planning to have Indian guests, remember that Hindus do not eat beef and Moslems do not eat pork, and that many Indians are strict vegetarians. India joined the UN on October 30, 1945.

Pakoras

FRIED APPETIZERS

1 cup yellow split peas	½ cup finely chopped onions
2 cups boiling water	½ cup finely chopped green
½ cup sifted flour	pepper
1 teaspoon curry powder	½ cup finely chopped celery
⅛ teaspoon allspice	1 teaspoon dried mint
1 teaspoon salt	Fine dry bread crumbs
⅛ teaspoon Tabasco sauce	Fat for deep-fat frying

Add the split peas to the boiling water in a 2-quart saucepan and simmer until peas are tender but not mushy, 2 to 3 hours. Drain thoroughly. Cool. Sift together the flour, curry powder, allspice and salt, and stir into the cooled, cooked peas. Add the Tabasco sauce, onions, green pepper, celery and mint. Drop the mixture by teaspoonfuls onto the bread crumbs and roll around to cover all sides. Deep-fat fry 6 or 7 of the balls at a time at 370°F. for 2 or 3 minutes, or until brown. Serve hot with the following mint chutney. Yield: 8 servings.

Pudiina Chutney

MINT CHUTNEY

1 cup firmly packed fresh mint
leaves
1 cup finely chopped onion
1 medium tomato, finely
chopped

4 tablespoons lemon juice
½ teaspoon salt
Dash of Tabasco sauce

Wash the mint leaves and chop very fine. Combine with all other ingredients. Yield: 2 cups.

Shrimp Bhaji

CURRIED SHRIMP

2 medium onions, ground
1 teaspoon minced garlic
¼ cup peanut oil
½ teaspoon crushed ginger
root or ¼ teaspoon ground
ginger
1 cup chopped fresh tomato
1 teaspoon vinegar

1 teaspoon salt
½ teaspoon chili powder
1 teaspoon curry powder
⅛ teaspoon turmeric
½ cup water
2 pounds cooked shrimp,
shelled, deveined and cut in
½-inch pieces

Combine onions and garlic and cook in hot peanut oil until golden brown. Stir the ginger, tomato, vinegar, salt, chili powder, curry powder, turmeric and water into the onion-and-garlic mixture. Stir only until blended; cover and simmer sauce for 10 minutes or until mixture is slightly thickened. Add shrimp to sauce; simmer for 5 minutes. Serve with boiled rice. Yield: 6 servings.

Bengali Kurma Mahi

BENGAL FISH CURRY

2 dried chili peppers, finely crushed

1 teaspoon turmeric

1 teaspoon salt

2 pounds halibut steak, cut in 1-inch cubes

3 tablespoons vegetable oil

Curry Sauce:

1 teaspoon coriander seeds

1 teaspoon cardamom seeds

1 teaspoon cumin seeds

2 teaspoons mustard seeds

2 pounds onions

1 teaspoon turmeric

½ teaspoon cinnamon

½ teaspoon chili powder

1 teaspoon salt

4 cloves garlic

¼ cup oil

1 pound tomatoes, peeled and sliced

1 cup yogurt, beaten

Mix chili peppers, turmeric and salt together. Sprinkle over halibut cubes and coat well. Heat oil in large frying pan and brown the fish on all sides. Remove fish from pan, drain and set aside.

To make curry sauce: Grind together coriander, cardamom, cumin and mustard seeds with half the onions. Add the turmeric, cinnamon, chili powder and salt to the ground onion-and-spice mixture. Slice remaining onions and cook with garlic in oil in frying pan until brown. Add the ground onion-and-spice mixture and the tomatoes to the browned onions and garlic. Cook gently until tomatoes are tender, about 10 minutes. Add yogurt and cook over medium heat for 5 minutes more.

Add fried fish to curry sauce and simmer for 10 minutes. Remove garlic. Serve hot with Tomato Chutney (page 108). Yield: 6 servings.

Note: For recipe to serve 50, see LARGE-SCALE BUFFET MENUS section, page 261.

Aam Ki Chutney

TOMATO CHUTNEY

3 dried chili peppers
5 cloves garlic
1 1-inch piece green ginger, peeled
1 cup vinegar

1 pound tomatoes, peeled and sliced
1 teaspoon salt
2 cups sugar

Grind the chili peppers, garlic and ginger, and put in heavy saucepan. Add vinegar, tomatoes, salt and sugar. Simmer gently for 2 to 3 hours or until mixture is thick. Yield: 2 cups.

Yakhni

SPICED LAMB

6 cups warm water
2 pounds lamb, cubed
3 whole cardamom seeds
2 whole cloves
1 1-inch cinnamon stick, broken

½ teaspoon whole black pepper
1 cup yogurt
1 tablespoon ginger powder
3 tablespoons coriander powder
Salt

Put the water in a saucepan. Add lamb, cardamom, cloves, cinnamon and black pepper. Cook until meat is tender and the liquid is reduced to 4 cups, about 1½ hours. Beat the yogurt well and add to the meat. Bring to a boil; add ginger, coriander and salt to taste and simmer for about 15 minutes. Yield: 4–6 servings.

Poori

TASTY BREAD

1 cup whole wheat flour
1 cup white flour, sifted
1 tablespoon vegetable oil

¾ cup ice water
1 pint vegetable oil

Blend the flours; add oil and mix with a fork. Gradually add ice water to make a stiff dough. Form into a firm ball and let stand for ½ hour. Place dough on lightly floured board and knead vigorously for 5 minutes. Pinch off balls of dough about the size of a walnut. Roll each ball into a thin circle about 3 inches wide. Fry in 1½ inches of very hot fat, 350° to 375°F. As each *poori* is placed in the fat, press the back of a tablespoon in the center and turn in a light, rapid, circular motion until the dough puffs. Turn and fry the other side until delicately browned. Cook one at a time. Drain on paper towels and serve hot. Yield: 2 dozen.

Dosa

PANCAKES

½ cup *urad dal,* or dried split peas	Water
1 cup rice	1 teaspoon mustard seed
Water	1 tablespoon vegetable oil
1 teaspoon salt	1 medium onion, chopped
	2 green chilis, chopped
Oil	1 tablespoon parsley
	½ teaspoon salt

Masala (Potato Filling):
3 medium potatoes

Preparation for this food should be started the morning of the day previous to its use. Place the *dal* and rice in separate bowls; cover with water and soak at least 8 hours. Drain and wash the *dal;* drain the rice and save 1 cup of the rice water. Blend the *dal* and rice separately until creamy, in an electric blender, if possible; use rice water as necessary while blending to keep the blades moving. Combine the *dal,* rice and salt. Cover and keep at room temperature for about 5 hours. When bubbles appear, mix well. (This batter can be kept for 2 days in the refrigerator.)

Heat a large skillet or electric frying pan on medium heat (325°F.). Brush a thin layer of oil on the surface. Reduce heat to low and pour a very thin layer of batter into the pan to make a pancake about 8 inches in diameter. Spread batter with a spoon or pastry brush and thin with a little water if necessary. Cover pan and cook over low heat for 5 minutes; it should have bubbles on the surface and be golden brown underneath. Turn the cake and cook for 3 to 5 minutes longer or until golden brown. Repeat.

To make masala filling: Boil potatoes in water to cover; when tender, peel and mash slightly. Fry mustard seed in hot oil until seeds start crackling; add onion and chilis. Stir over medium heat until the onion is transparent. Add the potatoes, stirring until heated. Remove from heat. Stir in parsley and salt.

Place 2 tablespoons of *masala* filling on each pancake; roll pancakes and serve hot (pancakes may be reheated in the oven). Yield: 6 servings.

INDONESIA

Indonesia has an unusual history within the UN; it joined the organization originally on September 28, 1950, but withdrew in January 1965 in opposition to the admission of Malaysia to the UN. It rejoined on September 28, 1966. It is an extraordinary country geographically, consisting of over 3,000 islands that stretch 8,000 miles east and west, 1,500 miles north to south. In population Indonesia ranks fifth in the world. Inhabited since prehistoric times, it was occupied over centuries by many small Indian, Malayan, Buddhist and Hindu kingdoms. The Portuguese were the first Europeans to control the area and the Dutch the last.

Semur

NOODLE STEW

1 3–4-pound stewing chicken or 2–3 pounds beef
Salt
Black pepper
¼ cup butter
2 large potatoes, peeled
2 cloves garlic, minced
1 teaspoon nutmeg

½ teaspoon powdered cloves or 4 whole cloves
4 tablespoons soy sauce
1–2 cups water
¼ pound transparent Chinese noodles (cellophane noodles)

Cut up chicken or beef as for a stew. Sprinkle with salt and pepper; then sear in butter. Add potatoes and all other ingredients except noodles and cook 2 to 3 hours. During the last 15 to 20 minutes of cooking, add noodles; add additional water, if necessary. Serve with hot rice. Yield: 6 servings.

IRAN

Iran, the former ancient empire of Persia, has existed as a nation for 2,000 years. The land is rich in oil, but most of the population is engaged in agricultural pursuits. Rug weaving, deftly painted miniatures and great pottery reveal Persian artistry, which is in turn reflected in the country cuisine. Of course, Iranian caviar is a natural attribute, but the Iranian treatment of rice is a great culinary contribution to all the Middle East and beyond. Iran became a member of the UN on October 24, 1945.

Khoreshe Karafs

BEEF-CELERY SAUCE

1 large onion, finely chopped
4 tablespoons butter
1½ pounds lean beef, cut in 1-inch cubes
1 teaspoon salt
½ teaspoon black pepper

1 teaspoon cinnamon
½ teaspoon nutmeg
¾ cup water
4 cups diced celery
1 cup chopped parsley
3 tablespoons lemon juice

Cook onion in 2 tablespoons butter in large frying pan until yellow. Remove onion from butter. Add beef, salt, pepper, cinnamon and nutmeg to butter and cook over low heat until meat is brown. Add water and cooked onions; cover and simmer until meat is tender, 1 to 1½ hours.

Melt remaining butter in another large frying pan and sauté celery and parsley for 10 minutes. Add celery and parsley mixture and lemon juice to the beef mixture and simmer for 15 minutes. Serve with *Chelo* (see following recipe) or steamed rice. Yield: 6 servings.

Chelo

GOLDEN RICE

1⅓ cups long-grain white rice   ¼ cup melted butter
2 teaspoons salt   1 tablespoon water
1 quart boiling water

Add rice and salt to water. Stir, cover, and reduce to low heat.
Cook for 15 minutes; drain in colander or sieve and rinse with
lukewarm water. Place half of the melted butter in a Dutch oven
or similarly heavy pan with a lid. Add the tablespoon of water and
spoon rice over bottom of pan and pile up in the shape of a cone.
Pour remainder of melted butter over the rice. Place several layers
of paper toweling over the top of the cooking utensil and cover
with tight-fitting lid. Cook for 10 to 15 minutes over medium heat
in order that rice may form a crisp, golden brown crust on the
bottom of the pan. Reduce heat and cook for 35 to 40 minutes.
More butter may be added before serving. Yield: 6 servings.

Morg Polo

CHICKEN WITH GOLDEN RICE

1 recipe *Chelo* (above)   ¼ teaspoon black pepper
1 large onion, finely chopped   3 pounds choice pieces of
6½ tablespoons butter   chicken
1 teaspoon poultry seasoning   ⅔ cup seedless raisins
¼ teaspoon cinnamon   ½ cup dried chopped apricots
1 teaspoon salt

Begin preparation of *chelo.*
    Cook chopped onion in 5 tablespoons butter until golden; re-
move onion. Mix poultry seasoning, cinnamon, salt and pepper,
and sprinkle over chicken. Brown seasoned chicken in butter remaining from cooking onions. Wash raisins and chopped apricots
and soak in cold water to cover for 5 minutes. Drain well and
cook over low heat in 1½ tablespoons butter for 5 minutes.
    When *chelo* is ready to be placed in butter in heavy pan, pro-
ceed according to directions until half of rice has been placed in
pan. Arrange chicken, onions and dried fruit over rice. Place re-

maining half of rice on top of mound and add butter as directed
for *chelo*. Cover top of utensil with paper toweling and with a
close-fitting lid. Follow directions for completing *chelo*. Yield: 6
servings.

IRAQ

*Iraq is based on the site of ancient Mesopotamia, the
area of the oldest-known civilization, which flourished
in 3000* B.C. *From this rich historical past there remain
excavations, mosques, tombs, ruins, the famous Hang-
ing Gardens and the Lion of Babylon to make this exotic
land a great tourist and archaeological mecca. Most
Iraqis are Arab, mainly employed in oil, with which
Iraq is greatly endowed. On December 21, 1945, Iraq
was admitted to the UN.*

Kubba Shalgum

TURNIP SOUP WITH MEATBALLS

5 turnips, peeled and sliced
1 large onion, chopped
2 tablespoons fat
8 cups water
1½ teaspoons salt
4 tablespoons tomato paste
2 pounds ground lean beef
1 cup plus 2 tablespoons
  farina, uncooked
Water

1½ pounds ground lamb
  shoulder
1 cup minced onion
¼ cup minced parsley
1 tablespoon butter
½ cup raisins
½ cup blanched almonds,
  sliced
⅓ cup lemon juice
6 spinach leaves or sprigs of
  parsley

Cook turnips and onion in hot fat in large heavy saucepan or
Dutch oven until onions are yellow. Add the water, salt and tomato
paste; bring to a boil and boil for 15 minutes. Reduce heat and
simmer for 30 minutes.

Combine the beef, 1 cup farina, and sufficient water to mold mixture with your hands. Set aside. Mix the lamb, onion and parsley; cook in butter until meat is brown and thoroughly cooked. Add raisins and almonds and mix with lamb.

Divide the mixture of beef and farina into 4 equal portions; divide each of these into 6 equal portions. Flatten each portion into about a 3-inch round or patty. Place 1 teaspoon of lamb mixture in the center of each patty. Shape into balls, keeping the lamb within the beef-rice mixture.

Add the remaining 2 tablespoons of uncooked farina, the lemon juice and spinach leaves or sprigs of parsley to the soup. Return soup to simmering point. Drop meatballs into the soup and simmer, uncovered, for 25 minutes. Serve soup with meatballs while piping hot. Yield: 8 servings.

Dolmas

MEAT AND VEGETABLE ROLLS

1½ cups rice	2 green peppers
1½ pounds ground lamb	1 large Spanish onion
½ cup butter, softened	½ teaspoon salt
1 teaspoon salt	½ cup tomato juice
¼ teaspoon black pepper	Water
½ cup water	1 tablespoon lemon juice
1 large cabbage	1 teaspoon sugar
Boiling water	

Mix rice with lamb and butter. Add salt, pepper and ½ cup water. Mix well. Remove cabbage leaves carefully from head. Wilt leaves in boiling water for 5 minutes. Remove center stem of each leaf and cut leaf in two. Place 1 tablespoon of meat mixture on each half leaf and roll into shape of cigar.

Cut tops off peppers; remove seeds. Fill peppers ¾ full of meat and rice. Cut off top of onion and slit 1 side. Wilt onion in boiling water sufficiently to remove each layer without breaking. Roll 1 teaspoon meat-and-rice mixture in each large onion leaf.

Place filled cabbage and onion leaves in alternate layers in deep skillet with green peppers in center. Add salt, tomato juice and water to cover. Press a plate on the *dolmas* to keep them from bursting while boiling; cover. Boil 15 minutes. Remove plate and sprinkle with lemon juice and sugar. Cover again and simmer 45 minutes. Yield: 6–8 servings.

Bulgur

CRACKED WHEAT

3½ cups cold water	2 medium eggplants
¼ pound butter	1 onion, chopped
1 teaspoon salt	2 tablespoons fat
1 pound bulgur, washed	½ cup chopped parsley

Bring the water to boiling point and add butter and salt. Slowly add the bulgur. Boil until most of the water is absorbed; cover and simmer slowly for 1 hour.

Peel the eggplants; cut into 1½-inch squares. Cook eggplants and onion in the fat until soft. Add the parsley to the eggplant-and-onion mixture; fold into the hot bulgur and serve as vegetable. Yield: 8 servings.

Note: Bulgur, a staple food in the Middle East, is available in parts of the U.S. as Redi-Wheat and as cracked wheat, as well as under its own name. It may be used in the same way as rice.

IRELAND

Ireland joined the UN on December 14, 1955, seven years after cutting her ties with the British Commonwealth. The official language is Irish, a Celtic Indo-European language (also called Gaelic or Erse), although English is universally spoken. Ireland exports dairy products and meat, including the famous Irish bacon, as well as Irish whisky, an essential component of the popular "Irish coffee."

Grilled Stuffed Trout

2 1½-pound trout, dressed
  and boned
4 tablespoons butter, melted
½ teaspoon salt
¼ teaspoon black pepper

1 cup minced parsley
⅓ cup chives
¾ teaspoon basil
1½ teaspoons lemon juice
2 tablespoons grated lemon

Stuffing:
1½ cups coarsely diced
  shallots

Lemon slices

Rinse the trout under cold water; dry with absorbent paper; brush the inside of each fish with 1 tablespoon of melted butter and sprinkle with salt and pepper.

To make the stuffing: Combine the shallots, parsley, chives and basil; sauté in remaining butter until shallots are tender. Add lemon juice and rind to the mixture.

Fill each fish with half of the stuffing. Place the stuffed fish in a well-greased baking pan; bake in a preheated 375°F. oven for 25 minutes or until the fish is tender. Garnish with lemon. Yield: 6 servings.

Sole Atchen

STUFFED FILLET OF SOLE SUPREME

¾ cup mushrooms, button or
  sliced
2 teaspoons chopped chives
¼ cup chopped fennel
½ cup butter

¼ teaspoon salt
6 cooked shrimp, chopped
½ cup heavy cream
2 pounds sole fillets

Cook mushrooms, chives and fennel in hot butter until mushrooms are done; add salt and shrimp. Continue cooking for 5 minutes; add cream; reduce heat and stir until cream is absorbed.

Place half the fillets in a shallow, greased baking dish; place stuffing on each fillet, then place a matching fillet on top of stuffing. Bake in a preheated 375°F. oven for 25 to 30 minutes. Yield: 6 servings.

Curaimir

VENISON CUTLETS

2½ pounds venison cutlets	½ teaspoon salt
1 pint elderberry wine	¼ teaspoon black pepper
4 tablespoons butter	½ pound mushrooms, button
3 tomatoes, halved	or sliced
¼ cup flour	

Marinate venison in wine overnight or for at least 3 hours. Drain and pan-fry in hot butter until meat is tender and brown. Remove meat to serving platter; add ½ cup of wine used for marinating to pan in which cutlets were cooked. Simmer to loosen bits of browned meat adhering to pan and pour hot sauce over cutlets.

Dredge tomatoes in flour seasoned with salt and pepper; arrange on a greased shallow pan with mushrooms. Place under broiler until surface is brown, then in hot oven for 3 to 5 minutes to complete cooking. Serve with venison. Yield: 6 servings.

ISRAEL

Israel today is a country of contrasts, the new side by side with historical evidence of past centuries. Verdant farms and orchards thrive where once there were swamps and deserts. New types of villages have been settled, especially the famous kibbutzim where the community owns the land and equipment. Modern factories have risen, and beautiful museums, the Israel Philharmonic, National Opera, and Habima Theatre provide cultural background. Vegetables and dairy foods are most popular with the Israelis. Israel became a member of the UN on May 11, 1949.

Boureka

MEAT SQUARES

3 cups flour
1 teaspoon salt
½ pound margarine
2 tablespoons oil
½ cup water

Filling:
1 onion, finely diced
2 tablespoons oil
1 pound ground lean beef

¼ teaspoon black pepper
1 teaspoon salt
½ teaspoon allspice
2 tablespoons chopped parsley
2 tomatoes, peeled and diced
½ cup ground or finely chopped nuts

1 egg, beaten
½ cup sesame seeds

Blend flour, salt and margarine together until mixture is similar to cornmeal; mix in oil and water; form dough into a ball. Place on wooden board; cover with a bowl; set aside for 2 to 3 hours. Divide dough in half; roll first half out on a cookie sheet into a 12-inch square.

To make filling: Sauté onion in hot oil in a 10-inch frying pan until onion is limp. Add beef and all other ingredients listed up to the nuts; cook until meat is thoroughly cooked and dry. Drain off all excess fat. Stir nuts into meat mixture; cool.

Spread filling evenly over the rolled-out square. Roll second half into a 12-inch square; place carefully on top of filling and press down gently. Brush top with egg; sprinkle with sesame seeds and cut into 36 squares. Bake in a preheated 350°F. oven for 30 minutes or until tops are brown. Serve as appetizers. Yield: 36 2-inch squares.

Levivot Gevina

CHEESE STEAKS

1 pound, small-curd pot cheese
2 eggs
4 tablespoons flour

½ teaspoon salt
½ teaspoon red pepper
Approximately 2 tablespoons vegetable shortening

Drain all excess moisture from pot cheese. Mix all ingredients except fat. Heat fat in iron skillet. Divide mixture into portions of 2 to 3 tablespoons each and drop into hot fat. Cook over low heat until golden brown on both sides. Yield: 4 servings.

Nezio Adashim

LENTIL CASSEROLE

1 cup lentils	1 tablespoon shortening
4 cups cold water	2 tablespoons flour
⅔ cup minced onion	2 teaspoons salt
1 tablespoon minced parsley	⅛ teaspoon black pepper
½ clove garlic, minced	2 tablespoons tomato purée
3 tablespoons minced celery	6–8 small beef frankfurters

Wash lentils and soak overnight in water. Drain; reserve lentil liquid. Heat 2 cups of this liquid to boiling point and add lentils, onion, parsley, garlic and celery. Cook until tender (about 1 hour). Drain. Measure lentil-onion-parsley liquid. Put drained lentil mixture into greased casserole.

To the lentil-onion-parsley liquid add enough of the lentil water to make 1¼ cups. Melt shortening in saucepan, add flour, salt and pepper, and stir in the 1¼ cups liquid. Cook until thickened. Pour over lentils, then cover with tomato purée. Arrange sausages in attractive design on the top of the mixture and bake in a preheated 350°F. oven 30 minutes. Yield: 6 servings.

Chocolate Date Nut Pie

1 8-ounce package pitted dates	½ cup chopped nuts
Boiling water	2 cups heavy cream
4 ounces milk chocolate	1 tablespoon sugar
2 tablespoons butter	1 tablespoon cocoa
1 10-ounce angel-food cake broken into small pieces	1 tablespoon instant coffee
	Chocolate for topping

Soak dates in boiling water for 5 minutes; remove from water and mash. Melt chocolate and butter over hot water; stir into the dates. Fold angel-food cake and nuts into chocolate mixture. Pour into 9-inch pie pan and refrigerate. Mix 1 cup cream, the sugar, cocoa and coffee; bring to a boil. Cool and refrigerate overnight. The next day, whip cream mixture until stiff and spread over top of pie. Whip remaining cream and spread over boiled cream mixture. Grate chocolate over top. Yield: 6–8 servings.

ITALY

Italy has many popular recipes that date back to the sixteenth century, a time of high gastronomic achievement in that country. In fact, many so-called traditional French dishes, including "French pastry," owe their origins to Italian chefs, who were brought to the French court by Catherine de' Medici when she became the wife of Henry II of France. Regional cooking is much in evidence, the northern area using a great amount of rice and cornmeal, and more butter than olive oil. Southern Italy is widely known for its tomato, garlic and pasta dishes. Italy is one of the world's largest producers of wine, consuming one third of her output and exporting the rest. Italy has been a member of the UN since December 14, 1955.

Funghi Ripieni

STUFFED MUSHROOMS

12 large mushrooms	1 clove garlic, minced
1 cup bread crumbs	Chicken bouillon
½ teaspoon salt	2 tablespoons olive oil
¼ teaspoon black pepper	½ cup dry white wine
2 tablespoons chopped parsley	

Cut off and chop stems of mushrooms. Combine bread crumbs, chopped stems and seasonings. Add enough bouillon to moisten. Stuff mushroom caps with mixture; brush caps with oil. Place in flat ovenproof dish. Pour wine in dish; bake in a preheated 350°F. oven for about 30 minutes. Baste several times, using additional bouillon or wine if needed. Yield: 6 appetizers.

Note: For recipe to serve 50, see LARGE-SCALE BUFFET MENUS section, page 115.

Carciofi Ripieni al Forno

BAKED STUFFED ARTICHOKES

6 artichokes
2 quarts boiling water
1 teaspoon salt
1 clove garlic
2 cups grated bread crumbs, made from Italian or French bread

½ cup grated Parmesan cheese
1 small onion, finely chopped
1 tablespoon chopped parsley
1 teaspoon salt
¼ teaspoon black pepper
1¼ cups chicken or beef broth
¼ cup olive oil

Cut off both ends of artichokes so that tops and bottoms are flat. Cook in boiling salted water, to which clove of garlic has been added, for 15 to 20 minutes. Cool. Drain upside down. Remove prickly chokes. Open leaves in circles and place in deep baking dish.

For stuffing, combine bread crumbs, cheese, onion, parsley, salt, pepper, and 4 tablespoons broth. Place some stuffing in each row of leaves. Tie each artichoke with string to hold in shape. Brush olive oil over top to moisten. Add remaining chicken broth to baking dish and cover tightly. Bake in a preheated 325°F. oven about 40 minutes, until dressing is lightly browned but not dry. Baste with broth from time to time. Yield: 6 servings.

Involtini

ROLLED VEAL WITH PÂTÉ

2 pounds veal cutlets, cut very thin
1 teaspoon rosemary
½ cup flour
½ cup grated Parmesan cheese
1 teaspoon salt
¼ teaspoon freshly ground black pepper

1 4-ounce can *pâté de foie gras*
2 tablespoons butter
1 tablespoon chopped parsley
2 tablespoons oil
1 cup Marsala or dry white wine

Sprinkle each slice of veal with rosemary and pound with meat mallet or edge of saucer. Dredge cutlets in mixture of flour, cheese, salt and pepper; pound both sides of meat again.

Combine *pâté de foie gras,* butter and parsley; spread thinly on 1 side of each piece of veal. Roll each piece tightly (with *pâté* mixture inside) and secure with toothpicks. Sauté gently in oil for 5 to 10 minutes—until veal is brown. Add the wine and simmer for 5 minutes, or until rolls are tender. Serve sliced, cold, as an appetizer or hot with rice. Yield: serves 12 as an appetizer, 6 as an entrée.

Note: For recipe to serve 50, see LARGE-SCALE BUFFET MENUS section, page 260.

Stracciatella

CHICKEN SOUP WITH EGG DROPS

2 pounds chicken wings, necks and backs	1 teaspoon salt
	½ teaspoon black pepper
2 quarts cold water	4 eggs, beaten
1 rib celery with leaves, sliced	½–1 cup Parmesan cheese, grated
2 carrots, sliced	
1 small onion, diced	1 tablespoon chopped parsley

Place chicken in large kettle with water. Cover and bring to a boil. Skim surface; add celery, carrots, onion, salt and pepper. Cover; cook slowly until meat is very tender, about 1½ hours. Strain broth into saucepan and keep hot. Keep chicken for another dish.

Combine eggs, cheese, and parsley. Bring 7 cups of chicken broth to the boiling point and gradually pour egg mixture into broth, stirring constantly with a fork or wooden spoon to prevent lumping. Simmer about 5 minutes until egg drops are cooked. Correct seasoning. Serve hot. Yield: 6 servings.

Gnocchi Leggeri

LIGHT CHEESE NOODLES

1 cup plus 2 tablespoons butter	⅛ teaspoon grated nutmeg
	2 teaspoons salt
4 egg yolks, beaten	⅛ teaspoon black pepper
1⅓ cups flour	4 egg whites, beaten stiff
½ pound Parmesan cheese, grated	Boiling salted water
	Melted butter

Cream butter with egg yolks, adding one at a time until mixture is well blended. Add flour, half of grated cheese, nutmeg, salt and pepper; blend well. Fold in egg whites and chill mixture thoroughly. Toss on lightly floured board and roll to ¼ inch thick. Cut in 1-inch strips and cut again to form small cubes. Boil in salted water until noodles float to top. Drain well. Alternate layers of noodles, remaining Parmesan cheese and melted butter to taste in serving dish. Yield: 6 servings.

IVORY COAST

Ivory Coast in a recent year was the world's third largest producer of coffee. Agriculture is important to the economy of this West African country: bananas, pineapple, manioc, rice and yams are all grown. Fishing is a new industry, and the breeding of cattle is also becoming of economic importance. Exports exceed imports by $50 million. Ivory Coast became independent on August 7, 1960 and entered the UN on September 20, 1960.

Chicken à la N'Gatietro

FRIED CHICKEN WITH PEANUT BUTTER SAUCE

1 2½- to 3-pound frying chicken, cut up	1 tablespoon tomato paste
3 tablespoons oil	1 teaspoon salt
½ cup chopped onion	1 teaspoon paprika
3 green onions, sliced	1 bay leaf
1 large tomato, diced	2 cups water
	1 cup peanut butter

Brown chicken in hot oil in frying pan or Dutch oven. Add chopped and sliced onions, tomato, tomato paste, salt, paprika and bay leaf to browned chicken. Cover; cook over low heat for 5 to 10 minutes. Add water to chicken and simmer until chicken is nearly tender, 15 to 20 minutes more. Remove chicken mixture from heat.

Cream peanut butter with some of the chicken stock in mixing bowl; add stock until peanut butter is a light, creamy, smooth sauce. Pour sauce over chicken; cover and cook over low heat for about 10 minutes or until chicken is tender. Yield: 6 servings.

JAMAICA

Jamaica has an average temperature throughout the year of 80°F., which contributes to its popularity as a resort— as do its beautiful beaches and mountainous areas where dozens of uniquely indigenous birds and orchids are found. Aside from tourism, agriculture and the mining of bauxite are the economic mainstays of this country, which achieved its independence from Britain on August 6, 1962, and joined the UN on September 18, 1962.

Sweet Potato Pudding

1 pound sweet potatoes, peeled and grated
¼ cup butter, melted
¾ cup brown sugar
¼ cup flour
¼ teaspoon nutmeg

¼ teaspoon ground ginger
⅛ teaspoon salt
2 cups Coconut Milk (pages 23 and 40)
½ teaspoon vanilla extract
½ cup raisins

Combine grated sweet potatoes with butter and sugar. Sift flour with nutmeg, ginger and salt, and add to potato mixture. Add 1 cup of coconut milk slowly; add vanilla and raisins. Pour mixture into oiled baking dish and bake in a preheated 375°F. oven for 1½ hours or until pudding is firm to touch. Serve as dessert, warm or cold, with remaining cup of coconut milk. Yield: 6 servings.

JAPAN

Japan takes a passionate interest in visual form, and an outstanding feature of the country's food is that it is beautiful to look at. Many restaurants in Japan specialize in some one food—tempura, chicken, sukiyaki, eels, vegetables or raw fish. Only 15 percent of the land can be cultivated, but the crop yield per acre is among the highest in the world. Since the Second World War, Japan's economic growth has been at the extraordinary rate of between 10 and 11 percent annually, its trade with the United States accounting for some 30 percent of both its exports and imports. Japan has been a member of the UN since December 18, 1955.

Chawan Mushi

CHICKEN AND SHRIMP CUSTARD

1 quart chicken broth or *Dashi* Sauce (page 127)	1 cup chopped chicken and shrimp
4 eggs, well beaten	½ cup cooked noodles
1 teaspoon salt	½ cup cooked green beans, peas or cut asparagus
1 tablespoon soy sauce	
1 tablespoon sugar	

Combine chicken broth or *dashi* sauce with eggs. Put mixture through fine strainer to blend. Add salt, soy sauce and sugar.

In each of 6 Japanese bowls with covers, or in 8 custard cups, place an equal portion of chicken and shrimp, noodles and green vegetable. Fill bowl or cup with broth mixture. If Japanese bowls are not available, cover custard cup tightly with foil. Set covered bowls or cups in baking pans; fill with hot water nearly to the top of cups and bake in a preheated 350°F. oven for 35 to 40 minutes or until knife blade inserted in custard comes away clean. Serve while hot, in place of soup, in the cups. Yield: 6 servings.

Note: Any combination of mushrooms, bamboo shoots, gingko nuts and water chestnuts also may be used. Proportion of egg used is 2 eggs for each pint of mixture.

Tempura

SEAFOOD AND VEGETABLES

12 medium or large shrimp	*Batter:*
2 flounder fillets	3 egg yolks
1 medium squid	2 cups cold water
6 scallops	2½ cups sifted flour
1 carrot	3 cups *Dashi* Sauce (page 127)
12 green beans	
1 sweet potato	Freshly grated ginger or powdered ginger, optional
3 cups vegetable oil	
1 cup sesame seed oil	Freshly grated Japanese white radish (*daikon*) optional

Preparation of shrimp: Insert small blade of scissors under the shell of each shrimp. Starting at the head portion, cut down to, but not through, the tail segment. Peel shrimp, leaving tail segment intact. Cut off lower half of tail. Wash peeled shrimp under cold running water and remove intestinal tract. Make 3 shallow cuts across the underside of each shrimp in equidistant places to permit "straightening" the shrimp lengthwise.

Preparation of flounder: Cut into small sections, each 2" x 3".

Preparation of squid: Remove tentacles and peel off outer and inner skins. Cut into bite-size pieces.

Preparation of scallops: Cut into quarters.

Preparation of vegetables: Cut carrot into slices about ⅛-inch thick. Cut green beans into 3-inch lengths. Peel and cut sweet potato into ⅛-inch-thick slices, then cut each slice in quarters.

Dry all seafood and vegetables well between paper towels. Heat oil in a deep-fat fryer to 330°F. (A deep-fat thermometer is necessary. Temperature of 330°F. must be maintained during entire frying process to obtain good results.)

To make batter: Combine egg yolks with water and mix well. Gradually stir in flour, stirring from bottom of bowl. The secret of light batter is not to overbeat. Some flour should remain floating on top of batter.

Hold shrimp by the tail, dip into batter and drop gently, one at a time, into hot fat. Fry for 30 seconds to 1 minute, or until golden brown. Dip each piece of remaining fish and seafood and the vegetables into batter, following same procedure, and fry until golden brown. Do not fry too many pieces of food at one time. Remove to paper towels as done and drain briefly. Serve some of each food to each person with an individual serving bowl of *dashi* sauce, with ginger and radish added to sauce to taste, if desired. Serve with hot rice. Yield: 6 servings.

Yosenabe

CHICKEN AND SEAFOOD WITH DASHI SAUCE

2 chicken breasts, boned and cut in 12 pieces
12 shrimp
12 oysters
12 clams
12 scallops
12 pieces of lobster
1 package frozen leaf spinach
12 strips Chinese cabbage
12 slices carrots
1½ cups cooked vermicelli
12 small mushrooms

12 gingko nuts or canned water chestnuts
12 sliced bamboo shoots, canned
1 teaspoon monosodium glutamate, optional

Dashi Sauce:
7 cups water
¾ cup bonito flakes
¾ cup Japanese soy sauce
¾ cup dry sherry

Place chicken, seafood and vegetables in a 12-inch skillet or heavy frying pan with the spinach, cabbage and carrots in the center, and the remainder of the ingredients surrounding them. Insofar as possible, keep all of each kind of food together, since each serving should consist of some of each kind of food used. If used, sprinkle the monosodium glutamate over all.

To make dashi sauce: Combine water and bonito flakes and boil for 3 minutes. Strain and discard the flakes. Combine strained liquid (known as *dashi*), soy sauce and sherry.

Pour *dashi* sauce over the chicken-seafood mixture and cook over moderate heat for about 20 minutes. Yield: 6 servings.

Note: Ingredients for *yosenabe* both in kind and amount may be varied according to preference. A *dashi* sauce mix is obtainable in specialty food shops.

Mizutaki

CHICKEN AND VEGETABLES

2 3-pound chickens
Water
Salt
12 scallions, cut in 1-inch
  lengths
2 medium onions, thinly sliced
2 bunches watercress, trimmed

Lemon-Soy Sauce:
1 cup lemon juice
1 cup soy sauce
1 cup sake (Japanese wine)
1 teaspoon monosodium
  glutamate, optional

6 cups hot cooked rice

Have the butcher cut chickens (with bone) into 1½-inch pieces. Place chickens in heavy 6-quart saucepan and cover with water. Add 2 teaspoons salt to each quart of water. Cover; bring to boil, reduce heat, and simmer for 45 minutes. Complete cooking at dining table in an electric skillet; transfer chicken and some broth to electric skillet and heat to 300°F. After guests are seated, add vegetables, a few at a time, to simmering chicken and broth. Cook vegetables only 1 minute.

To make lemon-soy sauce: Place all ingredients in small saucepan and bring to boil; reduce heat and simmer for 5 minutes.

Serve chicken and vegetables to each guest in individual bowls. Give each guest a small bowl of lemon-soy sauce for dipping chicken and vegetables. Serve with individual bowls of rice. Yield: 6 servings.

JORDAN

Jordan is located in the heart of the Arab world, and its food is typical of the area, hot and spiced, with great use of lamb, rice, vegetables—such as zucchini and eggplant —pine nuts, olive oil and yogurt. Believed to be inhabited since prehistoric times, Jordan for many centuries was occupied successively by Middle Eastern empires, the last of which was the Ottoman Empire. After World War I it was part of the Palestine Mandate administered by the British. Jordan became independent in 1946 and on December 14, 1955, joined the UN.

Kufta Soup

SOUR EGG DROP MEATBALL SOUP

1 pound finely ground lamb
   or mutton
2 tablespoons farina
1 teaspoon salt
½ teaspoon ground cinnamon
½ teaspoon ground allspice

4 tablespoons freshly chopped
   parsley
3 eggs
6–8 cups chicken broth
4 tablespoons lemon juice

Mix meat, farina, salt, spices and parsley in a large mixing bowl. Add 1 egg and mix thoroughly. Roll mixture into 1-inch balls. Drop balls into boiling chicken broth in a large saucepan and simmer for 30 minutes or until balls are cooked. Remove saucepan from heat. Beat 2 eggs with lemon juice and pour into the hot soup. Lift egg lightly with a fork so that it cooks in long strands. Serve immediately. Yield: 6–8 servings.

Kousa Mahshi

LAMB AND RICE-STUFFED ZUCCHINI

12 medium zucchini
2 pounds ground lamb
2 cups rice
1 tablespoon salt
1 tablespoon allspice

1 6½-ounce can tomato paste
1 tablespoon butter, softened
Water
1 clove garlic, minced
1 tablespoon lemon juice

Cut zucchini in half lengthwise and hollow out center. Dice this center portion and add lamb, rice, salt, and allspice. Mix well. Lightly fill zucchini with mixture and place in large pan. Combine tomato paste and butter; spread over rice-lamb stuffing. Add enough water to just cover zucchini. Heat until water boils. Cover. Reduce heat and simmer 20 to 25 minutes or until rice is tender. Uncover. Stir garlic and lemon juice into sauce and spoon over rice stuffing. Simmer 5 to 10 minutes, or until sauce is thickened. Place zucchini on serving dish and pour remaining sauce over them. Yield: 12 servings.

Mughle

SPICY RICE DESSERT

1 cup farina
1 tablespoon ground cinnamon
1 tablespoon caraway seeds,
   pulverized
2 teaspoons aniseed,
   pulverized

8 cups water
2 cups sugar
1 cup walnuts, almonds or
   pine nuts, chopped

Combine farina and spices in a saucepan. Add the water slowly.
Bring to boil and cook rapidly for 1 minute, stirring constantly.
Add the sugar and boil for 10 minutes or until mixture is the con-
sistency of custard. Pour into custard cups; garnish with nuts.
Serve hot. Yield: 6 servings.

KENYA

*Kenya has been independent of Britain since 1963, and
a UN member since December 16 of that year. The
country is largely agricultural, with coffee, tea, sisal, wine
and wheat her main crops. The magnificent wildlife
draws tourists from all over the world. The national
parks and game reserves for the protection of the wild
animals are a foremost concern of the government of this
beautiful East African country.*

Bean Stew

1 cup dried beans
5 cups boiling water
1 pound beef stew meat,
   tenderized and cut in 1-inch
   cubes
2 tablespoons oil
1 large onion, chopped
   coarsely
2 large potatoes, pared and
   cubed

3 celery ribs, cut in 1-inch
   slices
3 medium carrots, pared and
   cut in rounds
1 cup fresh or frozen corn
1 teaspoon curry powder
1½ teaspoons salt
½ pound fresh or frozen
   Brussels sprouts

Add beans to 4 cups of boiling water in a 3-quart saucepan or
Dutch oven; boil for 2 minutes. Remove from heat and let stand,
covered, for 1 hour. Return to heat and simmer in the same water
for 1 hour. Brown meat in hot oil; add onion and cook until brown.
Add meat-and-onion mixture and all other ingredients, except the
Brussels sprouts, to the beans; add remaining boiling water. Simmer stew for 1 hour. Add sprouts and continue cooking for 15
minutes. Yield: 6–8 servings.

KUWAIT

*Kuwait is an Arab sheikdom located on the west coast of
the Persian Gulf. It is estimated that one-fifth of the
world's known oil reserves are found on its land or off
its coasts. The country is using some of its oil royalties
to develop new industries in chemical products, food
canning and building materials. Kuwait also contributes
to the economic development of other Arab lands. The
country has been a member of the UN since May 14,
1963.*

Kharoff

STUFFED CROWN ROAST OF LAMB

1 pound lean lamb, cut in small cubes	¼ teaspoon powdered cloves
1 medium onion, chopped	¼ teaspoon powdered ginger
1 cup water	2 cups cooked rice
1 teaspoon salt	¼ cup raisins
¼ teaspoon black pepper	¼ cup toasted almonds
¼ teaspoon cinnamon	5-pound crown roast of lamb
¼ teaspoon powdered cardamom	3 hard-cooked eggs

Simmer cubed lamb and onion in water in covered saucepan for
20 minutes, or until liquid is reduced to about ¼ cup. Mix together all of the spices, rice, raisins and half the almonds. Add
lamb mixture and toss lightly.

Place crown roast on rack in a shallow roasting pan; half fill roast with stuffing. Cut 2 eggs in quarters lengthwise and arrange on top of stuffing. Add remaining stuffing. Cover top of roast and stuffing with aluminum foil. Bake in a preheated 325°F. oven for 2½ hours or until done. Remove foil during last 15 minutes of roasting. Garnish with remaining egg, sliced, and rest of almonds. Serve with curried rice. Yield: 8 servings.

Dakooss

COOKED TOMATOES

4 large fresh tomatoes or 2
  9-ounce cans tomatoes
½ teaspoon salt

2 cloves garlic, finely minced
3 or 4 dashes of Tabasco
  sauce

Combine all ingredients in a saucepan; bring to a boil, lower heat and simmer 10 minutes. Serve hot as a vegetable with fried fish or lamb. Yield: 5–6 servings.

LAOS

Laos, a kingdom in southeast Asia, joined the UN on May 14, 1963. Her people are mostly Buddhists and about half are Lao, a branch of the Tai people of southern China. The country is sparsely populated, with 90 percent of the people living in rural areas and engaged in subsistence agriculture. In addition to rice, vegetables, spices and fruits such as mangoes, bananas and pineapples are grown. The soil of the valleys of the Mekong river is very rich, and there are many forests with potentially valuable timber.

Kengphed

SPICED FISH CHOWDER

½ cup pimientos, mashed
1 clove garlic, minced
½ cup diced onion
2 tablespoons oil
1 pound swordfish steak or
  other fish steak or fillet, cut
  in small pieces

1 quart Coconut Milk (pages
  23 and 40)
2 medium potatoes, sliced and
  parboiled
1 teaspoon salt
¼ teaspoon black pepper

Sauté pimientos, garlic and onion in hot oil for 5 minutes or until onion is yellow. Add fish and cook over low heat about 5 minutes, or until fish is partially cooked. Add coconut milk and potatoes. Simmer for 20 minutes. Add salt and pepper. Serve hot. Yield: 4–6 servings.

Nham Salad

FRESH VEGETABLE-CHICKEN SALAD

1 medium head lettuce	1 cup diced cooked chicken
3 tomatoes, peeled and cut in eighths	4 tablespoons olive oil
	2 tablespoons vinegar
2 celery ribs, cut in ¼-inch slices	1 tablespoon pickle relish
	1 teaspoon monosodium glutamate, optional
3 scallions, cut in small pieces	
2 hard-cooked eggs	½ teaspoon black pepper

Tear lettuce into bite-size pieces. Add tomatoes, celery, scallions, chopped whites of eggs and chicken. Mash egg yolks and add oil, vinegar, pickle relish, monosodium glutamate, if using it, and pepper. Mix to a smooth paste. Add this dressing to salad ingredients and toss lightly until salad is well coated with dressing. Yield: 6 servings.

Sankhagha Makoû

PUMPKIN PUDDING

1 3-pound pumpkin	2 cups Coconut Milk (pages 23 and 40)
6 tablespoons sugar	
	5 eggs, well beaten

Stand pumpkin with stem end up. Cut off sufficient of the stem end to form a lid and to facilitate serving from the pumpkin. Scrape out seeds and fibrous flesh. Add sugar and coconut milk to eggs. Pour this mixture into the pumpkin and replace lid. Place pumpkin on rack in tightly covered kettle with water to reach just below bottom of pumpkin. Steam until custard is set and pumpkin is tender. (The pudding may also be baked in a preheated 350°F. oven about 1 hour or until pumpkin is thoroughly cooked and the custard is firm.) Serve from the pumpkin and include some custard and pumpkin in each serving. Yield: 4–6 servings.

LEBANON

Lebanon has mountains excellent for skiing, and beauti-
ful beaches as well; there are Roman ruins for sightsee-
ing, and Beirut, Lebanon's largest city, has many
nightclubs. All of these contribute to Lebanon's appeal
to tourists. The Lebanese are enormously hospitable
people. Approximately half are Moslem and half Chris-
tian, and for the most part Arab. Many Lebanese have
emigrated to North and South America, where one can
often find Lebanese food. It is a Middle Eastern cuisine
stressing rice, lamb, yogurt, pine nuts, chicken and very
sweet desserts baked with honey. Lebanon joined the
UN on October 24, 1945.

Sayadiah

FISH AND RICE CASSEROLE

1 pound fish fillets	½ cup pine nuts
(cod, halibut or sole)	1 cup rice
4 tablespoons butter	1 teaspoon salt
1 large onion, chopped	2 cups water

Cook fish fillets in 2 tablespoons of butter until light brown. Cook
chopped onion and pine nuts in the other 2 tablespoons of butter
in a second frying pan until onions are yellow but not brown.
Grease a 2-quart casserole; in it place a layer of onions and pine
nuts, a layer of fish, and a layer of rice. Repeat layers, using all of
the ingredients. Add salt to water and pour over all. Cover and
bake in a preheated 350°F. oven for 1 hour or until rice is cooked.
Remove cover for last 15 minutes of baking time. Yield: 6
servings.

Kibbeh Bissanieh

BAKED LAMB AND WHEAT

1 pound bulgur (cracked
wheat), finely crushed
Water
2 pounds ground lean lamb
⅓ cup grated onion
2 teaspoons salt
½ teaspoon black pepper
¼ teaspoon cinnamon

Filling:
⅔ cup chopped onion
4 teaspoons shortening
½ pound ground lean lamb
¼ cup pine nuts
½ teaspoon salt
¼ teaspoon black pepper

2 tablespoons shortening

Cover bulgur with water and soak for 30 minutes. Add the 2 pounds of lamb, onion and seasonings. Knead well.

To make filling: Sauté the ⅔ cup chopped onion in shortening until light brown. Add the ½ pound ground lamb, pine nuts, salt and pepper. Cook and stir until meat is browned.

Spread half of the bulgur-lamb mixture in well-greased 9″ x 12″ baking pan. Cover with filling. Cover with remaining bulgur-lamb mixture and press down firmly. With a sharp knife, cut diagonal lines across to mark diamond shapes. Dot top with the 2 tablespoons shortening. Bake in a preheated 400°F. oven for 30 minutes; reduce heat to 300°F. and bake 30 minutes longer. Yield: 8 servings.

Lebanie

YOGURT CHEESE

1 quart plain yogurt
1 teaspoon salt

Beat salt into yogurt; pour into a square of cheesecloth; bring corners together; suspend and let drain for 24 hours. Open cloth; place mold of cheese on serving plate. Serve with plain toast or with apricot marmalade. Yield: 6 servings.

Makbous Flaifleh

PICKLED STUFFED PEPPERS

6 green peppers	1 clove garlic
2½ cups finely chopped cabbage	3 tablespoons salt
½ cup chopped carrots	3 cups water, boiled and cooled
½ cup chopped celery	1⅓ cups vinegar

Cut tops off peppers carefully and remove seeds. Combine cabbage, carrots and celery. Stuff peppers very tightly with the mixture. Replace tops on stuffed peppers; secure with thread. Place peppers, top side up, in large-mouthed glass jar; place garlic in center of jar. Add salt to cooled water; stir to dissolve and add vinegar. Pour this mixture into jar to cover peppers. Seal jar and allow 2 weeks for peppers to pickle. Serve as a relish. Yield: 6 servings.

Tabbouli

WHEAT SALAD

½ cup bulgur (cracked wheat), finely crushed	1 onion, chopped
Water	1 tomato, chopped
1½ cups finely chopped parsley	¼ cup lemon juice
½ cup finely chopped fresh mint leaves	¼ cup olive oil
	½ teaspoon salt
	¼ teaspoon black pepper
	Lettuce

Soak bulgur in water to cover for ½ hour. Drain well; add parsley, mint, onion and tomato to drained bulgur. Mix lemon juice, oil, salt and pepper, and add to salad. Toss lightly, coating salad ingredients. Serve on lettuce Yield: 6 servings.

LESOTHO

Lesotho, a former British dependency, became independent on October 4, 1966. It is an African state without white settlers or landowners. The land is arid

*and mountainous with altitudes ranging from 5,000
to 11,000 feet. Heavy erosion has hindered agriculture,
although maize, sorghum, barley, beans and peas are
grown. The main industry is livestock raising, which
produces wool and mohair, the chief exports. Lesotho
was admitted to the UN on October 17, 1966.*

Bohobe Ba Poone E Tala

MEALIE BREAD

3½ cups water	2¼ cups white cornmeal
½ tablespoon salt	Shortening

Heat water with salt to a rapid boil. Slowly stir in cornmeal—it
will thicken rapidly. As soon as all cornmeal is in, turn off heat.
Beat vigorously with a wooden spoon without removing from heat.
Turn thick mass onto a breadboard to cool for 10 minutes.
Dampen hands with cold water. Knead approximately 15 minutes, until smooth and almost satiny. Form dough into balls about
the size of tennis balls and flatten to a thickness of about 1 inch.
Put on a greased warm skillet, several at a time, and cook until a
light crust forms. Regrease skillet when turning. Keep warm. When
all are done, arrange on baking sheets and bake 30 minutes in a
preheated 450°F. oven. Turn every 10 minutes until a thick crust
forms. Split and serve with butter. Yield: 18 servings.

LIBERIA

*Liberia was founded in 1822 by the American Coloniza-
tion Society to help those freed slaves return to Africa
who desired to do so. Until 1926 Liberia was heavily dependent upon its coffee production, but in that year
rubber plantations were established and today over 53
million tons of rubber are exported. Iron ore, gold, diamonds and lead are also found there. Liberia's government is modeled on that of the United States. In
addition to its membership in the Organization of African Unity, Liberia has belonged to the UN since November 2, 1945.*

Jollof Rice

CHICKEN AND MEAT WITH RICE

1 3-pound frying chicken, cut up	2 1-pound cans tomatoes
¼ cup oil	1 6½-ounce can tomato paste
½ pound smoked ham, cubed	1 tomato-paste can water
2 medium onions, sliced	¼ pound green beans, fresh or frozen
2 teaspoons salt	1 cup rice
¼ teaspoon black pepper	2 cups water
½ teaspoon ground allspice	

Cook chicken in hot oil in Dutch oven or large frying pan until chicken is brown. Add ham, onions, 1 teaspoon salt, pepper and allspice. Cook until onions are tender, stirring occasionally. Add tomatoes, tomato paste and water; stir to mix ingredients. Place green beans on top of meat mixture; cover and simmer for 20 minutes or until vegetables are tender. Cook rice for 10 minutes in water with remaining salt; drain in a colander. Add rice to meat and vegetables and continue to simmer for 15 minutes or until rice is tender and blended with sauce. Additional water may be added. Yield: 6 servings.

Note: For recipe to serve 50, see LARGE-SCALE BUFFET MENUS section, page 253.

Cassava Cake

1¼ cups raw grated cassava or minute tapioca	¾ cup grated coconut
½ cup milk	½ cup flour
1 egg, beaten	2½ teaspoons baking powder
6 tablespoons butter	Few grains of salt
1 cup sugar	1 teaspoon vanilla extract

Mix cassava or tapioca with milk and egg; let stand for 5 minutes. Cream butter and sugar; add cassava mixture and coconut to creamed butter and sugar. Mix batter well. Sift flour, baking powder and salt together; add to batter. Stir in vanilla and turn batter into an oiled and floured 8-inch-square cake pan. Bake in a pre-heated 400°F. oven for about 40 minutes or until done. Cut in squares or rectangles. It is delicious warm with vanilla ice cream. Yield: 8 servings.

LIBYA

Libya is almost entirely desert, with oil production the basis of its economy, but the largest part of the population is engaged in date-growing, cattle raising, and fishing and processing fish from the Mediterranean. For tourists there are lovely seashores, Roman antiquities and beautiful mosques. The UN admitted Libya to membership on December 14, 1955.

Abrak

STUFFED GRAPE LEAVES

⅔ cup rice
1½ cups boiling water
½ cup minced lamb
⅔ cup finely chopped onion
½ cup strained tomatoes
½ cup butter, melted

1 teaspoon salt
½ teaspoon black pepper
3 tablespoons chopped parsley
40 grape leaves, fresh or
    canned
Boiling water

Add rice to boiling water; boil 5 minutes; drain. Add the lamb, onion, tomatoes, 2 tablespoons butter, salt, pepper and parsley. Mix well.

Wilt the grape leaves, if fresh, in boiling water. Place about 1 tablespoon of rice mixture on each grape leaf, then fold sides of grape leaf over rice mixture and roll up loosely. Spread 4 tablespoons of the butter in a 10-inch frying pan and place grape-leaf rolls in pan, folded edges down. Pour remaining butter over top. Cover tightly and cook over low heat for 35 to 45 minutes. Yield: 40 appetizers.

Libyan Couscous

1½ pounds lean boneless
  lamb, cut in 2-inch cubes
¾ cup olive oil
7 large onions, sliced ½ inch
  thick
1 large tomato, cubed
1 tablespoon crushed red
  pepper
½ teaspoon allspice

2 teaspoons turmeric
2 teaspoons salt
1 6½-ounce can tomato paste
1 quart boiling water
4 medium potatoes, peeled
  and quartered
1 1-pound can chick-peas
½ pound cracked wheat or 1
  pound couscous or semolina

Brown the meat in hot oil in deep kettle or Dutch oven with a capacity of at least 3 quarts. Add 3 of the onions, and the tomato. Continue cooking over low heat for 10 minutes. Add the pepper, allspice, turmeric, salt, tomato paste, and water. Cover and simmer for 1 hour; add the remaining onions and potatoes; simmer for 30 minutes, adding water if needed. Add the chick-peas with their liquid and simmer for 10 minutes or until mixture is hot.

Cook the cracked wheat or couscous according to package directions. Turn the cooked cracked wheat or couscous into a large serving bowl; pour the meat stew or sauce over the wheat slowly; let the dish stand for 5 minutes before serving to permit wheat to absorb some of the sauce. Yield: 10 servings.

Note: Cracked wheat, semolina or couscous may be purchased in specialty food stores.

LUXEMBOURG

Luxembourg is one of the smallest countries of Europe (998 square miles) and a most enchanting one with ruins of fortresses and castles interspersed among wide rivers and deep ravines. A good Moselle is produced in its eastern vineyards. Wheat, potatoes and barley are farmed in the middle section of the country and iron mining and steel manufacturing take place in the southern part—all contributing to making Luxembourg one of the wealthiest countries per capita in the world. On

*October 24, 1945, Luxembourg became a charter mem-
ber of the UN.*

Potage Jardinière

VEGETABLE SOUP

3 carrots

3 parsnips

2 medium potatoes

6 leeks

3 tomatoes

1 cup cabbage

1 cup celery

¼ head lettuce

½ pound peas, shelled

½ pound lima beans, shelled

½ pound green beans

3 quarts boiling water

1½ teaspoons salt

½ teaspoon freshly ground
      black pepper

2 tablespoons butter

½ cup cream

Milk

Cut carrots, parsnips, potatoes, leeks, tomatoes, cabbage, celery
and lettuce into small pieces. Place all vegetables in boiling water and simmer for 3 hours. Press the vegetables through a sieve,
and return puréed vegetables to broth. Add salt, pepper, butter
and cream to soup. Thin with milk to desired consistency. Yield:
6–8 servings.

Bo'neschlupp

GREEN BEAN SOUP

1 pound green beans, cut in
      small pieces

2 quarts boiling water

2 medium potatoes, peeled
      and cut in ½-inch cubes

1½ teaspoons salt

Freshly ground black pepper

2 slices bacon, cut in ½-inch
      pieces

1½ tablespoons flour

1 cup sour cream

Drop green beans in water; cover and cook for 40 minutes. Add
potatoes, salt and pepper and continue cooking for 15 minutes.
Cook bacon until brown in small frying pan; remove bacon and
save. Brown flour in bacon fat; mix with ½ cup of cooled bean
liquid and add to the soup mixture. Simmer for 5 minutes; add
bacon bits to the soup and serve as luncheon soup with side dish

of sour cream; or add sour cream to soup, according to taste, just before serving. Yield: 6 servings.

Lieverkniddelen

LIVER DUMPLINGS

1½ pounds calf's or beef liver
1 large onion
1 small leek or 2 tablespoons minced chives
4–6 slices white bread, crusts trimmed
2 eggs

2 tablespoons flour
3 teaspoons salt
½ teaspoon black pepper
2 tablespoons chopped parsley, optional
6 cups water
¼ pound bacon, diced

Grind liver with onion, leek and bread. Add eggs, flour, 2 teaspoons salt, pepper and parsley. Mix well.

Boil water; add remaining salt. Drop liver mixture, 1 tablespoon at a time, into the boiling water. (Dip tablespoon in hot water each time before scooping up mixture.) Cover pan and simmer for 10 minutes. Remove dumplings from water and place on heated platter.

Fry bacon until light brown. Pour bacon and fat over the dumplings. Yield: 6 servings.

Crème Caramel

CARAMEL CUSTARD

2 eggs
5 tablespoons sugar
Pinch of salt
½ teaspoon vanilla extract

2 cups scalded milk

Caramel Sauce:
1 cup sugar
½ cup cold water

Beat the eggs slightly; beat in the sugar, salt and vanilla; stir in the scalded milk. Pour into 6 individual custard cups of oven glassware or earthenware. Set cups in a baking pan; pour hot water into pan nearly to the top of cups. Bake in a preheated 350°F. oven for 45 minutes or until mixture does not adhere to the blade of a knife when inserted in center of custard.

To make *caramel sauce:* Place sugar in heavy skillet over heat.

Melt sugar slowly, stirring constantly. When brown or caramelized, remove from heat and add cold water, stirring rapidly until syrup is smooth. If necessary to make smooth, replace over heat for a short time.

Serve custard warm or cool with the sauce. Yield: 6 servings.

Crème Vanille

FLOATING ISLAND

4 eggs, separated	3 cups milk
1 cup sugar	¼ package vanilla pudding
1 cup water	mix

Beat egg whites until they form peaks. Beat in 2 tablespoons of the sugar. Bring water to boiling in a deep pan and add egg whites, either all at once or by tablespoonfuls. Let boil, turning egg white over occasionally in water. Remove whites, drain and place on a plate until later.

Combine milk with rest of the sugar and bring almost to the boiling point. Beat egg yolks, combine with pudding mix; add some of the hot milk to pudding mix, stirring constantly. Pour egg mixture into balance of scalded milk; return to heat, cook over very low heat, stirring continuously, and bring just to the boiling point.

Pour custard into a glass casserole and place egg whites on top. Chill and serve. Yield: 6–8 servings.

MADAGASCAR

Madagascar, or the Malagasy Republic, is an island nation off the east coast of Africa. It has eighteen different ethnic groups. Dutch, French and British merchants on their way to India in the sixteenth century established trading and supply ports on the island. Eventually France controlled the island, but in 1956 French policy changed toward all her colonies and political activity was permitted, resulting in independence for Madagascar in 1960, and in membership in the UN on September 20 of that year.

Soupe à la Malgache

VEGETABLE SOUP

3 pounds veal bones
2 tablespoons salt
2 quarts water
2 large tomatoes, peeled and diced
1 large onion, diced

3 medium potatoes, peeled and diced
3 carrots, peeled and diced
1 small turnip, peeled and diced
1 leek, optional
1 cup green beans, optional

Place veal bones in a 5-quart saucepan. Add salt and water; bring to a boil and simmer for 1 hour. Add tomatoes and onion and simmer for 1½ hours. Add remainder of vegetables and simmer until vegetables are tender, about 1 hour. Remove the veal bones; sieve the vegetables and return to the liquid. Serve hot. Yield: 6 servings.

Varenga

BROWNED SHREDDED BEEF

2 pounds boneless chuck, cut in small pieces
Water

2 tablespoons salt
1 clove garlic
1 onion, sliced

Place beef in a 2-quart saucepan and cover with water. Add salt, garlic and onion. Cover; bring to a boil and simmer for 2 hours, or until the meat is tender enough to be shredded with a fork. Add water, if necessary, during the cooking period. Remove beef from liquid, shred and transfer to a 7" × 11" baking dish; roast in a preheated 400°F. oven for ½ hour or until meat is browned. Yield: 6 servings.

MALAWI

Malawi, formerly called Nyasaland, became independent of Britain in 1964, and a UN participant on De-

cember 1 of that year. Because of its many mountains, this Central African country has been referred to as "Switzerland without snow." Agriculture, especially the production of corn, millet, cassava, peanuts, rice, cotton, tobacco and tea, is the basis of the economy.

Supu Wa Nuemba Zolfiira

RED BEAN SOUP

2 cups red beans	2 tablespoons fat
4–6 cups boiling water	2 tomatoes, cut in small pieces
2 pounds beef soup bones	1 tablespoon flour
2 large onions, chopped	1 teaspoon salt

Wash beans. Cover with boiling water; boil 2 minutes. Remove from heat and soak 1 hour or more. Simmer beans and beef bones in same water until tender, about 1 hour. Remove the bones and reserve, and mash the beans in the broth. Sauté the onions in fat until tender; add flour, stir and cook over low heat until color changes to golden brown. Add onion mixture and the tomatoes to mashed beans; add salt, the reserved bones and more water, if necessary. Simmer for 30 minutes. Remove the bones and serve soup either as is or strained. It should be very hot. Yield: 6–8 servings.

MALAYSIA

Malaysia is the world's leading producer of natural rubber and tin. The country has a very interesting cuisine, influenced by East Indian settlers and by its Indonesian neighbors. Malaysians are great fish eaters, and although local fish is bountiful, some is imported from England, oysters and lobsters from Australia, trout from New Zealand and salmon from Canada. UN membership began September 17, 1957, at which time the country's name was the Federation of Malaya. On September 16, 1963, it was changed to Malaysia.

Kuwe Ikan

FISH PUDDING

1 pound fillet of sole,
  flounder, or haddock
1⅓ cups Coconut Milk
  (pages 23 and 40)
1 teaspoon salt
1 teaspoon ground turmeric
1 clove garlic, minced

¼ teaspoon ground Cayenne
  pepper
1 tablespoon paprika
2 tablespoons onion powder
5 eggs
Thinly sliced cucumbers,
  scored

Cut fish into ½-inch strips and place in a buttered 1-quart casserole
or baking dish. Combine coconut milk with the next 6 ingredients.
Beat eggs only until foamy. Fold eggs into the coconut-milk mixture. Pour over the fish. Place casserole in a pan of hot water.
Bake in a preheated 325°F. oven 50 minutes or until knife inserted in center comes out clean. Garnish with cucumbers. Yield:
6 servings.

Rindang Udang

SHRIMP WITH GREEN PEPPER

1 medium onion, finely diced
3 green onions, including
  tops, finely chopped
¼ cup vegetable oil
1 green bell pepper, cut in
  thin strips
3 tomatoes, peeled and cut
  in cubes
½ cup blanched almonds,
  slivered

¾ pound fresh shrimp,
  cleaned and deveined
½ teaspoon basil
½ teaspoon thyme
1 teaspoon salt
¼ teaspoon white pepper
2 tablespoons flour
1 cup Coconut Milk (pages
  23 and 40) or light cream

Sauté onions in oil for about 3 minutes. Add the rest of the ingredients except the flour and coconut milk or light cream; simmer for 3 minutes. Make a paste of the flour and ¼ cup of the
coconut milk; add the remaining coconut milk, mix thoroughly

and add to mixture. Cook, stirring constantly, until it boils. Serve over rice. Yield: 6 servings.

Note: For recipe to serve 50, see LARGE-SCALE BUFFET MENUS section, page 258.

Ayam Panggang

BARBECUED CHICKEN

2 tablespoons powdered ginger or 1½ inches fresh ginger, ground
¼ cup soy sauce
1 tablespoon sugar

1 teaspoon monosodium glutamate, optional
¼ teaspoon black pepper
Drumsticks and thighs of 3 chickens

Mix ginger, soy sauce, sugar, monosodium glutamate, if used, and pepper. Pour soy sauce mixture over chicken. Let stand 2 or 3 hours. Barbecue or broil. Yield: 6 servings.

Daging Goreng

FRIED BEEF STRIPS

2 pounds beef chuck or round steak, tenderized
1½ teaspoons turmeric
1½ teaspoons black pepper
1½ teaspoons garlic powder

1½ teaspoons onion powder
1½ teaspoons salt
1½ tablespoons sugar
1 cup cooking oil

Slice meat in strips about ¼ inch thick. Combine all seasonings and sprinkle on meat. Let meat stand for 1 hour; turn occasionally to coat all pieces. Heat oil in large frying pan. Put all the meat in hot oil and cook until brown, stirring and turning so that each piece browns. Drain well and serve hot. Yield: 6 servings.

Inti-puff

COCONUT SURPRISE

6 tablespoons brown sugar
6 tablespoons white sugar
2 tablespoons cornstarch
5 tablespoons water

1 4-ounce can shredded
  coconut
Plain pie dough, using 2 cups
  flour
1 egg, beaten

Combine sugars, cornstarch and water in saucepan. Bring to a boil while stirring; cook until thickened. Add coconut and stir until blended. Let mixture cool.

Roll pie dough on floured surface to ⅛-inch thickness. Cut out 18 4-inch circles, rerolling dough as necessary. Place 1 teaspoon of coconut mixture on half of each circle. Brush edges with egg; fold circle over and seal edges with fork. Place on cookie sheet; prick tops with fork and brush tops with egg. Bake in a preheated 400°F. oven, 20 to 25 minutes or until golden brown. Cool on wire rack. Yield: 18 Surprises.

Note: For recipe to serve 50, see LARGE-SCALE BUFFET MENUS section, page 259.

MALDIVE ISLANDS

Maldive Islands, comprising 2,000 islands, only about 220 of which are inhabited, include people of Ceylonese, Indian, Southeast Asian, Middle Eastern and African descent. Their economy is based on fishing and coconuts, and this fact is in evidence in the cuisine. On September 21, 1965, the country was admitted to the UN.

Hanaa Kuri Mas

FISH CURRY

1 coconut	Pinch of black pepper
6 dry red chili peppers	½ inch green ginger, cut in
Pinch of turmeric	pieces
1 teaspoon coriander seeds	1 small onion, sliced
½ teaspoon fennel	2 pounds fresh fish fillets, cut
¼ teaspoon cumin seeds	in ½" x 1" strips
1 small stick cinnamon	Cooked rice
2 cardamom seeds	

Grate coconut meat and mix with coconut liquid and enough warm water to make two cups liquid. Coconut should be mashed and squeezed in the liquid and then the mixture strained and pulp discarded.

Lightly brown chili peppers with turmeric in frying pan. Add coriander and continue browning. Add fennel and cumin. Grind these spices and chili peppers together with cinnamon, cardamom and black pepper.

Mix half of ginger with half of sliced onion and add to coconut milk. Bring to boil and remove from heat.

Combine fish with remaining onion and ginger and the ground spices, and let marinate for ½ hour. Add marinated fish to coconut mixture and simmer over low heat until fish is cooked, about 15 minutes. Serve with rice. Yield: 8 servings.

MALI

Mali, like many African nations, has an economy based on agriculture. The Niger River flows through the southern part of the country, irrigating the soil. Millet, rice and corn are raised for domestic consumption, but peanuts, cotton and fish are exported. There are deposits of salt, bauxite, phosphates, gold, zinc and other minerals, but industrial development has been hampered by lack of transportation. On September 28, 1960, Mali was admitted to the UN.

Le To

TWO-SAUCE STEW

First Sauce:
½ pound ground beef
¼ pound dried fish soaked in
  1 cup water or ½ pound
  fresh fish, flaked
½ teaspoon salt
2 medium onions, diced
  coarsely
Water
2 teaspoons filé (see Note) or
  1 tablespoon cornstarch
  mixed with ¼ cup water

Second Sauce:
½ pound beef, cut in ½-inch
  cubes
1 tablespoon oil
2 small onions, diced
3 tablespoons tomato purée
½ teaspoon salt
Water

Cornmeal Accompaniment:
1 cup cornmeal
½ teaspoon baking soda
3½ cups boiling water
½ teaspoon salt

To make first sauce: Combine beef, flaked fish, salt, and onion in a saucepan; cover with water. Cover and bring mixture to a boil; reduce heat and simmer for 20 minutes. If filé is used, stir into sauce immediately before serving and do not let sauce boil after adding filé. If cornstarch is used, let sauce simmer for 5 minutes.

To make second sauce: Brown beef in hot oil in frying pan. Add onions and cook for 5 minutes, stirring frequently. Add tomato purée, salt and water to cover. Cook, covered, over low heat for 20 minutes.

To make cornmeal accompaniment: Add cornmeal and soda to the boiling water, stirring constantly. Add the salt and cook until mixture is thick. Reduce heat and cook 20 minutes, stirring occasionally.

Combine the 2 sauces. Serve the cornmeal mixture in a shallow bowl with the 2 sauces in a separate dish. Yield: 6 servings.

Note: Filé, a green powder used in Creole cookery, is available in spice sections of food shops.

MALTA

*Malta has lost and gained population in recent years.
Many Maltese have emigrated from this Mediterranean
island of dense population, but in the last few years,
thousands of visitors have arrived to spend their holi-
days and retirement years in the sun. In addition to
tourism, Malta is concentrating on the processing of
farm products and on construction and ship repair, the
exporting of potatoes, wines, textiles and cut flowers.
Inhabited since prehistoric times, this strategic island
of limestone rock achieved independence in the British
Commonwealth in 1964 and became a member of the
UN on December 1 of that year.*

Timpana

MALTESE MACARONI DISH

¼ eggplant, peeled and cubed
¼ cup water with 2
   tablespoons vinegar
½ pound macaroni
Salted water
1 small onion, chopped
4 tablespoons lard
½ 6½-ounce can tomato paste
   or purée
½ cup water
½ pound ground beef or pork

⅛ pound liver, ground or
   chopped
¼ pound ricotta cheese
Puff pastry or plain pastry to
   line and cover 1½-quart
   casserole
⅛ pound Cheddar cheese,
   grated
1 hard-cooked egg, sliced
1 egg, well-beaten

Soak the eggplant in water and vinegar for 45 minutes; drain.
Boil the macaroni 9 minutes in salted water; drain and reserve.
Gently sauté the eggplant with the onion in the lard until cooked.
Dissolve the tomato paste or purée in the ½ cup of water and add
to the contents of the saucepan containing eggplant-onion mixture. Add the meat and liver; let simmer. Mix the meat sauce
with the ricotta.

Line the bottom and sides of a casserole with pastry. Place a layer of macaroni on the bottom of the casserole. Follow this with a layer of meat sauce. Sprinkle with grated cheese. Place some of the egg slices on the cheese. Repeat this procedure, finishing off with a layer of the meat sauce, but reserving a small amount of the grated cheese. Pour the beaten egg over the casserole, allowing it to seep down. Sprinkle remaining grated cheese on top and cover with pastry. Bake in a preheated 375°F. oven for 45 minutes or until the pastry is golden. Yield: 6 servings.

Note: The meat sauce should be rather thin. Pour another ½ cup of water over the top, if needed, in order that the finished *timpana* is not too dry.

MAURITANIA

Mauritania is two-thirds desert in the northern part, but is cultivated in the southern area of the Senegal River valley. Sheep, cattle, goats and camels are raised and exported live. Gum arabic, made from the acacia trees found in the central area, is an important export. Most of the people are nomadic Moors, of mixed Berber and Arab stock, speaking Arabic, and by religion Moslem. Mauritania joined the UN on October 17, 1967.

Michoui

STUFFED LEG OF LAMB

⅓ cup raisins
⅓ cup pitted dates, chopped
⅓ cup dried figs, chopped
1½ tablespoons pine nuts
¼ cup chopped onion
⅔ cup bulgur (cracked wheat)

1½ tablespoons chopped
  parsley
1 teaspoon salt
¼ teaspoon ground coriander
⅛ teaspoon black pepper
1 cup stock or bouillon
1 5-pound leg of lamb, boned

Combine the first 10 ingredients with ⅓ cup of the stock or bouillon; mix well. Stuff lamb with this mixture, filling bone cavity well; secure with skewers. Place stuffed leg on a rack in shallow roasting pan and roast in a preheated 325°F. oven for 2½ to 3 hours, depending upon how well done meat is preferred. Baste lamb occasionally during cooking period with the remaining ⅔ cup of broth and the meat juices. Yield: 6–8 servings.

Note: In Mauritania it is the stomach cavity of a whole young sheep that is stuffed.

MAURITIUS

Mauritius consists of several islands in the Indian Ocean, with an area of 790 square miles and an estimated population of 774,000. More than half the people are of East Indian background, the rest of Chinese, European, African and other origins. Although English is the official language, Creole, Chinese, Hindi, French and Arabic are all spoken. The processing of the chief crop, sugar cane, is the most important industry. Mauritius was accepted into UN membership on April 24, 1968.

Aubergine Orientale

ORIENTAL EGGPLANT

1 large eggplant, peeled and finely diced
1–2 tablespoons salt
2 small green peppers, cored and seeded

Olive oil
1 clove garlic, minced
3 firm tomatoes, peeled and thickly sliced
Black pepper

Sprinkle eggplant with salt and press between two plates for 1 hour. Rinse eggplant and wipe the pieces dry before using. Slice each pepper into five or six pieces. Cover the bottom of a medium frying pan with olive oil, and heat. Fry the garlic, peppers and eggplant until brown; add more oil if necessary. Add the tomatoes, and pepper to taste. Simmer gently until all of the ingredients are soft. Serve very hot. Yield: 6 servings.

MEXICO

Mexico has a cuisine that is far more varied than is supposed by those who think it is a series of roaring hot dishes. Mexican food today reflects Spanish, Indian and, to some extent, American and Continental influences. From early Aztec days corn has been of primary importance, as are dried beans, chocolate and chilis in great variety and degrees of hotness. Mexico's chief exports are cotton, sugar, coffee, fish, wheat and metals. Mexico became a member of the UN on November 7, 1945.

Pescado a la Veracruzana

FISH VERACRUZ

2 pounds red snapper or haddock, cut in serving pieces	4 tablespoons oil
	3 onions, sliced
Cold water	1 1-pound can tomatoes
2 teaspoons salt	3 tablespoons chopped ripe olives
½ teaspoon black pepper	
Juice of 1 lemon	2 tablespoons capers
2 cloves garlic, whole	6 Jalapeño chilis

Rinse fish with cold water; drain and rub with salt, pepper and lemon juice. Set aside. Cook garlic in the oil to extract flavor. Remove and discard garlic. Cook onions in same oil until yellow. Add the fish, tomatoes, olives, capers and chilis to the onions and oil. Simmer over low heat until the sauce is thick and the fish is tender. Yield: 6 servings.

Pollo Relleno con Nueces

CHICKEN WITH CHESTNUT DRESSING

1 roasting chicken, 4–5 pounds
1 cup white wine
1 clove garlic, minced
Juice of 1 lemon
1½ teaspoons salt
1 tablespoon chopped chives or green onion tops
1 tablespoon minced parsley
Giblets, chopped
1 tablespoon butter
⅛ teaspoon freshly ground pepper
⅛ teaspoon nutmeg
8-ounce can purée of chestnuts
4 slices bacon

Marinate chicken in mixture of wine, garlic, lemon juice, 1 teaspoon salt, chives and parsley 24 hours in the refrigerator. Drain and wipe chicken dry.

Cook chopped giblets in butter. Add pepper, nutmeg, chestnut purée and remaining salt. Place this mixture inside chicken. Close opening with skewers. Place slices of bacon over breast; wrap in foil and place in open roasting pan, breast side up. Cook in a preheated 375°F. oven for 2 hours; open foil covering to brown and complete cooking, about 30 minutes more. Yield: 4 servings.

Frijoles Refritos

REFRIED BEANS

1 teaspoon finely chopped onion
6 tablespoons bacon fat or lard
3 cups cooked cold red beans

Brown onion lightly in 3 tablespoons of fat in 10-inch frying pan. Add the beans and mash well with potato masher or wooden spoon. Stir continuously until mixture is dry and fat is absorbed. Beans are now fried. To refry beans, heat remaining fat in a frying pan; add beans and continue to fry and stir until beans are dry enough to shake loose from the pan. Shape beans into a loaf; remove to a hot platter and push a few crisp tortilla quarters into the loaf. Serve loaf with a Mexican hot sauce. Yield: 6 servings.

Note: To prepare tortilla crisps, cut tortillas into quarters and fry a few at a time (single layer) in deep hot fat until brown.

Ensalada de Nochebuena

CHRISTMAS EVE SALAD

4 oranges, cut in thin
  rounds with peel, seeded
8 apples, cored and cut in thin
  rounds with peel
4 limes, cut in thin rounds
  with peel, seeded
4 bananas, peeled and sliced
  diagonally
1 cup canned sliced beets
  with liquid
4 water chestnuts, sliced thin

½ cup sugar
1 teaspoon salt
3 tablespoons lemon juice
2 large heads lettuce,
  shredded
4 radishes, 2 cut in thin slices,
  2 cut in thin strips
1 cup roasted peanuts
2 tablespoons aniseed,
  preferably sugared

Arrange cut fruit, drained beets and water chestnuts in a bowl. Strain beet juice; mix with sugar, salt and lemon juice. Pour mixture over fruits and vegetables in the bowl; marinate for 10 minutes. Drain fruit carefully.

Place shredded lettuce on large platter or silver tray. Arrange fruits and vegetables artistically on lettuce bed. Garnish with radishes and peanuts. Serve with individual nut cups of aniseed, into which guests dip fruit. Yield: 12 servings.

Capirotada

BREAD PUDDING

12 slices day-old bread
¾ cup melted butter
2½ cups light brown sugar
1 teaspoon ground cinnamon

1 cup water
6 tablespoons butter
½ cup cottage cheese
½ cup pine nuts

Brush both sides of each slice of bread with melted butter and brown in oven. Make syrup by boiling the sugar, cinnamon and water for 3 minutes. Use 1 tablespoon of butter to grease a 9″ × 9″ × 2″ baking pan. Place a layer of bread in the pan; add some cheese, syrup, dots of butter and nuts. Continue layers until all ingredients are used. Place in a preheated 350°F. oven for 20 minutes or until top layer is brown. Serve hot with fruit or berry sauce. Yield: 6 servings.

Natilla

CUSTARD WITH CARAMEL SAUCE

4 cups milk	6 egg yolks, slightly beaten
½ cup sugar	1 teaspoon vanilla
½ cup sifted flour	½ cup light brown sugar
¼ teaspoon salt	

Scald 3 cups of milk in top of a double boiler. Mix sugar, flour and salt. Combine remaining milk and egg yolks and stir into sugar mixture. Add to scalded milk. Continue cooking over boiling water, stirring constantly until thick. Remove from heat; let stand a few minutes; add the vanilla. Pour custard into a shallow glass baking dish. When custard is entirely cold, sprinkle lumpless brown sugar over the top. Place the baking dish beneath the broiler until the sugar caramelizes all over the top. (Take care that the flame does not touch the sides of the dish.) Chill in the refrigerator for several hours before serving. Yield: 6 servings.

MONGOLIA

Mongolia, until recently called "Outer Mongolia," was united in 1206 by Genghis Khan, who led the Mongols in their conquest of northern China, eastern Russia and the Islamic lands of the Near East. His son and his son's successor went on to take Hungary, Poland, Vienna, the rest of China, Korea and much of Southeast Asia. As these rulers were less skillful at administering their acquisitions, the empire eventually disintegrated. Today Mongolia is a land of 604,249 square miles, independent since 1911, and a member of the UN as of October 27, 1961.

Ukheriin Chanasan Makh

MARINATED BEEF STRIPS

2 pounds top round steak, cut in ¼" x 2" x ½" strips	2 cloves garlic, minced
½ cup soy sauce	½ teaspoon black pepper
3 tablespoons sugar	2 green onions, finely chopped

Place strips of beef in mixture of soy sauce, sugar, garlic, pepper and green onions in a shallow dish. Let meat marinate at least 1 hour at room temperature; turn meat occasionally. Drain from marinade and reserve marinade.

Broil each strip for 3 to 5 minutes on each side, depending on how well done meat is preferred. Heat the remaining marinade with meat juices and pour over meat. Serve as entrée with rice, or cut into smaller pieces and serve with toothpicks as an appetizer. Yield: 6 servings as entrée.

MOROCCO

Morocco has been a constitutional monarchy since 1956, having previously been divided into a French protectorate, two Spanish zones and the international zone of Tangier. On November 12 of that year the country joined the UN. Its economy is primarily agricultural. The basic crops are wheat, barley, wine grapes, citrus and vegetables, and it is an important source of seasonal fruits and vegetables for Western Europe. Phosphate rock, iron ore, zinc and other minerals are mined and exported. Small, but of increasing importance, are its textile and leather industries. Many foreign visitors are intrigued with Morocco's principal cities—Rabat, its capital, Casablanca, an industrial and commercial center and port, Marrakech, and Tangiers—and tourism is booming.

Tagine

BRAISED CHICKEN WITH OLIVES

1 3-pound frying chicken, cut up (See Note)
3 tablespoons butter
1 cup water
2 medium onions, chopped
½ teaspoon ground ginger
⅛ teaspoon paprika
¼ teaspoon black pepper

¼ cup chopped parsley
1 7-ounce jar pitted whole green olives
Cold water
2 tablespoons lemon juice
2 tablespoons flour mixed with 2 tablespoons water

Brown chicken in hot butter in a 3-quart saucepan or in a Dutch oven. Add water, onions, ginger, paprika, black pepper and parsley to browned chicken. Mix well; cover and simmer for 45 minutes.

Drain olives; cover with water in small saucepan and bring to boil for 1 minute. Pour off water; repeat procedure and drain. Add to chicken shortly before serving. Place chicken with olives on serving dish. Pour lemon juice over chicken. Thicken remaining liquid with flour-and-water paste. (Add water, if necessary, to make 1½ cups.) Cook for 3 minutes over low heat, stirring constantly. Pour sauce over chicken and olives. Yield: 6 servings.

Note: Lamb may be used in place of chicken.

Gdra

CHICKEN OR LAMB WITH CHICK-PEAS

¾ cup butter
⅛ teaspoon saffron
1 tablespoon salt
1 teaspoon freshly ground
   black pepper
6 medium onions, finely
   chopped
2 3-pound stewing chickens,
   split lengthwise, or 4
   pounds shoulder of lamb,
   cut in serving pieces

2 1-pound cans chick-peas
Water
2 cups rice
Few sprigs of coriander or
   pinch of ground coriander
   seeds
1 large bunch parsley
Juice of 1 lemon

Melt the butter in a deep kettle or saucepan; stir in the saffron, salt, pepper and 1 chopped onion. Add chicken or lamb and chick-peas; cover with water and simmer for 1 hour.

Put rice in large muslin bag tied securely and place in the kettle containing the meat. Rice should be completely covered with broth. Remove bag of rice after 15 to 20 minutes and keep rice warm.

Continue cooking until meat is tender. During last hour of cooking, add remainder of onions, the coriander and parsley. Serve meat in the center of a large platter with the rice, chick-peas,

and sauce over the meat. Pour lemon juice over the entire surface.
Yield: 8–10 servings.

NEPAL

*Nepal is a land of spectacular mountain grandeur. Mt.
Everest, on its border, with an elevation of over 29,000
feet, is the highest in the world. Magnificent flora,
shrines and temples with rich carvings, and abundant
wild life make Nepal a marvelous place to visit. The
Nepalese are descendants of Mongols and East Indians.
They earned their living, until this decade, primarily
from agriculture. Now their rich resources of copper,
iron, sulphur, coal and other minerals are beginning to
be tapped. The UN voted Nepal into its organization
on December 14, 1955.*

Aluke Chop

POTATO CAKES

¾ cup finely chopped onion
2 tablespoons finely chopped
   green pepper
1 teaspoon salt
1½ teaspoons turmeric

1 quart freshly mashed
   potatoes
1 cup oil
2 eggs, slightly beaten

Add onion, green pepper, salt and turmeric to potatoes and mix
thoroughly. Cool mixture until it can be handled easily. Shape
into 12 round cakes, using about ⅓ cup of mixture for each cake.
Heat oil in a 12-inch frying pan to 380°F. or to sizzling point
when food is placed in it. Do not let oil smoke. Using a fork, dip
each cake into beaten egg and cover completely. Place in hot oil
and cook until brown on each side. Cakes will have light, crispy
crust. Lift each cake with spatula; drain on absorbent paper. To
keep warm until all cakes are fried, place on cookie sheet in a
preheated 250°F. oven. Serve hot with entrée. Yield: 6 servings
(12 cakes).

Aluko Achar

DRESSED BOILED POTATOES

2 pounds potatoes for boiling	1 teaspoon salt
Boiling water	4 tablespoons lemon juice
½ cup oil	2 tablespoons chopped hot
2 tablespoons dry mustard	green or red pepper

Boil potatoes until done, 20 to 40 minutes. Peel and cut in 1-inch cubes. Mix oil, mustard, salt and lemon juice. Pour over hot cubed potatoes and toss gently to coat each cube with dressing. Sprinkle chopped pepper over potatoes. Yield: 6 servings.

Kera Ko Misthanana

BANANA PUDDING

2 cups milk	1 tablespoon finely chopped
2 tablespoons sugar	almonds
¼ cup raisins	1½ cups diced bananas
	(3 medium)

Scald milk in a double boiler; add sugar, raisins, almonds and bananas. Cook for about 10 minutes, stirring constantly until mixture thickens, but remove from heat immediately if small curds show on spoon. Spoon into individual serving dishes, distributing fruit evenly. Cool and refrigerate. Serve cold with a garnish of tart red jelly. Yield: 6 servings.

NETHERLANDS

The Netherlands, though small in area—no town is more than 170 miles from Amsterdam, the capital—is a country rich in culture and tradition. The Hague is the seat of government of this constitutional monarchy, but Amsterdam is where the inauguration of sovereigns is held. Although The Netherlands is highly industrialized, 40 percent of the land is given to pasture, farming takes 30 percent, and the more than 4,000 miles of canals throughout the country are important in transportation.

Dutch cheese is famous throughout the world, as are the country's tulips and other flowering bulbs. Dutch food is notable, and the excellent Holland beer that accompanies it is enjoyed in many foreign lands. The Netherlands joined the UN on December 10, 1945.

Erwtensoep

PEA SOUP

2 cups green split peas	4 leeks, chopped
4¼ quarts water	1½ cups chopped celery
1½ teaspoons salt	½ pound smoked sausage,
2 pigs' feet	cubed or sliced

Soak the peas in 3 cups of the water for 12 hours. Drain; add remaining water to peas. Add salt and bring to a boil. Skim; add the pigs' feet, leeks and celery. Simmer for 3 to 5 hours, or until the pigs' feet are quite tender and the meat loosens from the bone. Lift out the pigs' feet and discard skin and bones. Add meat bits to soup. During the last half hour of cooking add the smoked sausage. Yield: 8 servings.

Gehaktnestjes

MEAT LOAF NESTS

½ pound ground beef	5 tablespoons butter, melted
½ pound ground veal	½ cup soft bread crumbs
½ pound ground pork	⅓ cup milk
¼ teaspoon black pepper	6 hard-cooked eggs
1½ teaspoons salt	½ cup dry bread crumbs
¼ teaspoon nutmeg	½ cup water
½ cup chopped onion	

Mix beef, veal, pork, pepper, salt and nutmeg. Brown onion in 2 tablespoons of the butter. Add soft bread crumbs to milk. Combine meat mixture, browned onions and bread crumbs and milk. Divide mixture into 6 equal portions; flatten each; place a hard-cooked egg in center of each and cover egg with meat, forming a ball. Roll balls in dry bread crumbs; brown in remaining melted butter on all sides. Add water and simmer 25 to 30 minutes or until meat is well done. Cut each ball in half; place cut side up. Yield: 6 servings.

Lofschotel

ENDIVE AND EGGS

12 stalks endive	6 hard-cooked eggs, halved
½ teaspoon salt	½ cup butter, melted
Water	Few grains of nutmeg

Wash endive in cold water. Boil stalks in salted water for about 15 minutes, keeping stalks whole. Drain. Place on hot platter; garnish with eggs, cut in halves. Serve with melted butter to which a few grains of nutmeg have been added. Yield: 6 servings.

NEW ZEALAND

New Zealand's climate is mild because the waters that surround its several islands moderate the temperature. At least 90 percent of the population is of British descent, the remainder mostly Maori, of Polynesian ancestry, who arrived in New Zealand around the tenth century. Rich grazing land is found on both North Island and South Island, the two main islands. The most important industries are sheep raising, both for wool and meat, and dairying. New Zealand joined the UN on October 24, 1945.

Roast Lamb with Mint Sauce

1 4- to 6-pound leg of lamb	*Mint Sauce:*
1½ teaspoons salt	½ cup chopped fresh mint or
½ teaspoon black pepper	¼ cup dried mint leaves
¼ cup flour	2 tablespoons sugar
	¼ cup hot water
	¼ cup mild vinegar

Wipe meat with damp cloth. Sprinkle with salt and pepper; rub well with flour. Place on rack in open pan, skin side up. Roast uncovered in a preheated 300°F. oven, allowing 30 minutes per pound for medium, and 35 minutes for well-done lamb.

To make mint sauce: Combine ingredients in a small saucepan over low heat; stir to dissolve sugar. Let stand in a warm place for 30 minutes.

Serve lamb with mint sauce. Yield: 8–12 servings.

Queen of Puddings

2 cups soft bread crumbs
2 cups milk, scalded
2 egg yolks
1 tablespoon sugar
1 teaspoon vanilla extract
2 teaspoons butter, softened

2 tablespoons raspberry jam

Meringue:
⅛ teaspoon salt
2 egg whites
2 tablespoons sugar
1 teaspoon lemon juice

Put crumbs in bowl and pour milk over them. Allow to stand 10 minutes. Beat yolks with sugar; add vanilla, soaked bread crumbs and butter. Turn into a buttered 1-quart casserole. Place dish in pan of hot water and bake slowly in a preheated 350°F. oven 45 minutes or until set. Remove from oven; allow to cool slightly. Spread top with raspberry jam.

To make meringue: Add salt to egg whites and beat until almost stiff. Gradually add sugar and lemon juice and beat until stiff. Spread over top of pudding. Place in a preheated 250°F. oven to brown slowly. Yield: 4 servings.

NICARAGUA

Nicaragua, the largest Central American republic, is fortunate in its rich deposits of gold, silver, copper, tungsten, mercury, bauxite, iron and other minerals, as well as in its valuable forests of mahogany, pine, cedar and rubber trees. The principal cities are Managua, the capital, and Granada, the oldest city in the country, with many Spanish landmarks from the sixteenth century. Nicaragua, a land of spectacular scenery, joined the UN on October 24, 1945.

Indio Viejo

OLD INDIANS

½ cup chopped onion
1 large tomato, chopped
2 tablespoons fat
4 cups cooked pork, cut in
small pieces
12–18 tortillas, warmed
(See Note)

½ teaspoon salt
¼ teaspoon red pepper
1 6-ounce can of tortilla sauce
or tomato sauce
1 egg, well beaten
1 banana, sliced
Grated rind of 1 orange

Cook onion and tomato in fat in large frying pan until onion is soft. Add meat, 1 tortilla cut in thin strips, salt, pepper and sauce. Simmer 10 to 15 minutes, stirring frequently. Add egg, banana and orange rind. Continue simmering for 10 minutes, stirring constantly. Place 1 to 2 tablespoons of mixture on each tortilla and roll; place on dish with rolled edge underneath. Pour remainder of meat mixture over tortilla rolls and serve hot as appetizers. Yield: 12–18 servings.

Note: Tortillas are available in cans.

NIGER

Niger is a land of desert and grassy lowlands, with volcanic mountains, yielding tin and tungsten. Its 3½ million people are primarily engaged in the raising of basic crops—millet, sorghum, rice, beans and wheat—and commercial crops of peanuts, cotton and tobacco. There are also cattle raising and incipient industrial mining. The Netherlands, France, Nigeria and the Ivory Coast are heavy traders with this country, which has been a member of the UN since September 20, 1960.

Bondo Gumbo

LAMB STEW

3 pounds lean stewing lamb,
cut in 2-inch cubes

2 tablespoons peanut or other
vegetable oil

½ cup minced onion

3 tablespoons flour

1 6½-ounce can tomato paste

1 4-ounce can pimientos

1½ teaspoons salt

1 quart water

1 pound fresh okra or 1
10-ounce frozen package

Whole Wheat Balls:

1 cup whole wheat flour

½ cup water

Boiling salted water

Brown lamb in hot oil in large skillet or Dutch oven. Add onion and flour to browned lamb; mix well and let flour brown. Add tomato paste, pimientos, salt and water. Simmer for 1½ hours. Add okra cut in thin rounds and continue simmering until okra becomes soft. Serve in deep dish with whole wheat balls.

To make whole wheat balls: Mix flour and water. Cook, covered, in top of double boiler for 30 minutes. Stir; form ¾-inch balls of dough and drop into pot of boiling salted water for 10 minutes. Remove with slotted spoon and drain. Yield: 6–8 servings.

NIGERIA

Nigeria, Africa's most populous country, became independent in 1960 and was admitted into the British Commonwealth in 1963. It comprises nearly 250 tribal and linguistic groups. Its rich natural resources include oil, coal, iron and natural gas. Cocoa is the main crop, and other exports include tobacco, tin, palm oil, cotton, hides and skins. Nigeria has been a member of the UN since October 7, 1960.

Ewa Dodo

SEAFOOD, PLANTAINS, AND BLACK-EYED PEAS

2 cups dried black-eyed peas
4 cups boiling water
½ cup chopped onion
1 large tomato, chopped
1½–3 teaspoons crushed red
  pepper
2 tablespoons tomato paste

3 tablespoons oil
1 7-ounce can tuna or 2
  4½-ounce cans shrimp
3 large plantains or bananas,
  cut in ¼-inch slices
½ teaspoon salt
1 cup oil for frying

Wash peas in cold running water. Cover with boiling water; boil 2 minutes. Remove from heat and soak 1 to 2 hours; simmer in the same water until tender, about 2 hours. Add onion, tomato and pepper to peas; cook for 15 minutes. Add tomato paste, oil and fish to peas; cover and simmer for 10 minutes without stirring. Remove cover; stir and simmer for 5 minutes.

Sprinkle plantains or bananas with salt; deep-fat fry in oil until golden brown. Drain on absorbent paper. Serve black-eyed peas (*ewa*) with plantains (*dodo*). Yield: 6 servings.

Fish with Coconut and Rice

3 cups Coconut Milk (pages
  23 and 40)
2 tablespoons chopped onion
3 medium tomatoes, peeled
  and quartered
1 teaspoon salt

½ teaspoon black pepper
1 pound crayfish or shrimp,
  cut in bite-size pieces (See
  Note)
1 cup rice

Combine coconut milk, onion, tomatoes, salt, pepper and crayfish in a saucepan; simmer for 5 minutes. Stir rice into milk mixture and simmer for 15–25 minutes or until fish and rice are done. Yield: 6 servings.

Note: Parboiled beef or chicken may be substituted for fish.

Okuku-Ngbolodi-Ogede

CHICKEN AND SPINACH MEDLEY

2 2½-pound frying chickens,
cut up
2½ teaspoons salt
2 small onions, 1 sliced and 1
chopped
1 cup plus 2 tablespoons
water
½ cup peanut oil
2 large tomatoes, chopped

2 tablespoons tomato sauce
1 tablespoon crushed red
pepper
1 12-ounce package frozen
chopped spinach, thawed
3 large plantains, sliced ¼
inch thick
1 cup oil for frying
Cooked rice

Cook chicken with 2 teaspoons salt, sliced onion and 2 table-spoons water until water has evaporated. Add ¼ cup peanut oil to chicken and fry until golden brown.

Combine chopped onion, tomatoes, tomato sauce, crushed red pepper and remaining peanut oil in small saucepan; add remaining water and simmer for 15 minutes. Pour sauce over chicken and simmer gently for 10 minutes. Squeeze water from spinach and add spinach to chicken mixture. Cook, uncovered, for 5 minutes.

Sprinkle plantain slices with salt and deep-fat fry until golden brown; drain. Serve chicken and fried plantains over hot rice. Yield: 6–8 servings.

Wolof Rice

STEAK STEW WITH RICE

2 pounds sirloin steak or
tenderized beef, cut in 12
pieces
4½ cups water
2 teaspoons salt
½ cup peanut oil

2 large tomatoes, chopped
1 large onion, chopped
2 tablespoons tomato paste
1½–3 teaspoons crushed red
pepper
1 cup rice

Simmer steak in ½ cup of water to which 1 teaspoon salt has been added, until water is evaporated. Brown steak in ¼ cup hot oil. Set aside and keep warm.

Combine in saucepan 1 tomato, ½ of the chopped onion, 1 tablespoon tomato paste, crushed red pepper, remaining oil and 2 cups water. Simmer until water is almost evaporated. Add browned meat to tomato mixture and simmer gently until mixture is thick and all water evaporated.

Cook rice in remaining water, to which 1 teaspoon of salt has been added, for 15 minutes. Add the remaining onion and tomato and remaining tomato paste, to the rice. Cover saucepan and simmer for 20 minutes. Combine steak and rice mixtures; simmer uncovered for 10 minutes. If desired, serve steak over rice rather than combining the 2 mixtures. Yield: 6 servings.

NORWAY

Norway has many delicious dishes in its cuisine. Among the specialties are game dishes, such as venison, elk and ptarmigan. Smoked meats and fish are also used extensively. There are fewer inhabitants to the square mile—about 30—than in almost any other European country. Most Norwegians live along the southern coast, inhabiting the main cities of Oslo, Bergen and Trondheim. Norway's economy has traditionally been concerned with shipping, fishing and forestry. Today her vast hydroelectric power is being tapped and there is an upsurge in her industries. Norway joined the United Nations on November 27, 1945. The first Secretary General of the UN, Trygve Lie, was a Norwegian.

Leverpostei

LIVER PASTE

1 pound pork liver	3 tablespoons butter
Cold water	3 tablespoons flour
4 tablespoons vinegar	½ cup milk
½ pound fresh fat pork	1 teaspoon salt
1 teaspoon chopped onion	½ teaspoon black pepper
2 anchovies, optional	1 egg, beaten

Soak liver in cold water and vinegar for 2 hours. Cube and pass through fine grinder with fat pork, onion and anchovies. Melt butter in saucepan and gradually add flour, mixing thoroughly. Add milk, cook over low heat and stir constantly to prevent lumping. Add salt and pepper. Continue cooking until thickened. Add egg to meat mixture; mix. Combine with white sauce. Pour mixture into greased, oblong baking pan, 9" x 5", and bake in a preheated 350°F. oven for 1 hour. Cool. Turn out. Yield: Serves 18 as an appetizer.

Note: This makes a delicious sandwich spread.

Fersk Suppe og Kjott

BEEF WITH CARROTS AND CABBAGE

3 pounds beef bones, preferably with marrow
3 quarts water
3 pounds beef chuck in 1 piece
1 package dried vegetable or meat soup mix
2 teaspoons salt
½ teaspoon black pepper
6 large carrots, cut in ¼-inch slices

1 small head cabbage, cut in eighths
2 tablespoons chopped parsley

Sauce:
1 cup stock
1 small onion, chopped
4 teaspoons cider or wine vinegar
2 teaspoons sugar
1 tablespoon flour mixed with 3 tablespoons cold water

Boil the bones with water in a 6-quart Dutch oven or heavy kettle for 1½ hours. Remove the bones. Add meat and dried soup mix to stock; simmer until meat is tender, about 2 hours. Remove meat from stock. Drain stock and chill; remove fat. Reserve 1 cup of stock for sauce. Return meat to stock; add salt, pepper, carrots and cabbage; cook until vegetables are tender, about 20 minutes. Remove meat, carrots and cabbage.

Serve soup garnished with parsley as first course. Slice meat; serve with carrots, cabbage and sauce as entrée.

To make sauce: Simmer stock and onion until onion is tender. Add vinegar and sugar. Add flour-and-water mixture; stir until sauce thickens.

Yield: 6–8 servings.

Rompudding

RUM PUDDING

1 tablespoon unflavored
  gelatin
¼ cup cold water
¼ cup boiling water
2 eggs, separated
⅓ cup sugar

¼ cup rum
½ cup heavy cream
Whipped cream for garnish
Maraschino cherries, red or
  green

Soften gelatin with cold water for 5 minutes; add boiling water. Cool until thick, but do not allow it to stiffen. Beat egg yolks until lemon-colored; add sugar and beat well. Add rum. Beat egg whites to a soft peak and fold into egg-yolk mixture. Beat the ½ cup cream to a soft peak and fold into egg mixture. Fold gelatin into egg-cream mixture.

Pour ½ cup of mixture into each of 6 individual molds rinsed in cold water, or pour all into quart mold. Place in refrigerator to congeal. Garnish with whipped cream and/or maraschino cherries. Yield: 6 servings.

Kong Haakon's Kake

KING HAAKON'S CAKE

1 cup butter
1 cup sugar
4 eggs, separated
1 cup flour, sifted
1 cup potato starch
1 teaspoon baking powder

Cream Filling and Topping:
3 egg yolks
6 tablespoons sugar
2 teaspoons cocoa
2 squares unsweetened
  chocolate, melted
2 teaspoons flour
1 cup heavy cream

Cream butter and sugar together with electric beater until light and fluffy. Add egg yolks, one at a time, beating on high speed after each addition. Use rubber scraper to clean sides of bowl at intervals. Blend in, using low speed, the flour, starch and baking powder. Beat egg whites until stiff; fold into batter with a gentle motion. Spoon mixture into a greased and floured 8-inch springform pan. Bake in a preheated 350°F. oven for 25 minutes. Cool.

Divide cake into three layers; fill and top with cream mixture. *To make cream filling and topping:* Whip egg yolks with sugar until light and fluffy. Blend in cocoa and chocolate. Add flour; place mixture in top of double boiler. Cook over low flame until mixture is thickened. Cool thoroughly. Whip cream; blend approximately 3 tablespoons whipped cream with cooled chocolate. Fold in remaining whipped cream and spread between layers and on top.

Norwegians decorate the cake with marzipan, with an *H* and a 7 (for King Haakon VII) and with small Norwegian flags. The cake should be kept chilled. It freezes well. Yield: 12 servings.

Fyrstekake

CAKE ROYAL

½ pound butter
2 cups flour
2 teaspoons baking powder
½ cup granulated sugar
1 egg, beaten

½ pound blanched almonds, finely chopped
2 cups confectioners' sugar
1 egg white
2–3 tablespoons white wine

Cut butter into flour. Add baking powder, sugar and egg. Mix. Divide dough in 2 parts. Roll out 1 part to cover bottom of a greased 9″ x 12″ baking pan. Combine almonds, confectioners' sugar, egg white and wine. Spread over bottom layer of cake. Roll out second part of cake dough. Cut in strips 1½ inches wide with cookie wheel and place side by side on top of the filling. Bake in a preheated 375°F. oven 30 to 35 minutes, until lightly browned. Yield: 12 servings.

PAKISTAN

Pakistan, consisting of two distinct geographical units, East and West Pakistan, separated by 1,000 miles of Indian territory, was formed in 1947 and became a UN member on September 30 of that year. Ninety percent of the population is Moslem, the rest is mostly Hindu, residing in East Pakistan. The food of this country is spicy. No pork is eaten, but lamb and chicken are very popular. Fruit is often served, sometimes in combination with meat.

Murgh-I-Mussalam

STUFFED CHICKEN

1 small onion
1 medium green ginger root
2 tablespoons black pepper
1 teaspoon salt
1 cup yogurt
1 3½- to 4-pound roasting
    chicken

Stuffing:
4 small boiled potatoes, diced
2 hard-cooked eggs, diced
Juice of 1 lemon
2 tablespoons blanched
    chopped almonds
¼ cup seedless raisins

¼ cup butter

Shred onion and ginger together. Mix with pepper, salt and yogurt. Stab chicken all over with fork and rub the mixture into it well. Allow to stand 1 hour or longer.

To make stuffing: Sprinkle potatoes and eggs with lemon juice. Add almonds and raisins. Mix.

Stuff and truss chicken. Melt butter in deep heavy pot; put chicken in with marinade; cover and cook very slowly until tender, about 2 hours, turning frequently. Yield: 4 servings.

Murgh Qorma

CHICKEN CURRY

2 large onions, sliced
¼ cup butter, melted
2½ cups water
2 teaspoons ground coriander
¼ teaspoon garlic salt
¼ teaspoon ground ginger
¼ teaspoon ground turmeric
⅛ teaspoon ground red pepper

1 2½-pound frying chicken,
    cut up
2 tablespoons yogurt
1 bay leaf
1 teaspoon salt
2 tablespoons cornstarch
    mixed with 3 tablespoons
    water

In a 10-inch skillet, cook the onions in butter until yellow. Add ½ cup water, coriander, garlic salt, ginger, turmeric and red pepper. Stir mixture until water is absorbed. Add the chicken and brown.

Then add the yogurt, bay leaf, salt and remaining 2 cups water. Cover and simmer until tender, 40 to 45 minutes. Add cornstarch paste to liquid, stir constantly, and simmer until sauce is thickened and clear. Remove bay leaf. Yield: 4 servings.

Baigan awr Dahí

EGGPLANT IN SOUR CREAM

1 small eggplant	¼ teaspoon garlic salt
3 tablespoons butter	1 cup sour cream
¼ teaspoon chili powder	

Peel eggplant and cut in ½-inch cubes. Sauté in butter until soft and golden brown; remove from pan. Blend chili powder and garlic salt with sour cream and pour over eggplant. Mix gently; chill before serving. Serve as a side dish with a curry. Yield: 1½ cups or 6 servings.

PANAMA

Panama, which means "abundance of fish," has big game fish—tarpon, marlin and tuna—in its coastal waters as well as trout in the mountain streams. In addition to income from the Canal Zone and the registry of world shippers, Panama derives income from an enormous production of bananas and the export of coffee and sugar. Panama has been a UN member since November 13, 1945.

Carimanolas

STUFFED SWEET POTATO BALLS

½ pound lean pork	½ teaspoon crushed red pepper
1 small tomato	2 teaspoons chopped parsley
1 small onion	1 hard-cooked egg, chopped
1 tablespoon oil	1 egg, beaten
¼ teaspoon oregano	2 pounds sweet potatoes,
½ teaspoon salt	steamed and mashed
¼ teaspoon black pepper	Fat for deep-frying

Grind pork, tomato and onion in a food chopper, using medium blade. Cook this mixture in oil in heavy frying pan about 15 minutes or until pork loses its pink color. Add the seasonings, parsley and chopped egg; mix well but gently.

Add the beaten egg to sweet potatoes and knead to make a dough. On floured board, pat or roll flat about 3 tablespoons of potato dough. Fill the dough with 1 teaspoon of the meat mixture, bringing the dough up, over and around the meat, shaping it somewhat like a football. Repeat until all of dough and filling are used. Fry the balls in deep fat at 375°F. for 4 or 5 minutes or until golden brown. Serve hot. Yield: 6 servings or 18–20 balls.

Note: The original recipe calls for yuca, which is not readily available. A dry, starchy type of sweet potato is an excellent substitute.

PARAGUAY

Paraguay, along with Bolivia, is one of the two South American countries without a coastline. The terrain was discovered in 1524 by a Portuguese explorer, but Spain established settlements soon thereafter. In 1811 Paraguay overthrew Spanish rule. Spanish remains the official language but Guarani, the language of its native Indians, is also spoken widely. Food crops include corn, which is prevalent in a wide variety of Paraguayan food. On October 24, 1945, Paraguay became a member of the UN.

Chipá Guazú

CORN PIE

2 large onions, chopped	1 egg
¼ cup oil	¾ cup milk
2 tomatoes, peeled and sliced	¼ cup melted shortening
1 cup sifted flour	1 1-pound can creamed corn
¾ cup yellow cornmeal	3 egg yolks
2 teaspoons baking powder	½ pound Bel Paese or other
¾ teaspoon salt	soft cheese, coarsely grated
2 tablespoons sugar	3 egg whites

Sauté onions in oil, stirring slowly until they begin to get soft. Add tomatoes and continue cooking for 5 minutes.

Sift together the flour, cornmeal, baking powder, salt and sugar. Add egg, milk and shortening. Stir only until blended. Add corn, egg yolks, cheese and onion-tomato mixture to cornmeal mixture. Beat egg whites stiff and fold in. Turn into a greased baking dish and bake in a preheated 300°F. oven for about 1 hour, or until firm. Serve immediately. Yield: 8 servings.

Kiveve

SQUASH CREAM

1 pound butternut squash or other winter squash
Boiling water
¼ teaspoon salt
2 tablespoons butter

¾ cup cornmeal
2 tablespoons sugar
¼ pound mild Cheddar cheese, diced

Peel squash and cut into small pieces. Place in 1½-quart saucepan; cover with boiling salted water. Cover pan. Cook until tender 15 to 20 minutes; drain and mash the squash. Stir in the butter, cornmeal and sugar. Cook in top of double boiler over direct heat for 5 minutes, stirring constantly. Cover and place over bottom of double boiler which is ⅓ full of boiling water. Cook over low heat for 30 minutes. Add the cheese to the cooked mixture; blend. Serve either hot or cold, with milk, or as a side dish with broiled fish. Yield: 6 servings.

Chipá Paraguay

BREAD

6 tablespoons butter
1 teaspoon aniseed
3 eggs
1 cup grated Parmesan or Cheddar cheese

6 tablespoons milk
2½ cups potato flour, sifted
½ teaspoon salt

Cream butter with aniseed. Add the eggs, one at a time, and beat well. Fold in grated cheese; alternately add milk, flour and salt. Mix until dough is smooth. Shape dough into a long roll; cut into

12 equal portions. Form each portion by hand into a smaller roll, shaped like a doughnut, and place on greased baking sheet. Bake in a preheated 375°F. oven about 35 minutes or until lightly browned. Yield: 6 servings.

Note: 2 teaspoons of baking powder may be added with the flour to make a lighter bread.

PERU

Peru was the center of the great Inca civilization which dominated the western coast of South America from the thirteenth to the sixteenth centuries. Spain then destroyed the Inca empire and continued to rule the territory until 1824. Mining and agriculture are the backbone of the Peruvian economy. Llamas, vicuñas, tigers, condors and other species of birds make Peru an exciting and picturesque country. Peruvian food is often seasoned with hot pepper; seafood is abundant and exceptionally good. Corn is believed to have originated in Peru. Peru was admitted to UN membership on October 31, 1945.

Arroz Jimeno

VEAL AND PORK WITH RICE

12 thin slices of veal (about 1½ pounds)
6 thin slices of pork
1 teaspoon salt
½ teaspoon black pepper
¼ cup flour
6 tablespoons oil
½ cup sherry
1 cup water
1 tablespoon cornstarch mixed with 4 tablespoons water
1 medium onion, diced
1 medium green pepper, diced
1 medium sweet red pepper, diced
1 clove garlic, crushed
2 tablespoons butter
2½ cups cooked rice
2 tablespoons raisins
2 tablespoons sliced almonds
2 hard-cooked eggs, chopped
½ cup cooked peas
2 tablespoons minced parsley

Season veal and pork with salt and pepper; dust lightly with flour. Brown veal quickly in 4 tablespoons of hot oil. When brown, add sherry; simmer for 5 minutes; remove veal. Add half of water to wine sauce; thicken with cornstarch paste. Simmer for 5 minutes. Return veal to sauce and keep warm.

Brown pork in remaining oil in separate pan; add remaining water and simmer until water evaporates and pork is tender and well cooked. Add more water if necessary.

Cook onion, green and red peppers and garlic in butter slowly until tender, but not browned. Add rice, raisins, almonds and eggs. (If necessary, cover and place in a preheated 250°F. oven, or over hot water, to keep warm.)

Place rice mixture in a mound in center of serving platter; place meats around rice; pour sauce over meat. Garnish rice with green peas and the meat with chopped parsley. Yield: 6 servings.

Note: For recipe to serve 50, see LARGE-SCALE BUFFET MENUS section, page 256.

Lomo de Cerdo a la Peruana

SWEET ROAST PORK

3-pound loin of pork	½ cup fine bread crumbs
1 tablespoon salt	¼ cup butter
1 cup sweet wine	1 cup milk
4 whole cloves	½ teaspoon ground cinnamon
⅓ cup brown sugar	1 cup seedless raisins

Rub loin of pork with salt and allow to stand 30 minutes. Mix the wine, cloves and brown sugar in a roasting pan. Place loin of pork in pan, turning several times to soak well in marinade, and let stand overnight in refrigerator. In morning, sprinkle pork with bread crumbs and dot with half the butter. Mix the remainder of butter, the milk, cinnamon and raisins with the marinade in the roasting pan. Bake in a preheated 325°F. oven 35 to 40 minutes per pound, or use a thermometer and bake until internal temperature is 185°. Baste frequently with marinade. Serve on platter and pour gravy over roast. Yield: 4 servings.

Ají de Gallina

CHICKEN IN PEPPER SAUCE

¼ pound hot red peppers
¾ pound white bread
2 cups light cream
1 2½–3-pound frying chicken,
  cut up
1 cup olive oil
1 large onion, minced
1 clove garlic, minced

1 tomato, peeled and
  quartered
2 cups chicken broth
1½ teaspoons salt
¼ teaspoon black pepper
6 tablespoons grated
  Parmesan cheese
2 hard-cooked eggs, quartered
6 ripe olives

Wash peppers, remove centers, soak in water overnight. Grind peppers. Remove crusts from bread. Break up bread and soften in cream. Brown chicken in oil. Remove chicken; brown onion and garlic in same pan. Add tomato, ground peppers and bread-and-cream mixture to pan. Add chicken broth, salt and pepper. Bring to boiling point and add chicken. Simmer over low heat for 1 hour. Sprinkle with cheese and garnish with eggs and olives. Yield: 6 servings.

Anticuchos

MARINATED BROILED MEAT

2 dried hot chili peppers,
  crushed
1 bay leaf, crumbled
1 small clove garlic, crushed
¼ cup lemon juice
2 tablespoons lime juice
2 tablespoons oil
2 tablespoons water
½ teaspoon salt
1 pound beef sirloin, cut in
  1-inch cubes
1 calf heart, trimmed of veins
  and fat, cut in 1-inch cubes,
  optional

½ pound chicken livers

Sauce:
1 tablespoon chopped onion
1 small clove garlic, crushed
3 tablespoons oil
3 tablespoons flour
2 tablespoons chili powder
  (or more, to taste)
2 cups hot chicken stock
3 tablespoons tomato purée
Salt, optional

Combine the first 8 ingredients and marinate beef and heart cubes in the mixture for 6 hours or longer. Turn meat in the marinade occasionally. If chicken livers are large, cut them in half; marinate with the other meats during the last ½ hour. Drain, and thread meats on skewers, using 4 cubes each of beef and heart and 2 pieces of chicken liver to each skewer. Broil in a preheated 450°F. broiler 5 inches from heat, turning to brown on all sides, for about 15 minutes or until done to your taste. Serve with the sauce below as a dip.

To make sauce: Cook onion and garlic in oil until tender, but not browned. Stir in flour and chili powder. Add stock and tomato purée and stir until thickened. Taste and add salt if needed. Reduce heat to a low simmer and cook for 30 minutes.

Yield: 6 as an entrée, 12 or more as an appetizer.

Leche Asada

CUSTARD WITH COGNAC

⅓ cup water
1 14½-ounce can evaporated milk
4 tablespoons cognac

4–6 tablespoons sugar
3 eggs, slightly beaten
⅛ teaspoon ground cinnamon
⅛ teaspoon nutmeg

Add water to evaporated milk; scald. Combine other ingredients. Add the hot milk. Pour into individual molds of oven glassware or earthenware. Set the molds in a baking pan; pour hot water into pan nearly to the top of the molds. Bake in a preheated 350°F. oven for 45 minutes or until inserted knife comes out clean. Serve cold as dessert, plain or with cream or fruit sauce. Yield: 6 servings.

Note: For recipe to serve 50, see LARGE-SCALE BUFFET MENUS section, page 264.

PHILIPPINES

The Philippines consists of some 7,000 islands off the southeast coast of Asia in the Malay Archipelago. Named for King Philip II of Spain, the islands were a Spanish possession from the mid-sixteenth century until they were ceded to the United States after the Spanish-American War. The Philippines achieved independence on July 4, 1946. The cuisine of the islands reflects their four cultural elements: Chinese, American, Spanish and Filipino—and delicious meals in all these styles are to be found in Manila, the capital, as well as elsewhere throughout the islands. The Philippines joined the UN on October 24, 1945.

Pancit Guisado

MEAT AND SEAFOOD WITH NOODLES

¾ cup cooked shrimp
¾ cup cooked pork cubes
¾ cup cooked ham cubes
¾ cup cooked chicken cubes
4 cloves garlic, peeled
1 medium onion, sliced
2 tablespoons fat
3 tablespoons soy sauce

1 teaspoon salt
½ teaspoon black pepper
1½ cups chicken stock
1 cup coarsely shredded
   cabbage
1 6-ounce package home-style
   noodles
1 lemon, thinly sliced

Cook shrimp, pork, ham, chicken, garlic and onion in fat until onions are yellow. Remove a small portion of each meat for garnishing, and set aside. To the remaining mixture add the soy sauce, salt, pepper, ½ cup chicken stock and cabbage. Stir; cover and simmer about 10 minutes, or until cabbage is cooked but still crisp.

Boil the noodles according to directions on package until almost done. Drain and add to meat-and-cabbage mixture. Add remainder of chicken stock; cover and simmer for 15 minutes. Remove garlic. Serve in deep platter, garnished with reserved seafood and meat and with lemon. Serve with additional soy sauce, if desired. Yield: 6 servings.

Note: Amount and kind of meat can be varied according to taste and available leftovers.

Sinigand Na Baka

BOILED BEEF WITH VEGETABLES

1 cup long-grain rice
6 cups boiling water
1 tablespoon plus 1 teaspoon
   salt
3 tomatoes, quartered

1½ pounds lean, boneless
   stewing beef
4 large radishes, sliced
3 cups spinach, cut in 1-inch
   pieces
Juice of 2 lemons

Add rice to water with 1 teaspoon salt. Cover tightly and cook over low heat for 20 minutes. Pour off rice water and reserve. (There should be about 4 cups of rice water.) Put rice aside to heat when meal is to be served. Place tomatoes and 2 cups rice water in saucepan. Bring to boil and add the beef. Season with remaining salt, and simmer until meat is tender, about 1½ hours. Add the radishes, spinach, lemon juice and as much of the remainder of the rice water as is necessary. Cook until the vegetables are tender, about 5 to 8 minutes. Yield: 6–7 servings.

Asado de Carajay

PORK PAPRIKA

1½ pounds boneless pork
   shoulder butt, cut in long
   slices
¼ teaspoon freshly ground
   black pepper
1½ teaspoons salt
1 clove garlic, crushed

3 tablespoons oil
1 bay leaf
¼ cup vinegar
1 tablespoon paprika
1 cup water
4 medium onions, quartered
1 medium tomato, sliced

Brown pork with pepper, salt and garlic in oil. Add bay leaf, vinegar and paprika. Continue browning for about 10 minutes; add water, onions and tomato. Cover; simmer mixture for 1 hour or until pork is done, checking occasionally and adding water if necessary. Yield: 4–6 servings.

Note: For recipe to serve 50, see LARGE-SCALE BUFFET MENUS section, page 258.

POLAND

Poland has survived many partitions, and although its borders have changed from century to century, it has kept its distinctive culinary achievements. There is a trace of Slavic heritage in the cooking, but national characteristics are very much in evidence. Yeast is often used; nuts are substituted for flour in the favored rich pastries; recipes often call for mushrooms, dill, garlic, onions and cabbage. With bigos, *probably Poland's most famous dish, one should drink the delicious Polish vodka, ice cold. Poland came into the UN on October 24, 1945.*

Bigos Myśliwski

HUNTER'S STEW

1 cup chopped onion
2 tablespoons butter
1 small head white cabbage, finely shredded
1 quart sauerkraut
6 large whole mushrooms, sliced
4 cups diced Polish sausage and any combination of roast beef, veal, pork or lamb
2 bouillon cubes dissolved in 1 cup water or 1 cup gravy from roast

2 sour apples, peeled and diced
1 tablespoon plum marmalade or 4 pitted prunes
1 cup tomato purée
1 bay leaf
1 teaspoon salt
½ teaspoon freshly ground black pepper
¾ cup red wine
1 clove garlic, crushed

Cook onion in butter until golden brown. Using a 3-quart casserole or baking dish, add all of the ingredients as listed, except the wine and garlic, to the casserole. Place covered casserole in a preheated 300°F. oven and cook for 2 hours. Add the wine and garlic and continue cooking for 20 minutes. Yield: 8 servings.

Note: Bigos should be prepared at least 3 days in advance of serving, and reheated once or twice a day during this period. Refrigerate in a glass or nonmetal container.

Chlodnik

COLD VEGETABLE AND YOGURT SOUP

1 1-pound can beets
1 fresh cucumber, diced
1 pickle, diced
½ cup diced radishes
1 clove garlic, minced
½ teaspoon salt
1 quart yogurt
1 bouillon cube

12 shrimp, cooked and
   deveined, or ½ pound roast
   veal, cubed
2 hard-cooked eggs, sliced
½ teaspoon sugar, optional
1 tablespoon chopped onion
2 tablespoons chopped parsley
2 tablespoons chopped dill

Drain canned beets and cut in fine strips; save beet liquid. Add beets, cucumber, pickle, radishes, garlic and salt to yogurt in a 2-quart bowl. Dissolve the bouillon cube in beet juice and add to the yogurt mixture; add the shrimp or veal, hard-cooked eggs, sugar and onion. Serve cold with parsley and dill sprinkled on top. Yield: 6 servings.

Note: This soup is usually served in Poland during the harvest season.

Grzyby w Smietanie

MUSHROOMS WITH SOUR CREAM

1 medium onion, sliced
¾ pound mushrooms, sliced
4 tablespoons butter
1 tablespoon flour
2 tablespoons milk

1 cup sour cream
½ teaspoon salt
⅛ teaspoon black pepper
⅛ teaspoon paprika

Brown onion and mushrooms lightly in hot butter in frying pan. Sprinkle with flour; blend and continue to cook until flour is slightly browned. Add milk and ½ cup sour cream. Continue cooking over low heat until onions and mushrooms are tender. Add seasonings and remainder of sour cream. Heat and serve as an appetizer on small toast rounds. Yield: 24–30 appetizers.

Sliwki w Pianie

PLUM FLUFF

1 cup red wine	4 egg whites
1½ cups sugar	½ teaspoon vanilla extract
2 pounds plums	

Combine wine and 1 cup of the sugar in a saucepan; bring to a boil, stirring until sugar is dissolved. Add plums; cover and simmer for 20 to 25 minutes, or until plums are soft. Beat egg whites until they stand in soft peaks; gradually add remaining sugar and vanilla, beating until mixture is stiff and glossy. Pour hot plums and juice into a 2-quart baking dish or into 6 individual casseroles; spread meringue over fruit. Bake in a preheated 375°F. oven for about 12 minutes. Serve hot. Yield: 6 servings.

Babka

GRANDMOTHER'S DELICIOUS CAKE

1 teaspoon salt	¼ cup butter, melted
14 egg yolks	1 cup sugar
3 envelopes dry yeast	¼ teaspoon almond extract
1 cup lukewarm milk	1 teaspoon vanilla extract
5½–6 cups flour	½ cup fine bread crumbs

Add salt to the egg yolks and beat until lemon-colored. Add yeast, milk and half the flour. Mix well and leave standing until double in bulk. Add remaining flour, butter, sugar, almond and vanilla extracts. Knead thoroughly. Let rise until double in bulk. Punch down and let rise again. Butter a 10-inch tube pan, sprinkle with bread crumbs and fill with dough to ⅓ of capacity. Let rise about 1 hour and bake in a preheated 350°F. oven for 40 minutes. Yield: 1 *babka*.

PORTUGAL

Portugal is the home of the great after-dinner drink port, which is red wine fortified with brandy, as well as of the world-famous Madeira wine. Madeira is used in making

*sauces that often combine tomatoes, garlic, oil and
onions—à la portugaise, as the French describe them.
Portugal exports an enormous quantity of fish—oysters,
sardines and tuna being most popular. Its various dishes
using codfish must be included in any gourmet's reper-
toire. Portugal joined the UN on December 14, 1955.*

Bacalhau do Céu

HEAVENLY CODFISH

2 pounds potatoes of uniform size, boiled in jackets	¼ cup flour
	½ teaspoon salt
2 tablespoons butter	⅛ teaspoon white pepper
¼ cup milk	1½ cups hot chicken stock
2 onions, sliced	1 cup scalded milk
¼ cup olive oil	2 tablespoons tomato paste or
2 pounds codfish	1 egg yolk
Béchamel Sauce:	8 hard-cooked eggs, sliced
¼ cup butter	1 egg yolk, beaten

Drain, cool and peel boiled potatoes. Slice about ¾ of the potatoes; mash remaining potatoes and season with butter and milk.
Cook onions in hot oil in 12-inch skillet until they are yellow; add
codfish, cut in small pieces. Cook for 30 minutes over low heat.

To make béchamel sauce: Melt butter; add flour, salt and pepper; gradually add chicken stock and milk. Stirring constantly,
cook over low heat 3 to 5 minutes. Add tomato paste to give flavor
and color, or add 1 slightly beaten egg yolk if a yellow sauce is
desired.

Grease a 2-quart casserole. Place a layer of codfish and onions
in the casserole, then a layer each of sliced potatoes, eggs and
béchamel sauce. Continue layers in order given, using all ingredients; top with mashed potatoes. Brush with beaten egg yolk. Bake
in a preheated 350°F. oven for 45 minutes or until potatoes are
golden brown. Yield: 6–8 servings.

Carne Assada à Portuguêsa

PORTUGUESE POT ROAST

1 4–5-pound boned rump roast	¼ teaspoon black pepper
2 cups red wine	¼ cup fat
3 large onions, sliced	Water
1 clove garlic, minced	2 large tomatoes, thickly sliced
2 teaspoons salt	

Marinate the roast (in refrigerator) for at least 24 hours with red wine, 2 of the onions, garlic, salt and pepper. Turn meat occasionally. Cook remaining sliced onion in hot fat in Dutch oven or heavy kettle with lid, until onion is brown; remove onion and save. Brown drained and dried roast on all sides in hot fat; add browned onion and marinade to roast. Add water to cover approximately ⅔ of the meat. Cover tightly; simmer, turning meat occasionally, for 4 to 4½ hours or until meat is fork tender. During last hour of cooking, add sliced tomatoes; remove cover during last 30 minutes. Sauce can be strained and thickened, if desired. Yield: 8–10 servings.

ROMANIA

Romania (Rumania is a common alternate spelling) lies in the northern part of the great vine-growing regions of Europe and has produced vines since before 700 B.C. on its rolling hills and sunny sheltered slopes. Only in recent years has Romania begun to expand its wine-export potential. It is also one of the world's largest producers of natural gas, and the second largest European oil producer. Romania joined the UN on December 14, 1955.

Vinete Conservate în Saramura

PICKLED EGGPLANT

1 medium eggplant	3 tablespoons vinegar
1 teaspoon salt	1 bay leaf
½ cup flour	1 clove garlic, minced
½ cup oil	½ teaspoon powdered ginger
3 tablespoons water	

Cut eggplant in ½-inch slices, leaving skin on; salt and let stand ½ hour. Dry with paper towels. Dip slices in flour and sauté in hot oil until lightly browned and tender. Drain on paper towels. Combine water, vinegar, bay leaf, garlic and ginger. Heat for 5 minutes. Remove bay leaf; pour sauce over eggplant. Refrigerate and serve very cold. Yield: 6–8 servings.

RWANDA

Rwanda, like Burundi, to which it once was joined as Rwanda-Urundi, is mainly composed of the people of the Hutu and Tusi ethnic groups. The Tusi, who are believed to have come from Ethiopia, invaded the area in the sixteenth century and established a kingdom. The country was colonized by the Germans and then by the Belgians, until it became a UN trust territory in 1946. Independent since July 1, 1962, Rwanda became a member of the UN on September 18 of that year.

Beef Stew à la Rwanda

1½ pounds stewing beef, cut in 1-inch cubes	4 tablespoons lemon juice
	4 tablespoons tomato sauce
1 medium onion, diced	1 teaspoon salt
2 tablespoons oil	½ teaspoon ground sage
4 green plantains (available in Spanish food shops)	¼ teaspoon black pepper
	Water

Cook meat and onion in hot oil in heavy saucepan or Dutch oven until brown. Add plantains, cut crosswise into 4 pieces and rubbed with lemon juice. Cook for 5 minutes over low heat, stirring constantly. Add tomato sauce and seasonings; cover mixture with water and simmer for 1½ to 2 hours. Add water, if needed. Yield: 6 servings.

SAUDI ARABIA

Saudi Arabia occupies four-fifths of the Arabian Peninsula. The form of government is a hereditary monarchy, and its people are almost entirely Moslem. Mecca, the Prophet Mohammed's birthplace, is visited by more than 300,000 Moslems annually. Saudi Arabia possesses one of the greatest oil reservoirs in the world. An agricultural country except for oil, its chief products are dates, wheat, barley and fruit. Camels, horses, donkeys and sheep are raised. The country became a member of the UN on October 24, 1945.

Tadjin Ahmar

LAMB WITH SAFFRON

1 cup large dried prunes	¼–½ teaspoon saffron
Cold water	1 small stick cinnamon
3 pounds lean lamb, cut in 2-inch strips	1 tablespoon salt
3 tablespoons butter	⅛ teaspoon black pepper
1 large onion, finely chopped	1 tablespoon grated orange peel
2 tablespoons flour	1 tablespoon sugar
Hot water	

Soak prunes in cold water for 1 to 2 hours.

Brown the lamb in the butter; remove the meat and add onion to remaining fat and cook until brown. Add the flour to the onion and continue cooking until mixture is deep brown, stirring continuously.

Add onion-and-flour mixture to the meat in a 2-quart casserole. Cover with hot water; add saffron, cinnamon, salt and pepper. Cook in a preheated 325°F. oven for about 2 hours or until meat is almost tender. Add prunes. Continue cooking meat for another hour; add orange peel and sugar. Serve immediately. Yield: 8–10 servings.

Fouja Djedad

CHICKEN STUFFED APPLES

6 baking or cooking apples
1 cup cooked chicken, chopped

¼ teaspoon ground cloves
6 teaspoons sugar
½ cup buttered bread crumbs

Wash and core the apples, making a cavity for the filling. Combine chicken with the clove; fill the apple cavities with the chicken. Place stuffed apples in baking dish. Sprinkle each apple with 1 teaspoon sugar; top with bread crumbs. Cover and bake in a preheated 375°F. oven for 45 minutes or until apples are tender. Remove cover and cook for 5 minutes to brown bread crumbs. Yield: 6 servings.

Munkaczina

ZESTY ORANGE SALAD

3 large oranges
2 sweet onions
3 tablespoons oil
3 tablespoons vinegar

⅛ teaspoon Cayenne pepper
½ teaspoon salt
12 pitted ripe olives, sliced

Peel oranges and onions; slice thinly. Arrange the slices alternately in a serving bowl; pour over slices dressing of oil, vinegar, pepper and salt. Let salad marinate for 1 hour at room temperature. Top with slices of ripe olives before serving. Yield: 6 servings.

SENEGAL

Senegal, whose capital, Dakar, was once the capital of French West Africa, has been a member of the UN since September 25, 1960. Between 400 and 200 B.C. the peoples of Senegal first started to trade with the Carthaginians, then with the merchants of Ghana and Mali, and in recent centuries with Portugal, France, Hol-

*land and Britain. Senegal has rich phosphate deposits,
which are processed and exported; other exports are
peanuts and fish.*

Beignets

FRITTERS

1½ cups sifted flour	⅔ cup milk
1½ teaspoons baking powder	1 teaspoon vanilla extract
¼ teaspoon salt	2 drops orange extract
1 egg, well beaten	Fat for deep frying

Sift dry ingredients together. Add egg mixed with milk, vanilla
and orange extracts. Stir until smooth; drop from a spoon into
deep fat heated to 375°F., and fry a deep golden brown.

For fruit fritters, use 6 bananas, cut in thick slices, or sections
of 3 oranges with seeds and pith removed. Add fruit to batter just
before frying. Yield: 6 servings.

Boulettes

FISH BALLS IN SAUCE

3 cloves garlic, peeled	Oil for frying
½ cup chopped parsley	*Sauce:*
2 large tomatoes	1 onion, chopped
3-inch slice French bread	3 tablespoons tomato paste
2 pounds cod or haddock fillets	2 cups water
1 onion	1 teaspoon salt
2 teaspoons salt	Few grains of Cayenne pepper
¼ teaspoon black pepper	2 tablespoons vinegar

Put first 6 ingredients through food chopper, using fine blade. Add
salt and pepper. Blend mixture well; form into balls about 1½
inches in diameter. Fry in 1 inch of oil heated to 375°F., until
well browned.

To make sauce: Fry onion in 2 tablespoons oil left from frying
fish balls. Add tomato paste, ¼ cup water, salt and pepper; mix
well. Add remaining water and cook until reduced to desired con-

sistency. Add vinegar and fish balls; simmer for 1 hour. Serve as appetizers. Yield: 6–8 servings.

SIERRA LEONE

Sierra Leone, bordered by Liberia and Guinea, is populated by various tribes as well as several thousand Creoles who are descendants of freed slaves, most of whom live in Freetown, the nation's capital and largest city. Sierra Leone is one of the world's major diamond producers, and it is not an unusual sight to see workers panning for alluvial diamonds along a riverbank. Rice and cassava are basic food crops, but palm kernels, cacao, ginger and coffee are commercial crops. Sierra Leone entered the UN on September 27, 1961.

Coconut Delight

2 cups milk
½ cup sugar
3 tablespoons farina
1 cup flaked or grated coconut

¼ teaspoon salt
1 teaspoon vanilla extract
6 teaspoons strawberry
  preserves

Scald milk in top part of a double boiler. Add sugar; blend farina into hot milk mixture and place over bottom of double boiler which is ⅓ full of boiling water. Cook over low heat for 15 minutes, stirring occasionally. Add coconut and salt; continue cooking for 10 minutes. Remove from heat; cool slightly; add vanilla. Chill and serve with 1 teaspoon of strawberry preserves over each portion. Yield: 6 servings.

Banana Akara

BANANA FRITTERS

6 bananas, well ripened
1 cup rice or wheat flour
¼ cup sugar dissolved in ¼
  cup water

½–1 teaspoon nutmeg
Fat for frying

Mash bananas with a fork or use blender to make pulp; add the flour, sugar-water mixture and nutmeg. Add water, if needed, to make batter of pancake consistency. Mix well. Fry like pancakes in oiled frying pan until golden brown. Yield: 24 small pancakes.

SINGAPORE

Singapore is where East meets West gastronomically. Many cuisines are represented: Malaysian, Indian, Indonesian, European and Chinese—the latter style has been specially developed in a manner known as "Straits Chinese." A tiny island off the Malay Peninsula, Singapore became a sovereign state in 1965 (and a UN member on September 21 of that year) after two years as part of Malaysia and 150 years as a British possession.

Nasi Goreng

FRIED RICE

3 tablespoons peanut oil
3 fresh red chili peppers,
  seeded and finely chopped
6 shallots, chopped
1 cup shelled shrimp
4 ounces (¾ cup) cooked lean
  pork, cubed
4 ounces (¾ cup) cooked
  white chicken meat, cubed
4 ounces mushrooms, sliced

2 or 3 chicken livers, cut in
  small pieces
8 cups cold boiled rice
Salt
2 eggs, beaten
2 Chinese parsley sprigs
  (coriander leaves), finely
  chopped
2 green onions, chopped

Heat the oil. Sauté the peppers and shallots until they are cooked through and the shallots are golden. Add the shrimp, pork, chicken, mushrooms and chicken livers. Continue to simmer gently until the livers and mushrooms are cooked, about 15 minutes. Add the boiled rice. Mix all the ingredients together, making sure the rice grains are separated. Season with salt. Pour eggs over the rice. Stir continuously until the eggs are cooked and the rice is dry. Add the chopped Chinese parsley and green onions. Serve immediately on a very hot platter. Yield: 8–10 servings.

SOMALIA

Somalia, adjacent to Ethiopia on the East African coast, has inhabitants of mixed Ethiopian, Arab and Indian ancestry. Many are herdsmen, raising camels, sheep and goats for export, both alive and as hides or skins. There are irrigated plantations in the southern part of the country, where many tons of bananas are grown. In 1963 a five-year plan was inaugurated to develop transportation, communications, agriculture and industry. This was but three years after Somalia's emergence as an independent nation—and a UN member as of September 20, 1960.

Huris Hilib

VEAL WITH TOMATO TOPPING

½ green pepper, sliced
2 small potatoes, pared and
   quartered
Water
½ cup chopped onion
1 pound veal, cut in ½-inch
   cubes

2 tablespoons oil
1 teaspoon salt
¼ teaspoon white pepper
1 teaspoon basil
½ teaspoon crushed garlic
1 fresh tomato, peeled and
   sliced

Boil pepper and potatoes in a saucepan with water to cover until vegetables are half cooked, about 15 minutes. Grind in a food chopper, using fine blade. Cook the onion and the veal in the oil for 15 minutes or until brown; add the potato mixture and the seasonings to the meat. Put into greased casserole; place slices of tomato on top of mixture. Cover and cook in a preheated 325°F. oven for 20 minutes. Yield: 6 servings.

SOUTH AFRICA

South Africa's cooking reflects a number of influences. The Dutch pioneers in this country combined many of their familiar spices such as cumin and saffron with local ingredients, producing a distinctive cuisine. The British adapted their native ways of cooking to an unusually large selection of luscious fruits and vegetables. The tastes of other groups are evidenced in the Indian curries and the Bantu corn dishes. South Africa has been active in the UN since November 7, 1945.

Bobotee

MEAT TIMBALES

1 medium onion, chopped
2 tablespoons butter
1 slice white bread
1 cup milk
2 eggs, beaten
1 pound ground beef
1½–3 teaspoons curry powder
Juice of 1 lemon

12 almonds, chopped
8 dried apricots, soaked and chopped
¼ cup chutney
Salt
Black pepper
2 bay leaves, broken in pieces

Sauté onion in butter until golden brown. Soak bread in milk, remove and squeeze dry. Add eggs to milk. Mix the meat with the bread, onion, curry powder, lemon juice, almonds, apricots, chutney, salt and pepper. Add half of egg mixture and blend well.

Place in a greased shallow baking dish or 6 individual casseroles. Hollow center slightly to allow for rising. Stick pieces of bay leaves on top. Bake in a preheated 350°F. oven for 20 minutes. Remove bay leaves and pour rest of egg mixture on top. Return to oven and continue baking until custard sets, about 25 minutes. Yield: 6 servings.

Sosaties

SKEWERED LAMB WITH SAUCE

1 leg of lamb	½ teaspoon curry powder
1 teaspoon salt	2 tablespoons sugar
½ teaspoon black pepper	2 cups water
1 cup vinegar	½ pound fat salt pork, cut in
1 medium onion, thinly sliced	1-inch squares, ½ inch thick
12 dried apricot halves, cut in	2 tablespoons cornstarch
small pieces	½ cup cold water

Cut lamb crosswise in 1½-inch slices; cut again into 1½-inch squares for skewering. (Reserve poorly shaped pieces for another dish.) Salt and pepper cubes.

Prepare a marinating sauce of vinegar, onion, apricots, curry powder, sugar and water. Boil for 3 minutes; cool and pour over lamb in a deep container. Add water, if needed, to cover lamb. Refrigerate lamb with marinade for 2 days.

Remove lamb and drain. Use 12 skewers and alternate lamb and fat salt pork. Grill over red-hot coals or broil under direct oven heat until meat is brown and tender, about 15 minutes.

Heat marinating sauce to which paste of cornstarch and water has been added. Cook until sauce thickens; serve the *sosaties* with the sauce and with chutney or yellow peach pickle (recipe follows). Yield: 12 *sosaties.*

Yellow Peach Pickle

1 29-ounce can sliced yellow
  peaches
⅔ cup peach juice
1 cup vinegar
1 teaspoon peppercorns
1 teaspoon coriander seeds
1 teaspoon whole allspice
½ teaspoon salt

⅓ cup brown sugar
½ teaspoon turmeric
1 teaspoon curry powder
1 teaspoon cornstarch
½ cup chopped onion
1 hot chili pepper, chopped, or
  ½ teaspoon crushed red
  pepper

Drain peaches and measure ⅔ cup peach juice. Simmer peach juice and vinegar with peppercorns, coriander and allspice, spices tied loosely in a muslin bag, for 10 minutes. Mix salt, sugar, turmeric, curry powder, and cornstarch. Add ½ cup of peach juice pickle mixture; blend and return to pickle mixture. Cook until thickened, stirring constantly. Add onion, peaches and chopped chili pepper or crushed red pepper; cook for 10 minutes. Remove spice bag. Fill pint jars and seal, if not to be used soon. Serve as a relish with chicken, turkey, lamb or fish. Yield: 2 pints.

Note: For recipe to serve 50, see LARGE-SCALE BUFFET MENUS section, page 254.

SOUTHERN YEMEN

Southern Yemen is an Arab state in the southwestern Arabian Peninsula. There are mountains in the western part of the country, but the major area is a desert plateau almost devoid of rain. The population, composed almost entirely of Moslem Arabs, is concentrated along the coast, particularly in its largest city, Aden. Herding and farming are the principal occupations of the citizens, with sheep and goats grazing along the edges of the desert. Cotton, grains and fruits are cultivated. Also important to the economy are soap and cigarette manufacturing and salt and oil refining. Southern Yemen has been a UN member since December 14, 1967.

Bint Assahn

PASTRY WITH HONEY

¼ pound butter	¼ cup melted butter
2¼ cups flour	½ cup finely chopped nuts,
½ teaspoon salt	optional
3 eggs, beaten	Honey
½ cup milk	Additional melted butter

Work butter into flour; add salt. Add the eggs and milk to the flour and mix well. Divide the dough into small balls about the size of an egg. Work each ball into a very flat, wafer-thin circle. Place a circle on a round pie tin or on a cookie sheet; cover with melted butter; sprinkle with nuts, if you are using them. Lay another circle lightly on the first, spread with melted butter and sprinkle with nuts. Continue until all circles form one stack. Bake in a preheated 350°F. oven about 45 minutes or until golden brown. Serve hot with honey and more melted butter. Yield: 6 servings.

SPAIN

The cuisine of Spain varies from region to region, mirroring varied historical developments and geographical differences. Moorish and Arabic influences are noted in the south, Greco-Roman in the east. Along the Mediterranean coast much use is made of fish and seafood, while meat, fowl and game are more popular inland. The abundance of olives makes the oil widely available for cooking and seasoning. Spain is equally famous for its sherry, produced from vineyards in Jerez. Industrially, Spain is a world leader in the production of mercury and cork. Since 1965 there has been a phenomenal rise in tourism. Spain joined the UN on December 14, 1955.

Carbonada

SWEET AND SOUR BEEF WITH FRUIT

4 medium onions, sliced
¼ cup butter
1 large tomato, peeled and
   sliced
1½ pounds ground beef
1 teaspoon salt
¼ teaspoon black pepper

1 cup beef stock
2 pears, peeled and sliced
2 peaches, peeled and sliced
4 plums, sliced
4 medium potatoes, peeled and
   diced
¼ cup seedless raisins

Sauté the onions in butter until lightly browned. Add the tomato
and cook for 2 minutes. Add the beef, stir well and cook for 2
minutes. Add salt, pepper and stock. Cover and simmer slowly
for 1 hour. Add the pears, peaches, plums and potatoes; cook until potatoes are tender, 15 to 20 minutes. Do not overcook. Add
raisins. Stir. Allow to stand for 1 minute. Serve hot. Yield: 6
servings.

Pollo a la Pepitoria

CHICKEN WITH SHERRY AND ALMONDS

1 3-pound frying chicken, cut
   up
½ cup flour
1 teaspoon salt
¼ teaspoon black pepper
1 egg, beaten
1 cup dry bread crumbs
1 cup oil for frying
½ cup chopped onion
1 cup dry sherry

3 cups chicken broth
½ teaspoon saffron
1 tablespoon chopped parsley
1 bay leaf
1 clove garlic, minced
12 dry almonds, finely
   chopped
2 hard-cooked egg yolks
2 tablespoons flour mixed
   with 4 tablespoons broth

Coat chicken with flour seasoned with salt and pepper; dip each
piece in beaten egg and then into bread crumbs. Place breaded
chicken in hot oil in large frying pan and cook until brown. Remove chicken from oil and fry onion in remaining oil until brown;
drain off excess oil and reserve. Return chicken to pan with on-

ions; add sherry and heat slowly; add broth to cover chicken. Add saffron, parsley and bay leaf; cover tightly and cook over low heat or in a preheated 325°F. oven for 30 to 40 minutes or until chicken is tender. Stir occasionally during cooking period.

Brown garlic in reserved oil. Make a paste of garlic, almonds and egg yolks; add flour-and-broth mixture to paste. Mix well.

Remove chicken from pan when tender and stir paste into remaining broth slowly, stirring constantly. Bring to boiling point; reduce heat and simmer for 5 minutes. Return chicken to sauce; simmer until thoroughly heated. Yield: 6 servings.

Langosta Diablo

DEVILED LOBSTER

1¼–1½ pounds lobster tails
½ cup olive oil
1 clove garlic, minced
3 tablespoons butter
½ cup chopped mushrooms
¼ cup chopped pimiento
⅛ teaspoon tarragon
3 tablespoons sliced ripe olives
3 tablespoons grated onion
½ teaspoon salt
⅛ teaspoon freshly ground black pepper
3 tablespoons sherry

Sauce:
2 tablespoons butter
4 tablespoons chopped scallions
1 teaspoon dry mustard
1 teaspoon anchovy paste
1 hard-cooked egg yolk
2 tablespoons olive oil
1 tablespoon tarragon vinegar
2 tablespoons sherry
¼ teaspoon salt
Dash of Tabasco sauce

Cut the underside of lobster tails down the center. Heat oil in a large skillet. Add garlic. Place lobster split side down in the oil. Cover and cook over medium heat for 5 minutes. Turn lobster, cover, and continue cooking for 10 minutes. Let lobster cool. Remove meat from shell and cut into bite-size pieces. Reserve shell. Heat butter in skillet and add mushrooms, pimiento, tarragon, olives, onion, salt, pepper and lobster meat. Mix thoroughly and cook 5 minutes; add sherry. Fill shells with mixture.

To prepare sauce: Heat butter, add scallions, and cook slowly for 5 minutes. Add remaining ingredients and spoon over stuffed lobster. Brown under broiler about 5 minutes. Yield: 4 servings.

SUDAN

Sudan became an independent republic in January 1956 and joined the UN on November 19 of that year. For 50 years before, it had been ruled jointly by Britain and Egypt. It is the largest country in Africa. Most of its northern area consists of the Sahara desert. The Nile river flows through central Sudan, creating a fertile region. The economy is largely agricultural, the principal crops being peanuts, millet, sesame seeds, castor beans and dates. Cotton is the largest cash crop. Most of Sudan's trade is with Britain, West Germany and Italy. The Sudanese are very fond of lamb, which is often served with a fiery hot sauce on the side.

Shorba

PEANUT BUTTER SOUP

2 pounds beef bones	1½ teaspoons salt
½ pound ground lean beef	½ cinnamon stick
6 cups water	2 cardamom seeds
1 onion	2 tablespoons peanut butter
2 cloves garlic	Juice of ½ lemon
6 black peppercorns	

Bring bones, ground meat and water to a boil; add onion, garlic, peppercorns and salt. Boil for ½ hour; add cinnamon and cardamom and continue boiling for 1 hour more; drain. Combine peanut butter and ¼ cup of the stock, and add to remaining drained stock; simmer for 3 minutes; add lemon juice and serve. Yield: 6 servings.

Shorbat Robe

YOGURT AND CUCUMBER SALAD

2 cucumbers   ⅛ teaspoon garlic powder
1 pint yogurt   ⅛ teaspoon black pepper
½ teaspoon salt

Peel and chop cucumbers. Combine with yogurt, salt, garlic powder and pepper. Serve on lettuce. Yield: 6 servings.

Note: For recipe to serve 50, see LARGE-SCALE BUFFET MENUS section, page 263.

SWAZILAND

Swaziland, a former British territory in Southeast Africa, achieved full independence on September 6, 1968, and joined the UN on September 27 of that year. The economy is based primarily on agriculture, the chief crops being corn and sorghum. Sugar cane, rice, citrus and other fruits and vegetables are also grown. Cattle are raised all over the country; formerly a symbol of social status, they now have economic importance. The leading exports are iron ore, asbestos and sugar, which go chiefly to South Africa, Britain and Japan.

Mealie Pudding

½ cup corn, cut from the cob   Salt
2 eggs, beaten   Black pepper
4 tablespoons melted butter   ¼ teaspoon nutmeg
1 teaspoon sugar   ½ cup milk

Chop or pound the corn. Add the eggs, butter, sugar, salt, pepper, nutmeg and milk. Mix well. Butter a shallow ovenproof dish and bake in a preheated 350°F. oven for 20 minutes. Yield: 4 servings.

SWEDEN

Sweden has adopted the cuisine of many lands, but there are many characteristics of its food which are distinctly Swedish. Gravad lax *and* Jansson's Frestelse *are exemplary, as is* kokt lamm med dill sås. *Swedes toast each other at a dinner party with little glasses of aquavit, saying* Skal *and looking into the eyes of the person being toasted. At a large party, this uses up a lot of aquavit and creates the necessary appetite for the wide range of delicious dishes displayed. Sweden joined the UN on November 19, 1946. The second Secretary General of the UN was a Swede, Dag Hammarskjöld, who died tragically in a plane crash while on special duty.*

Gravad Lax

MARINATED SALMON

3 pounds center-cut fresh
  salmon
3 bunches fresh dill
½ cup salt
½ cup sugar
1 teaspoon freshly ground
  black pepper

Dressing:
6 tablespoons olive oil
3 teaspoons vinegar
1 teaspoon prepared mustard
½ teaspoon salt
Dash of pepper

Fresh dill for garnishing

Wipe the salmon with a damp cloth. Cut fish in half lengthwise. Place ⅓ of dill in bottom of dish or pan (enameled, glass or china, not metal). Mix salt, sugar and pepper and rub into fish; place one piece of fish, skin side down, on dill in pan; place second bunch of dill on top of fish and sprinkle with any remaining mixture of seasonings. Place second piece of fish, skin side up, on top of first piece. Put remaining dill on top. Cover fish with a very heavy weight; refrigerate for 16 to 24 hours. Remove dill; cut salmon in either thin or portion-size slices; arrange on platter garnished with fresh dill and serve with dressing.

To make dressing: Put all ingredients in bottle or small jar. Shake until well blended.

This salmon is served in Sweden as an entrée with dressing, poached eggs, spinach and boiled potatoes. Yield: 6 servings. It may also be served as an appetizer.

Kokt Lamm med Dill Sås

BOILED LAMB WITH DILL SAUCE

1 2- to 2½-pound breast or shoulder of lamb
Boiling salted water
3 or 4 black peppercorns
1 bay leaf
12 sprigs of fresh dill
Black pepper

Dill Sauce:
2 tablespoons butter

2 tablespoons flour
2 cups stock from cooking lamb
2 tablespoons chopped dill
1½ tablespoons vinegar
½–1 tablespoon sugar
Salt
1 egg yolk, beaten

Place meat in kettle and cover with boiling salted water. Bring to boil, skim; add peppercorns, bay leaf, few sprigs of the dill, and pepper. Cover and simmer 1 to 1½ hours or until meat is tender. Cut in pieces, place on hot platter, and garnish with remaining dill sprigs. Serve the dill sauce separately.

To make the dill sauce: Melt butter, add flour and stir until well blended. Add stock gradually, stirring meanwhile; then cook slowly 10 minutes, stirring occasionally. Add dill, vinegar, sugar and salt. Remove from heat. Mix a little of the hot sauce with the egg yolk. Mix with remaining sauce. Yield: 4–6 servings.

Note: For recipe to serve 50, see LARGE-SCALE BUFFET MENUS section, page 262.

Rågsiktbröd

SWEDISH RYE BREAD

1½ cups lukewarm water
¼ cup molasses
⅓ cup sugar
1 tablespoon salt
2 tablespoons shortening

Finely shredded rind of 1 or 2 oranges
2 envelopes dry yeast
2½ cups sifted rye flour
2½–3 cups sifted white flour

Mix together the water, molasses, sugar, salt, shortening and orange rind. Crumble the yeast into the mixture and stir until it is dissolved. Mix in, first with spoon, then with hand, the rye flour and the white flour, in 2 stages, using enough to make a soft but manageable dough. Turn dough onto lightly floured cloth-covered board, cover and let stand 10 minutes to tighten up, then knead until smooth and elastic. Place in greased bowl. Cover with damp cloth and let rise until double in bulk, about 2 hours. Punch down dough. Round up and let rise again until not quite double in bulk, about 45 minutes. Punch down and divide in half. Form into 2 round loaves. Place on lightly greased baking sheet. Cover with damp cloth and let rise until double in bulk, about 1 hour. Bake in a preheated 375°F. oven about 35 minutes. Cool on rack. Yield: 2 loaves.

Jansson's Frestelse

JANSSON'S TEMPTATION

2 onions, thinly sliced	14 anchovy fillets
3 tablespoons butter	1½ cups light cream
5 medium potatoes, peeled	

Cook onions in 1 tablespoon of butter until yellow. Cut potatoes into lengthwise strips about ¼ inch thick. Butter a 2-quart casserole or baking dish; place layers of potatoes, anchovies and onions alternately in the casserole, ending with a layer of potatoes. Dot with remaining butter. Pour cream over top; bake in a preheated 350°F. oven for 1 hour or until potatoes are done. Serve hot. Yield: 6 servings.

Rödkål

RED CABBAGE

1 large head red cabbage	2 pounds apples, peeled, cored
Salt	and finely diced
3 tablespoons butter	⅘ quart red wine
1 cup seedless raisins	

Remove outer leaves and stem of cabbage. Shred cabbage finely and salt lightly. Melt butter in 3-quart saucepan; add cabbage.

Cook over low heat until all fat is absorbed; add raisins and apples. Add wine, cover cabbage with brown paper and lid and cook 1 to 1½ hours. Yield: 4–6 servings.

SYRIA

The food of Syria is very similar to that of its neighbor Lebanon. Turkish overtones are strong, as Syria was part of the Ottoman Empire for many years. Much use is made of zucchini and eggplant. The economy is basically agricultural, Syria's leading crops being cotton, wheat and barley. International trade is also important, just as it was in ancient times when Syria was at the center of prosperous trade routes. Fees and taxes are paid to Syria on all oil from Iraq carried to the Mediterranean by pipelines across the country. Syria was one of the original members of the UN, joining the organization on October 24, 1945.

Menazzeleh

MEAT-TOMATO MIXTURE

1 pound chopped beef	2 tomatoes, peeled and
1 large onion, chopped	chopped, or ¾ cup stewed
1 clove garlic, minced	tomatoes
2 tablespoons oil	⅓ cup finely chopped parsley
½ teaspoon salt	½–1 teaspoon cumin
1 teaspoon black pepper	2 tablespoons chopped mint
	4 eggs, beaten

Brown the beef, onion and garlic in hot oil in a frying pan. Add salt, pepper, tomatoes, parsley, cumin and mint. Cook over low heat until the mixture is well blended. Stir eggs into the meat mixture; cook over low heat until eggs are set. Serve in pie-shaped wedges. Yield: 6 servings.

Ma'alubi

VEAL WITH RICE AND EGGPLANT

1½ pounds veal, sliced thin	1 medium eggplant
3 large onions, cut in quarters	2 cups rice
2 tablespoons plus ⅓ cup of oil	1 cup tomato sauce
	3 cups water
1½ teaspoons salt	2 teaspoons salt
½ teaspoon black pepper	2 tablespoons sliced almonds
1 cup water	2 tablespoons pine nuts

Brown veal and onions in 2 tablespoons hot oil in Dutch oven or heavy saucepan. Add salt, pepper and water; simmer gently until meat is tender, about 15 minutes.

Peel eggplant and slice into ¼-inch slices; let stand for 20 minutes and then fry in ⅓ cup hot oil. Remove eggplant as it browns and keep warm. Fry rice in remaining oil until yellow; add tomato sauce, water and salt. Cover and simmer until liquid has been absorbed.

When meat is tender, place fried eggplant slices carefully over it until surface is completely covered, and simmer for about 10 minutes without stirring. Place cooked rice on top of eggplant; smooth top surface of rice. Place a large serving plate over the top of the pan; turn pan upside down on plate to unmold. Sprinkle almonds and pine nuts on top of meat. Serve hot with Yogurt and Cucumber Salad (page 202). Yield: 8–10 servings.

Sheik el Mah'shi

STUFFED ZUCCHINI

8 zucchini, uniform size	⅛ teaspoon black pepper
1 pound ground beef or lamb	½ cup water
1 medium onion, finely chopped	*Yogurt Sauce:*
4 tablespoons butter	2 cups yogurt
½ cup pine nuts	2 teaspoons cornstarch
1 teaspoon salt	¼ teaspoon salt
	Few grains of black pepper

Wash zucchini and cut off ends; core, being careful to leave whole and with unbroken peel.

Brown the meat and onion in 1 tablespoon of butter. In a small pan, brown pine nuts in 1 tablespoon of butter. Combine meat and nuts; add salt and pepper. Cool mixture slightly and stuff into the cored zucchini.

Fry the stuffed zucchini in the remaining butter until all sides are browned. Add water; cover and simmer until zucchini are tender, about 35 minutes.

To make yogurt sauce: Combine yogurt and cornstarch; heat to boiling point, but do not boil; add salt and pepper. Serve with stuffed zucchini. Yield: 6 servings.

TANZANIA (UNITED REPUBLIC OF)

The United Republic of Tanzania was formed in 1964 by a political union of Tanganyika and the island of Zanzibar. Each of those countries belonged to the UN, and when they merged they became a single member. The admission date of the Republic to the UN is re-corded as December 14, 1961—the date when Tangan-yika originally joined the organization. The economy of the mainland is primarily agricultural, basic crops being corn, rice and sorghum. Cotton, coffee and sisal are pro-duced in significant amounts. Large quantities of cloves are grown on Zanzibar and coconuts are an important commercial crop there.

Mchuzi We Kuku

CHICKEN CURRY

1 2½- to 3-pound frying
   chicken, cut up
3 cups water
2 carrots, peeled and sliced in
   circles
2 medium onions, sliced
2 tomatoes, peeled and sliced,
   or 1 cup canned tomatoes

1 teaspoon salt
2 cups milk
1 teaspoon curry powder, or to
   taste, mixed with 1 tablespoon milk
2 tablespoons flour

Simmer chicken in water over low heat for 15 minutes. Add vegetables, salt, milk and curry mixture to chicken. Continue to simmer 30 to 40 minutes or until chicken is tender but not falling
from the bones. Lift chicken and vegetables to serving dish and
keep warm; thicken remaining liquid with flour mixed with ½ cup
of cooled liquid. Simmer for 5 minutes. Serve sauce over chicken
or in separate dish. Yield: 4–6 servings.

Ugali

SEMOLINA DISH

1½ cups semolina   1½ cups boiling water
½ cup flour

Mix semolina and flour. Sprinkle a little over the rapidly boiling
water. When it foams, add remaining semolina mixture and cook,
stirring constantly with a wooden spoon, for about 5 minutes,
adding more boiling water as needed. The *ugali* should be very
stiff, as it is the custom to gather a ball of it in the hand, poke a
hole in it with the thumb, and use it to dip up broth or sauce.
Ugali can also be served sliced. Yield: 4 servings.

Ndizi Na Nyama

BANANA MEDLEY

8 bananas, peeled, and sliced in   1 cup coconut milk (pages
  circles   23 and 40)
1 cup chopped onions   1 tablespoon butter
2 medium tomatoes, peeled   ½ teaspoon salt
  and chopped   ¼ teaspoon turmeric

Combine all ingredients in a 2-quart saucepan. Bring to a boil;
reduce heat and simmer for 15 minutes. Serve with beef. Yield:
6–8 servings.

THAILAND

The food of Thailand is quite spicy, frequent use being made of little hot red peppers. Chinese influence on the cuisine is obvious, as it is in many Oriental countries. The Thais raise a great deal of excellent rice, Malaysia, Indonesia and Hong Kong being major importers. Coconuts abound in Thailand, which is why all Thai curries are made with coconut milk; this results in their being less fiery than some of the Indian ones. No one can think of Thailand without praising her colorful silks, which have become world famous. The country's international trade is also concerned with the export of large quantities of ribbon, tin and teak. Thailand joined the UN on December 14, 1946.

Tom Yum Gai

HOT AND SOUR CHICKEN SOUP

6 cups chicken broth (See Note)
2 teaspoons lemon juice
¼ teaspoon crushed red pepper

1 tablespoon soy sauce
Salt, optional
1 large chicken breast, cooked and cut into shreds

Bring broth to a boil; add lemon juice, pepper and soy sauce. Add salt, if needed. Add shredded chicken breast; simmer for 3 minutes. Serve with fried noodles. Yield: 6 servings.

Note: Bouillon cubes are not satisfactory for this soup.

Moo Tang

SPICY ROAST PORK WITH PINEAPPLE

1 3-4-pound pork loin roast
2 teaspoons ground coriander
1 clove garlic, minced
½ teaspoon salt
1 teaspoon black pepper

3 tablespoons soy sauce
1 tablespoon wine vinegar
1 tablespoon sugar
1 20-ounce can sliced pineapple (See Note)

Have backbone separated from meat to make carving easier. Combine coriander, garlic, salt and pepper; rub this mixture into the pork on all surfaces. Place pork in a shallow roasting pan; cover loosely with foil and roast in a preheated 300°F. oven for 2½ hours. Remove foil. Baste with mixture of soy sauce, vinegar and sugar several times; continue cooking uncovered for 30 minutes. Remove roast to hot serving platter and garnish with pineapple slices. Pour roast juices into a saucepan; remove excess fat; heat and serve in sauceboat. Yield: 6 servings.

Note: A fresh pineapple may be used. In that case, lay the strips of peel close together over the pork, just before roasting, in place of foil as directed above.

TOGO

Togo has been an independent republic since April 27, 1960, and a member of the UN as of September 20 of that year. Previously, part of the country had been administered by the Germans; later France assumed supervision and it became a UN Trusteeship. This West African country has an agricultural economy, with yams, rice, corn, millet and sorghum the main crops. Cacao, coffee and phosphate are important commercially. The population of 1,725,000 is composed of many ethnic groups, including the Ewe, whose ancestors traded with the Portuguese in the fifteenth century.

Sauce au Poisson et Boeuf

SEAFOOD AND BEEF SAUCE

1 pound beef, cut in 1-inch pieces

1 cup diced onion

3 tablespoons oil, preferably peanut

1 teaspoon salt

¼ teaspoon black pepper

2 cups water

2 10-ounce packages frozen chopped spinach

1 pound shrimp, cooked and deveined

2 7-ounce cans crabmeat

4 tomatoes, peeled and diced

1 teaspoon crushed red pepper

¼ teaspoon ground ginger

2 tablespoons flour mixed with 2 tablespoons water

1 onion, sliced

Cook beef and onion in oil in 12-inch frying pan over low heat for 15 minutes. Add salt, pepper and water; simmer until meat is tender.

Cook spinach and drain well. Add spinach and all other ingredients to the meat mixture. Cover and cook over low heat for 10 minutes or until onion is tender; stir occasionally. Serve as entrée with rice. Yield: 6 servings.

TRINIDAD AND TOBAGO

Trinidad and Tobago are two islands in the West Indies, seven miles from Venezuela, and are well known and beloved by tourists. Sugar cane is the most important commercial crop in Trinidad, and cocoa in Tobago. Most of the population is of African descent, but there are also people of East Indian, Near Eastern, European and Chinese origin. All these groups have had an influence on the cuisine. Trinidad and Tobago received its independence from Britain in 1962, and joined the UN on September 18 of that year.

Almond-Chicken Arima

½ cup chopped onion
½ cup chopped cucumber
½ cup chopped carrot
1 8-ounce can water chestnuts, sliced
1 4-ounce can mushrooms, drained
1 8-ounce can bamboo shoots, drained

2 cups boiling water
2 cups diced raw chicken
3 tablespoons olive oil
1 teaspoon salt
¼ teaspoon monosodium glutamate, optional
½ cup almonds or walnuts

Combine the first 6 ingredients in a bowl; pour water over the vegetables; cover and let stand 10 minutes. Uncover; drain. Cook chicken over low heat in ⅔ of the olive oil for 15 to 20 minutes; add vegetables, salt and monosodium glutamate, if used. Mix and cook 5 minutes. Cook almonds or walnuts in remaining oil until crisp and slightly brown. Serve topped with browned nuts. Yield: 6 servings.

Note: For recipe to serve 50, see LARGE-SCALE BUFFET MENUS section, page 212.

TUNISIA

Tunisia, a republic in Northern Africa between Algeria and Libya, received its independence from France on March 20, 1956, and joined the UN on November 12 of that year. Most of the population is Moslem, descended from Berber-speaking people and from later Arab immigrants. The economy is primarily agricultural. Tunisia is one of the world's largest producers of olive oil. In addition to olives, Tunisia grows wheat, barley, citrus fruits, figs and wine grapes. Sheep, goats, cattle and camels are raised by nomads. Since independence, there has been an upsurge in the processing of the agricultural and mineral products.

Tunisian Couscous

1 cup semolina, farina or couscous
1 cup water
½ teaspoon salt
1 tablespoon butter
1 onion, chopped
2 pounds lamb shoulder, cubed
1 2½-pound frying chicken, cut up
2 tablespoons oil
Water

1 large tomato or 1 cup canned tomatoes
1 green pepper, sliced
1 carrot, sliced
1½ teaspoons salt
¼ teaspoon Cayenne pepper
1 cup chick-peas or ½ of 1-pound can, drained
½ 10-ounce package frozen green peas
½ pound yellow summer squash, cubed

Combine semolina, farina or couscous with water, salt and butter in a bowl; stir and let stand until water is absorbed. Brown onion, lamb and chicken in oil in 6–8-quart kettle; add enough water to cover meat. Add tomato, green pepper, carrot, salt and pepper.

Place cereal mixture in large colander and place colander over meat and vegetables in the kettle; cover kettle and cook over low heat for 1½ hours. Uncover, remove colander containing cereal; add chick-peas, green peas, and squash to meat mixture. Replace colander, cover and simmer for 45 minutes more.

To serve, place cereal in the center of a large bowl; mold in cone shape; make opening in top of mold. Pour broth from meat and vegetables into the opening; surround with meat and vegetables. Yield: 6–8 servings.

Market-Zeïtun

MECHANIC BRAISED BEEF WITH OLIVES

1½ pounds round steak, cut in 1-inch cubes	1 1-pound can tomatoes
Salt to taste	1 tablespoon minced parsley
2 tablespoons oil	1 clove garlic, minced
½ cup water	¼ teaspoon black pepper
	1 4½-ounce jar pitted green olives, sliced

Brown salted beef cubes in oil in 10-inch skillet; add water to loosen browned bits in pan. Combine tomatoes, parsley, garlic and pepper and simmer for 5 minutes; add to meat and simmer for 1 hour. Add olives and continue to simmer for 30 minutes or until beef is tender. Sauce should be thick. Yield: 4–6 servings.

Note: For recipe to serve 50, see LARGE-SCALE BUFFET MENUS section, page 253.

Pasha's Chakchouka

MEAT AND VEGETABLE MELANGE

1 medium onion, finely chopped	1½ teaspoons salt
½ pound mutton sausages, cut in bite-size pieces	1 cup water
	4 medium tomatoes, sliced
2 tablespoons olive oil	1 medium green pepper, cut in rings
1 medium eggplant, peeled and cubed	

Sauté onion and sausages in oil until delicately browned. Combine eggplant, salt and water with sautéed onion and sausages, tomatoes and green pepper in a saucepan. Cover and cook over low heat, 20 to 30 minutes. Serve over rice. Yield: 4–6 servings.

TURKEY

Turkey is located in both Asia and in Europe, on the land which was once the heart of the great Ottoman Empire. It is a fascinating land where history extends back 4,000 years through Greek and Byzantine periods to the civilization of the Hittites. Almost the entire population is Moslem. It will surprise no one who smokes to learn that tobacco is the most important commercial crop. The Turks like sweets; their coffee is usually heavily sugared and sweet pastries like baklava *are typical of Turkish desserts. Turkey was a founding member of the UN, joining on October 24, 1945.*

Salçali Köfte

BEEF BALLS IN TOMATO SAUCE

1½ pounds ground beef	1 teaspoon salt
1 large onion, grated	¼ teaspoon black pepper
1 teaspoon chopped parsley	3 tablespoons flour
2½ slices dry whole wheat bread, soaked in water and squeezed dry	3 tablespoons butter
	2 medium tomatoes, chopped, or ¼ cup tomato paste and
2 eggs, slightly beaten	1 cup water

Combine meat, onion, parsley, bread, eggs, salt and pepper; mix thoroughly. Shape into balls the size of a walnut. Dust with flour; brown in hot butter in large skillet. Add tomatoes or tomato paste thinned with the water to meatballs; simmer for 25 minutes. Serve hot as appetizers. Yield: 36 balls.

Zeytinyağli Enginar

ARTICHOKES IN OLIVE OIL

8 artichokes
Salted water
1 tablespoon flour
Juice of 2 lemons
3 onions, sliced
Salt
1 cup olive oil

1 cup water
1 cup green peas and diced
   carrots
2 teaspoons sugar
2 tablespoons fresh minced
   dill

Remove and discard the outer leaves of the artichokes. Cut away the fuzz or choke and spoon out pinkish center of the artichoke. Place each prepared artichoke in salted water with flour and the juice of 1 lemon to prevent discoloration. Drain artichokes and arrange them in a large saucepan. Add onion, salt, remaining lemon juice, olive oil, water, peas and carrots, and sugar.

Cook over medium heat with lid on for about 30 minutes, or until tender. Serve cold, with or without the other vegetables, in the oil; sprinkle with dill. Yield: 8 servings.

Baklava

TURKISH PASTRY

Pastry: (See Note)
2 cups flour
1 teaspoon salt
½ cup shortening
2 eggs, slightly beaten
2 tablespoons water

Filling:
1½ cups finely chopped
   walnuts or almonds

½ cup brown sugar, firmly
   packed
1 cup melted butter

Syrup:
1½ cups sugar
1 cup water
1 tablespoon lemon juice

Combine flour and salt. Cut shortening into flour until mixture is consistency of cornmeal. Blend eggs and water; add to dry ingredients and mix until thoroughly dampened. Turn onto wax paper. Knead lightly 6 to 8 times to make a smooth ball; let rest ½ hour. Divide pastry into 5 portions; roll each portion paper-thin, on a lightly floured pastry cloth, into 8″ x 8″ squares. Place one square in bottom of 8-inch-square pan.

To make filling: Mix all ingredients together and divide into 4 portions. Spread ¼ of filling over pastry. Place 2nd layer of pastry on top of filling. Spread with another ¼ of filling. Continue making layers until 4 portions of pastry and all of filling have been used. Place 5th portion of pastry on top. Cut *baklava* into diagonal sections across the pan; then cut to form diamonds.

To make syrup: Combine syrup ingredients and boil for 5 minutes. Pour ½ of the syrup over *baklava*. Bake in a preheated 350°F. oven for 35 to 40 minutes. Serve remaining syrup, cooled, over warm *baklava*. Yield: 9–12 servings.

Note: Filo dough, thin sheets of prepared pastry, can be used in place of the pastry in this recipe; it can be bought at stores that sell Near Eastern or Greek foods.

Note: For recipe to serve 50, see Large-Scale Buffet Menus section, page 252.

UGANDA

Uganda received its independence from Britain on October 9, 1962, and became a member of the UN on October 25 of that year. Most of the country lies at elevations from 3,000 to 6,000 feet above sea level, making the tropical climate comfortable the year round. Corn, beans and cassava, together with cotton and coffee, are the most important cash crops. Stews are characteristic of the cooking of this region, and chicken and plantains are much used.

Plantains with Chicken Stew

2 pounds plantains, peeled
   (See Note)
Water
½ teaspoon salt
Few grains of black pepper

Chicken Stew:
1 3-pound frying chicken,
   cut up
¼ cup oil

1 large onion, sliced
2 tomatoes, peeled and cut in
   wedges, or 1 cup canned
   tomatoes, drained
2 potatoes, peeled and sliced
1 teaspoon salt
½ teaspoon of black pepper
2 cups water

Place plantains on a rack in the bottom of a saucepan. Add water, leaving the plantains above the level of the water. Add salt and pepper. Bring contents to boiling point; reduce heat and steam plantains until soft, 30 to 45 minutes. Remove and mash well. Place in top of double boiler over simmering water until ready to serve with chicken stew.

To make chicken stew: Fry chicken in hot oil in heavy frying pan or Dutch oven until brown. Add onion, tomatoes, potatoes, salt, pepper and water. Cover tightly and simmer about 1 hour or until chicken is tender.

Pour chicken stew over plantains. Yield: 6 servings.

Note: Plantains are closely related to the "sweet" bananas more commonly known in the United States, and they are increasingly imported from the Antilles and Central America. They are used as a vegetable, must be cooked to be edible, and in their green state (as contrasted with semiripe or ripe) they taste like mashed white potatoes when prepared as above.

UKRAINIAN SOVIET SOCIALIST REPUBLIC

The capital of the Ukrainian Soviet Socialist Republic is Kiev, which is situated on the Dnieper River about 450 miles southwest of Moscow. Founded in 860, it is an educational and cultural center with museums and a national library. Lvov, another Ukrainian city, is an important railroad junction and commercial center. Some

Ukrainian food, such as borsch, is similar to that of the USSR, but there are distinctive contributions such as the dumpling recipes which follow. Geographically the most western of the Soviet Socialist Republics, the Ukrainian Soviet Socialist Republic joined the UN as an independent member on October 24, 1945.

Borsch

SPRING BEET SOUP

1 teaspoon salt
¼ medium cabbage, finely chopped
1 medium carrot, cubed
1 teaspoon chopped parsley
2 cups diced celery
1 medium onion, grated
4 cups water

1 pound young beets, peeled and grated
1 clove garlic, minced
4 tablespoons lemon juice
1 tablespoon sugar
1 tablespoon flour
1 cup sour cream
Salt
Black pepper

Add salt and vegetables, except beets, to water. Simmer for 30 minutes or until vegetables are just tender. Add grated beets and cook 10 to 15 minutes. Add the garlic and lemon juice to sugar; add to soup. Blend flour with sour cream, add to soup, and bring to boil. Adjust seasoning. Serve hot. Yield: 8–10 servings.

Varenyki

COTTAGE CHEESE DUMPLINGS

2 cups flour
½ teaspoon salt
1 egg
Water

2 tablespoons sour cream
2 eggs, beaten
¼ teaspoon salt
3 tablespoons sugar

Cheese Filling:
½ pound cottage cheese

Boiling water
1½ cups sour cream

Sift flour and salt into mixing bowl; make a depression in center, drop in egg, mix and moisten with water to make a stiff dough.

Knead until smooth; cover and let stand for 30 minutes. Divide dough in half and roll to ⅛-inch thickness. Cut into 2½- to 3-inch circles with cookie cutter.

To make cheese filling: Mash cottage cheese with a fork; add sour cream, eggs, salt and sugar. Mix well.

Place 1 heaping teaspoonful of cheese filling on lower half of circle; moisten edge of top half with water and fold. Press edges together firmly. Drop dumpling in large kettle, ¾ filled with boiling water. Cook for 5 to 7 minutes, counting time after water returns to boiling point. Serve as appetizer with sour cream. Yield: 12 servings.

Pyrohy

POTATO AND CHEESE DUMPLINGS

Dough:
1¾ cups flour
1 egg, well beaten
½ cup water
¼ teaspoon salt

Filling:
1½ cups mashed potatoes
½ cup cottage cheese

½ small onion, chopped
½ tablespoon fat
½ teaspoon salt
Black pepper

3 quarts boiling water
3 slices crisp bacon
Sour cream

Combine flour, egg, water and salt. Knead until smooth. Divide into 2 or 3 balls. Roll each ball thin on floured board and cut in circles about 3 inches in diameter.

To make filling: Mix potatoes and cheese. Sauté onion in fat until brown; add to potato mixture. Add salt and pepper and blend well.

Place 1 rounded tablespoon of filling in center of each circle and form dumpling, being sure to seal well. Place dumplings at the bottom of a kettle filled with boiling water; do not crowd. Continue to boil for 4 minutes after dumplings float. Remove to a colander, drain, and spray dumplings with cold water to set them. Place dumplings on platter, garnish with crumbled bacon and serve with sour cream. Yield: 20–24 dumplings.

Schnicel

CHICKEN FILLETS A LA MINISTER

3 large breasts of chicken, cut in halves and boned	1½ cups julienne strips or small cubes of fresh French-type bread
½ cup flour	1 cup oil
1 egg, beaten	
½ teaspoon salt	

Remove skin from chicken; split each breast half sufficiently so that fillet lies flat. Coat each fillet with flour; dip in egg mixed with salt. Cover both sides of fillets with thin strips or small cubes of bread; press bread into egg mixture. Place breaded fillets in hot oil and brown quickly on both sides. Remove from oil; place on shallow baking sheet and bake in a preheated 325°F. oven for 15 minutes. Yield: 6 servings.

USSR (UNION OF SOVIET SOCIALIST REPUBLICS)

The USSR was a charter member of the UN, membership commencing on October 24, 1945. This vast country has produced some very fine cooks (Georgians are considered preeminent) and interesting, unusual food, reflecting the varied climatic conditions. Many of the foods have a touch of great elegance; some are splendid peasant fare. Great use is made of sour cream, especially with soup. Vodka, the traditional Russian drink, is now internationally popular, prized for its neutrality of taste and smell and its great adaptability in combining with nonalcoholic beverages as well as other liquors.

Okroshka Soup

COLD RUSSIAN CREAM SOUP

½ pound boiled beef, ham or
tongue, or combination
2 cucumbers, peeled and thinly
sliced
1 dozen green onions, chopped
and mixed with ½ teaspoon
salt
2 hard-cooked eggs
½ cup sour cream
1 teaspoon sugar
¼ teaspoon prepared mustard

½ teaspoon salt
1 quart *kvas* or dry ginger ale
½ cup chopped fennel

Kvas:
2 tablespoons pulverized rye
bread crumbs
2 tablespoons sugar
3 raisins
1 pint water
½ teaspoon yeast

Cut boiled meat in small thin strips; combine meat, cucumbers,
salted onions and chopped whites of eggs. Combine mashed egg
yolks with sour cream, sugar, mustard and salt.

To make kvas: Combine crumbs, sugar, raisins and water; bring
to boiling point and cool. Add sufficient water to make 1 quart;
add yeast. Allow mixture to ferment for 1 or 2 days. When fer-
mented, bottle and cap until used. Yield: 1 quart.

Add *kvas* or ginger ale to egg-yolk mixture and stir well. Add
meat mixture to *kvas* mixture; mix and chill thoroughly before
serving. Garnish with fennel. Yield: 6–8 servings.

Zharenya Riba

FRIED FISH FRITTERS

1½ pounds flounder or halibut
fillets
½ teaspoon salt
⅛ teaspoon black pepper
2 tablespoons chopped parsley
Juice of 1 lemon
1 tablespoon oil

Fritter Batter:
1⅓ cups flour
½ teaspoon salt
2 teaspoons baking powder
⅔ cup milk
2 eggs, yolks and whites
beaten separately
1 tablespoon oil

Fat for deep-fat frying

Cut fish in strips, 1 inch wide and 5 to 7 inches long. Salt and pepper fish and add parsley, lemon juice and oil. Turn fillets to coat well and allow to marinate for 30 minutes.

To make fritter batter: Sift flour, salt and baking powder into mixing bowl; add milk, beaten egg yolks and oil. Mix well; when ready to fry fish, fold beaten egg whites into batter.

Coat each fillet with fritter batter and fry in deep fat until brown. Serve fillets hot with tartar or hot tomato sauce. Yield: 6 servings.

Chzarenaya Ryba Po-Moskovski

BAKED FISH, MOSCOW STYLE

6 fillets of fish, each weighing 6–8 ounces
½ teaspoon salt
¼ teaspoon black pepper
½ cup flour
½ cup oil
2 cups Béchamel Sauce (page 186)

½ cup chopped onions, sautéed
½ cup sliced mushrooms, sautéed
1 cup cooked crab meat or lobster, flaked
3 hard-cooked eggs, quartered
3 medium potatoes, peeled, sliced and fried
¼ cup grated cheese

Coat each fillet with mixture of salt, pepper and flour; fry in hot oil until both sides are brown. Spread a thin layer of béchamel sauce in a baking dish, about 9″ x 14″. Place fillets on top. Add the onions, mushrooms, seafood and eggs. Cover with fried potato slices. Pour remaining sauce on top of potatoes and sprinkle with cheese. Cook in a preheated 350°F. oven for 15 to 20 minutes or until thoroughly heated. Yield: 6 servings.

Phazar Ro-Gkuzinski

GEORGIAN PHEASANT

1 2½-pound pheasant
1 teaspoon salt
¼ teaspoon black pepper
6 thin slices salt pork
1 cup walnuts, coarsely
    chopped

1½ pounds white seedless
     grapes, chopped
1 cup orange juice
½ cup muscat wine
½ cup strong green tea
¼ cup flour, browned in oven
¼ cup butter

Rub inside of pheasant with salt and pepper. Skewer thin slices of salt pork over breast of pheasant. Place in a 2½-quart casserole. Add walnuts, grapes, orange juice, wine and tea to pheasant; cover and bake in a preheated 350°F. oven for 1½ hours. When done, remove pheasant from casserole and place in shallow baking pan; remove salt pork and return pheasant to oven for 10 minutes to brown. *To make sauce:* Mix flour and butter into a smooth paste; stir in ¼ cup of liquid in which pheasant was cooked. Blend and add to remaining broth in casserole. Cook and stir until sauce is thickened. Serve sauce with pheasant. Yield: 2–3 servings.

Ovotchnoy Salat

HEALTH SALAD

1 cucumber
1 carrot, peeled
1 apple
2 cups salad greens
2 teaspoons lemon juice

½ teaspoon salt
¼ cup sour cream
3 medium tomatoes, peeled
    and quartered

Cut the cucumber, carrot and apple into very thin strips. Tear salad greens into bite-size pieces. Place the greens and vegetable strips in a large bowl; add lemon juice and salt to vegetables and toss to mix well. Add sour cream and toss to coat all vegetables. Garnish with tomato. Chill and serve. Yield: 6 servings.

Mazurki

FRUIT BARS

1 cup dried currants
1 cup raisins
1 cup blanched almonds,
  chopped
1 cup walnuts, chopped
1 cup dried apricots, chopped

1 cup thick jam, raspberry or
  strawberry
2 eggs
1 teaspoon vanilla extract
2 cups flour, sifted

Mix all ingredients except flour, until well blended. Sprinkle the flour over the mixture and mix again. Spread ½ inch deep in a buttered 11″ x 15″ shallow pan. Bake in a preheated 300°F. oven about 35 minutes. Remove from oven, cut into diamond shapes and return pan to oven for 5 minutes to dry out cut edges. Cool on a cake rack. Yield: 24–32 bars.

UNITED ARAB REPUBLIC

The United Arab Republic (formerly called Egypt) is a major center of Arab culture. Most of the people live in the area of the Nile valley and the delta. The economy depends essentially upon agriculture; cotton is the most famous export. The cooking of the UAR is similar to that of its neighbors, but with distinctive touches of its own. As throughout the area, very sweet desserts are prized—the UAR produces a large amount of sugar— and much honey is used. The United Arab Republic, as Egypt, joined the UN on October 24, 1945.

Eggah

EGYPTIAN LAMB OMELET

1½ cups chopped cooked lamb
1 medium onion, minced
4 tablespoons oil
2 tablespoons flour
6 large eggs, beaten
1 small clove garlic, minced

1 teaspoon cumin
⅛ teaspoon black pepper
2 tablespoons finely chopped
  parsley
¾ teaspoon salt

Cook lamb and onion in 2 tablespoons of oil until browned: add the flour and set aside.

Combine eggs, garlic, cumin, pepper, parsley and salt. Add onion-and-lamb mixture; pour into skillet in which the remaining oil has been heated. If electric frying pan is used, turn heat to 300°F.; or cook over low heat. When the eggs are no longer liquid, increase heat for a few seconds to brown the bottom. To turn omelet, place a plate over the omelet and turn omelet out onto the plate; return omelet to skillet to finish cooking and brown on the other side. Yield: 6 servings.

Tagin Orz

BAKED RICE WITH CHICKEN LIVERS

1 large onion, thinly sliced	⅛ teaspoon black pepper
2 tablespoons butter	1½ cups rice
½ pound chicken livers,	2 cups chicken broth
rinsed with cold water and	½ teaspoon salt
dried	

Cook onion in 1 tablespoon butter in frying pan until golden brown. Remove onion and reserve. Place livers in pan; add pepper and cook slowly until livers are brown, about 10 minutes. Place onion and livers in a 2-quart buttered casserole.

In same frying pan, fry rice in remaining tablespoon of butter until rice is slightly brown. Add chicken broth and salt to rice and boil for 5 minutes. Mix rice and broth with liver mixture in casserole; cover and bake in a preheated 325°F. oven for 20 minutes. Remove cover and brown slightly. Yield: 6–8 servings.

Lokmet Elkadi

FRIED PASTRY

1 teaspoon sugar	1 cup water
1 package yeast	1 tablespoon lemon juice
¾ cup warm water	1 teaspoon vanilla extract
1 cup flour	2 cups oil for frying

Syrup:
1½ cups sugar

Dissolve sugar and yeast in warm water. Add flour. Mix together. Dough should be somewhat thin. Let stand in warm place 30 minutes.

To make syrup: Combine sugar and water in saucepan. Boil until it is threadlike when poured from a spoon, about 30 minutes. Add lemon juice and vanilla.

Heat oil to 365°F. Drop dough into hot fat by the teaspoonful. Fry until golden brown. Drain on paper towels. Dip into the syrup. Yield: 6–8 servings.

Khoshaf Shahira

DRIED FRUIT COMPOTE

½ cup dried apricots
½ cup dried pitted prunes
½ cup dried figs, preferably black
½ cup seedless raisins
4 cups water

¼ cup sliced blanched almonds
2 tablespoons honey
1 teaspoon lemon juice
Rose water, optional
½ cup heavy cream, whipped, optional

Cut apricots, prunes and figs into bite-sized pieces. Cook each fruit separately in 1 cup of water until tender, 1 to 1½ hours. Each fruit should have ½ cup syrup when cooking is completed. Mix fruits and juices together; add almonds, honey, lemon juice and rose water, if used. Chill; decorate each serving with whipped cream, if desired. Yield: 6 servings.

Grabie

SHORTBREAD COOKIES

1 cup butter
1 cup confectioners' sugar

2 cups flour

Cream the butter; add the sugar gradually, cream thoroughly. Stir in the flour. Roll the dough about ¼ inch thick on a lightly floured board. Cut with a doughnut cutter. Bake on cookie sheet in a preheated 300°F. oven for about 25 minutes. The cookies should be dry but still white in color. Do not remove from baking pans until thoroughly cool. Yield: 3–4 dozen cookies.

UNITED KINGDOM OF GREAT BRITAIN AND NORTHERN IRELAND

The United Kingdom of Great Britain and Northern Ireland has made many contributions to culinary pleasure, not the least of which is the English breakfast. That hearty meal has included, since the Middle Ages, meat or fish, though beer or wine as an accompaniment has been abandoned. Much of what is prized at British tables is hardly obtainable elsewhere—the salmon of Scotland, the sole of Dover, the thick, rich cream of Devonshire, the oysters of Colchester. But one can taste typical British fare abroad, as the English pioneers have carried such recipes as Lancashire Hot-Pot and Christmas Pudding to all parts of the Commonwealth, along with high tea, a small meal served with tea at about five in the afternoon. The United Kingdom joined the UN on October 24, 1945.

Lancashire Hot-Pot

1 pound lean, tender beef	2 tablespoons chopped parsley
5 medium potatoes, pared	½ teaspoon mixed dried herbs
2 medium onions	(thyme, bay leaf, rosemary,
2 medium carrots	etc.)
2 celery ribs	2 cups beef stock (canned
1 teaspoon salt	bouillon or cubes may be
½ teaspoon black pepper	used)

Cut the meat and vegetables into very thin slices. Place a layer of potatoes on the bottom of a 2-quart greased casserole; add a layer of meat, onions, carrots and celery. Sprinkle some salt, pepper, parsley and dried herbs on each layer. Repeat layers of potatoes, meat, onions, carrots, and celery. Top layer should be potatoes. Pour stock in casserole until ¾ full. Cover casserole and bake in a preheated 350°F. oven for about 2 hours. Remove cover during last 30 minutes to brown potatoes. Yield: 4–6 servings.

Christmas Pudding

1½ cups currants
1 cup raisins
¼ cup chopped mixed candied
  fruit peels
¼ cup coarsely chopped
  almonds
¾ cup finely chopped apple
1 cup chopped suet
½ cup flour
¼ teaspoon salt

1 teaspoon nutmeg
¾ cup sugar
1¾ cups soft bread crumbs
2 egg yolks
1 egg white
1 teaspoon almond extract
1 teaspoon lemon juice
1 teaspoon grated lemon rind
2 tablespoons brandy

Combine currants, raisins, candied fruit peels, almonds, apple and suet. Mix flour, salt, nutmeg, sugar and bread crumbs. Beat the egg yolks and white until light, and add to flour mixture; stir in fruit mixture. Add almond extract, lemon juice, rind and brandy.

Fill 1 medium and 2 small well-oiled pudding molds or tins ⅔ full of mixture. Cover each mold or tin with greaseproof paper and then cover with several layers of cheesecloth. Tie paper and cloth securely. Place molds in saucepan of boiling water; cover and steam 3 to 3½ hours. Add water as needed. Let cool. These puddings are best when allowed to ripen for about 2 months. Store in cool place. To serve, steam again for an hour and turn out on serving plate; pour slightly warmed brandy over the pudding; light with a match. Serve with brandy or hard sauce. Yield: 2½ pounds or 12 servings.

Old English Christmas Fruit Cake

1 11-ounce package dried
currants
½ pound dark seedless raisins
½ pound light seedless raisins
1 cup diced candied cherries
⅓ cup diced candied citron
⅓ cup diced candied orange
peel
1 cup ground walnuts
¾ cup ground blanched
almonds
1 cup brandy

½ pound butter
½ pound dark brown sugar
3 eggs, beaten
2 tablespoons dark molasses
1 teaspoon vanilla extract
1½ teaspoons glycerine
1½ teaspoons rose water
3 cups flour
½ teaspoon baking soda
1 teaspoon cinnamon
¼ teaspoon powdered ginger
¼ teaspoon ground cloves

Mix fruits and nuts in a large bowl—at least 5-quart size—and soak in brandy overnight, covered.

Cream butter and sugar together; add eggs and beat very well. Add molasses, vanilla, glycerine and rose water and mix thoroughly.

Sift flour, soda and spices together twice. Add to the fruit-and-nut mixture and stir well. Add egg mixture to fruit-and-flour mixture. Mix well. Pour into 10-inch springform pan lined with a double layer of wax paper. Spread evenly. (If smaller cake pans are used, fill ¾ full and bake shorter length of time.) Bake in a preheated 250°F. oven for 1½ hours, or until firm to touch. Cool slightly and remove from pan. Do not remove wax paper from cake. Cool completely. Wrap in wax paper and place in tightly covered tins or plastic bags. Store for at least 6 weeks to season. Before serving, remove wax papers and slice thinly with very sharp knife. These cakes will last up to a year if properly sealed and stored in cool, dry place. Do not store in refrigerator. Yield: 1 10-inch cake.

Baked Apple Dumpling

Rough Pastry:
2 cups sifted flour
½ teaspoon salt
¾ cup butter
½ cup cold water

6 medium cooking apples

6 cloves or ½ teaspoon grated
   nutmeg
¾ cup sugar
1 egg, beaten
½ cup confectioners' sugar

To make pastry: Mix and sift flour and salt; work butter into flour; add water and mix with hand until dough forms a ball. Roll out between sheets of wax paper or on a lightly floured board until ¼ inch thick. Cut pastry into 6 6-inch squares.

Peel and core apples, keeping them whole. Lay an apple in the center of each square of pastry; stick a clove in each apple or sprinkle with nutmeg. Fill each apple center with sugar. Bring the four corners of the pastry to the top of the apple; press lightly on the top to hold pastry together; pinch the corners. Brush top with beaten egg and sprinkle with confectioners' sugar. Place in shallow baking pan; bake in a preheated 450°F. oven for 10 minutes. Reduce heat to 350°F. and continue baking for 25 minutes or until done. Test apple with a skewer for tenderness. Serve with cream. Yield: 6 servings.

Tipsy Cake

2 eggs
¼ cup sugar
¼ teaspoon salt
1 teaspoon vanilla extract
1½ cups milk
1 12-ounce package sponge-
   cake ladyfingers
½ cup good quality sherry

1 tablespoon brandy
½ cup strawberry or raspberry
   jam
1 cup heavy cream, whipped
¼ cup slivered toasted
   almonds
6 glacé cherries, quartered

Beat eggs in top of double boiler. Add sugar, salt and vanilla. Add milk and simmer over hot water until custard coats spoon thinly. Remove from heat and allow to cool.

Cover the bottom of a shallow glass dish with the ladyfingers.

Moisten with combined sherry and brandy. Cover with the cooled custard; spread jam over custard. Top with whipped cream and garnish with the slivered almonds and cherries. Refrigerate until serving time, covered to prevent evaporation of the liquor. Yield: 6 servings.

UNITED STATES

The United States has been a member of the UN since October 24, 1945. As a nation, it is one of the great producers of food—fruits, vegetables, grains, livestock and fish abound. The cuisine of the U.S. is as varied as the ethnic groups that have settled in every part of the country. At the same time, there are regional culinary distinctions which are unique to this country, such as the Southern fried chicken recipe which follows. But traditional at Thanksgiving the last Thursday in November are roast turkey and pumpkin pie.

Southern Fried Chicken

1 2½–3-pound frying chicken, cut up	Pinch of salt, or salt to taste
Cold water	Vegetable fat or bacon fat for frying (half and half) or all
2 cups of flour	vegetable fat

Cover chicken with water. Remove chicken and shake off excess water. Sift flour and salt together and put into a deep bowl or into a paper bag. Add several pieces of chicken at a time to either the bowl or bag and coat well with flour. Have no more than 2 inches of very hot fat in a heavy skillet. Drop coated chicken in and cook uncovered. When underside is golden brown, about 5–7 minutes, reduce heat a little and turn the chicken over and cook until the other side is golden brown. Remove chicken and drain on paper towels. Yield: 4 servings.

Roast Turkey with Chestnut-Sausage Dressing

1 10- to 12-pound turkey	3 green onions, chopped
Salt	1 cup diced celery
Dressing:	2 tablespoons butter
1 pound chestnuts	1 pound bulk pork sausage
2 cups day-old bread, cubed	¼ pound butter, softened
1½–2 cups milk	

Prepare turkey for roasting. Sprinkle inside of cleaned, dry turkey with salt. (Save giblets and neck to make a broth for the gravy.)

To make chestnut-sausage dressing: Peel the chestnuts by making a slit in each shell with a pointed knife. Bake the nuts in a preheated 400°F. oven for 15 minutes, or boil for the same length of time in water to cover, then drain. When nuts are cool, remove shells and inner skins. Cook chestnuts in water until tender. Put through food mill using fine blade, or chop finely. Soak bread in milk. Cook onions and celery in butter until transparent but not brown. Add sausage meat to onion-and-celery mixture; combine well and cook over low heat until sausage is slightly browned. Combine bread, chestnuts and sausage mixture.

Stuff turkey with this mixture. Use poultry pins or short skewers to keep opening closed, lacing the skewers with twine to make secure. Press thighs of the bird close to the body; tie with twine. Rub the outside of the bird with butter; place, breast side up, on a rack in a shallow pan. Cover loosely with aluminum foil; roast in a preheated 350°F. oven for 4–5 hours basting occasionally. Remove foil during last 30 minutes for bird to brown. Keep bird warm while making a pan gravy, using broth in which giblets and neck were simmered. Yield: 12–15 servings.

Notes: Dressing can be baked separately in covered casserole and served with turkey.

For recipe to serve 50, see LARGE-SCALE BUFFET MENUS section, page 262.

Indian Corn Stew

1 medium onion, chopped
½ cup diced green pepper
2 tablespoons butter
1 pound ground beef
1 17-ounce can whole kernel
  corn

1 or 2 10¾-ounce cans condensed tomato soup (See
  Note)
2 teaspoons sugar
1 teaspoon salt

Sauté onion and green pepper in butter over low heat for 10 minutes. Add beef and cook slowly until beef browns slightly. Add the entire contents of the can of corn, 1 can of tomato soup, the sugar and salt. Simmer gently until the stew is heated thoroughly. Freezes well. Yield: 6 servings.

Note: Add 2nd can of soup to increase servings to 8.

Hush Puppies

3 celery stalks with leaves
1 green pepper
2 medium onions
1 cup cornmeal
½ cup flour

1 teaspoon salt
3 tablespoons sugar
1 egg, beaten
3 tablespoons baking powder
Fat for deep-fat frying

Grind celery, green pepper and onions together. Add cornmeal, flour, salt, sugar and egg. Add baking powder to batter just before cooking. Drop a teaspoonful at a time into fat heated to 370°F. Cook until golden brown. Yield: 6 servings.

Shrimp-Avocado Salad

1½ pounds shrimp, cooked,
   peeled, deveined and cut in
   half lengthwise
1 cup diced celery
2 avocados, cut in 1-inch cubes
1 3½-ounce can pitted ripe
   olives, drained
6 ounces olive salad oil

Salad Dressing:
1 cup mayonnaise

⅓ cup green pickle relish
⅓ cup chili sauce
⅓ cup French dressing
3 tablespoons minced green
   onions
1 teaspoon oregano
1 teaspoon caraway seeds,
   optional
½ teaspoon garlic powder

Combine salad ingredients just before serving.

To make salad dressing: Combine all ingredients in a pint jar; shake well and refrigerate.

Add dressing to salad ingredients, tossing lightly. Yield: 6 main-course servings or 12 appetizers.

Eggplant Casserole

1 large onion, chopped
4 tablespoons butter, melted
2 small eggplants, peeled and
   diced
1 28-ounce can tomatoes,
   drained

1 teaspoon salt
½ teaspoon black pepper
¼ cup cornflake crumbs
Chopped parsley

Sauté onion in 1 tablespoon melted butter until golden; remove from pan. Sauté eggplant in same pan with 2 tablespoons melted butter until golden brown. Add sautéed onion, tomatoes, salt and pepper to eggplant and mix thoroughly. Turn into casserole. Combine cornflake crumbs with remaining melted butter and cover eggplant mixture with this. Bake in a preheated 325°F. oven for 30 minutes. Serve hot, garnished with parsley. Yield: 6 servings.

Brownie Pudding

½ cup sifted flour
1 teaspoon baking powder
½ teaspoon salt
⅓ cup sugar
3 tablespoons unsweetened
   cocoa
¼ cup milk

1 tablespoon melted butter
½ teaspoon vanilla extract
¼ cup chopped pecans or
   walnuts
½ cup brown sugar
¾ cup boiling water

Sift flour. Add baking powder, salt, sugar, and 1 tablespoon cocoa. Sift mixture. Add milk, butter and vanilla and mix only until smooth. Add nuts. Turn into a greased 1½-quart casserole or baking dish.

Combine brown sugar with remaining cocoa and sprinkle over batter. Pour water over top. Bake in a 350°F. oven 30 to 35 minutes. There will be a little chocolate sauce lining the dish, which you serve with the pudding either at lukewarm or room temperature. Yield: 6 servings.

Pumpkin Chiffon Pie

3 egg yolks, beaten
¾ cup brown sugar
1½ cups cooked pumpkin
½ cup milk
½ teaspoon salt
1 teaspoon cinnamon
½ teaspoon nutmeg

1 envelope unflavored gelatin
¼ cup cold water
¼ cup sugar
3 egg whites, beaten
1 large pie shell or
   8 individual shells, baked
Whipped cream

Combine egg yolks, brown sugar, pumpkin, milk, salt and spices. Cook in double boiler until thick, stirring constantly. Soak gelatin in water until softened and stir into hot mixture until dissolved. Chill until partly set. Add sugar to beaten egg whites and beat until stiff. Fold into gelatin mixture. Pour into pie shell and chill until set. Garnish with whipped cream. Yield: 8 servings.

Mrs. Truman's Ozark Pudding

1 egg	Dash of salt
¾ cup sugar	½ cup chopped apple
2 tablespoons flour	½ cup chopped pecans
1¼ teaspoons baking powder	

Beat egg well. Add sugar and beat until creamy. Sift flour, baking powder and salt into the egg mixture. Mix well. Add apple and pecans and mix. Pour into buttered 8-inch pie plate and bake in a preheated 350°F. oven 35 minutes or until golden brown. Serve plain or with whipped cream or vanilla ice cream. (May be served hot, warm or cold.) Yield: 4–5 servings.

Note: Do not be dismayed when this "pudding" rises high, then falls before time to remove it from the oven. It is supposed to do so.

UPPER VOLTA

Upper Volta, formerly part of French West Africa, received its independence from France in August 1960 and became a member of the UN on September 20 of that year. The economy is agricultural. Millet, sorghum, peanuts and cotton are grown. Cattle, sheep and goats are raised throughout the country. There are deposits of manganese, bauxite and gold, but mining is still underdeveloped. Many of the people earn their living in neighboring Ghana or the Ivory Coast.

Maan Nezim Nzedo

FISH STEW WITH VEGETABLES

½ cup oil	1 10-ounce package frozen okra pods, cut in halves
2 8-ounce cans tomato sauce	
1 onion, thinly sliced	3 carrots, cut in ¼-inch slices
¼ teaspoon red pepper	1 small head cabbage, quartered and sliced
2 teaspoons salt	
1½ pounds freshwater fish, catfish preferred	1 10-ounce package frozen green beans
	1 cup rice

Combine oil, tomato sauce, onion, pepper and salt in a 12-inch skillet and bring to a boil. Add to this mixture the fish cut into 6 serving pieces, and the okra, carrots, cabbage and beans. Cover; bring mixture to a boil, then cook over low heat for 5 minutes. Add rice and continue cooking for 25 minutes, adding water during cooking if necessary. Yield: 6 servings.

URUGUAY

Uruguay, the smallest of the South American countries, has some 200 miles of beach resorts that make it a very popular vacation spot for the entire continent. One of its most valuable exports is beef, which is also consumed domestically in large quantities, often in combination with fruit. Fertile land is almost Uruguay's sole natural resource and on 70 percent of it cattle and sheep are raised for wool, hides and meat. The people of Uruguay are mostly of Italian and Spanish descent, the native Indians having been almost completely driven out during the Spanish colonial period. Uruguay was elected to membership in the UN on December 18, 1945.

Chupin de Pescado a la Uruguaya

URUGUAYAN FISH SOUP

1½ pounds fish bones
4 bay leaves
1 teaspoon allspice
1 tablespoon salt
5 cups water
¾ cup olive oil
3 medium onions, chopped
2 cups chopped celery
1 cup chopped green or red pepper
3 cloves garlic, minced
2 small hard-shelled crabs, cracked

1 pound shrimp, cleaned and deveined
1 dozen mussels in their shells
1 dozen clams in their shells
1 pound sea bass, cut into pieces
1 29-ounce can peeled tomatoes
¼ teaspoon sugar
1 teaspoon pepper
¾ cup dry sherry

In a very large kettle, combine the fish bones, bay leaves, allspice, 1½ teaspoons salt and water. Bring to a boil. Reduce heat and simmer for 20 minutes. Strain and reserve the stock for later; discard the bones.

Heat olive oil in the same kettle; add the onions, celery, green or red pepper and garlic. Sauté for 5 to 10 minutes or until vegetables are tender. Add the crabs, shrimp, mussels and clams to the vegetables. Cook for 5 minutes, stirring often. Add the sea bass, tomatoes, sugar, remaining salt, pepper and the fish stock. Simmer for 10 minutes. Add the sherry; bring to a boil. Serve hot. Yield: 6–8 servings.

Pastel de Carne

BEEFSTEAK PIE

1 medium onion chopped	1 teaspoon sugar
2 tablespoons oil	1 cup grated Cheddar cheese
1 pound ground round steak	2 cups well-seasoned mashed
1 cup seedless raisins	potatoes
3 hard-cooked eggs, chopped	½ cup dried bread crumbs
1 teaspoon salt	

Cook onion in hot oil until yellow. Add meat to onion and brown meat lightly; add raisins, eggs, salt, sugar, and ½ cup cheese to meat-and-onion mixture. Put into a 2-quart casserole; cover with mashed potatoes. Sprinkle remaining ½ cup cheese and the bread crumbs over potatoes. Bake in a preheated 350°F. oven for 20 minutes. Serve hot. Yield: 6 servings.

VENEZUELA

Venezuela's greatest natural resource is petroleum, making up over 90 percent of her exports. Sugar cane, corn, bananas, rice, coffee and cocoa are important crops. Caracas, the capital, was the birthplace of South America's famous liberator, Simón Bolívar. Venezuela, which was discovered by Christopher Columbus in 1498, has been active in the UN since November 15, 1945.

Pepitoria de Carne Picada

SPICY CHOPPED MEAT DISH

¼ cup butter
2 tablespoons olive oil
½ cup water
1 teaspoon salt
½ teaspoon black pepper
1 pound beef, chopped fine
  or ground
½–1 teaspoon crushed red
  pepper

½ teaspoon tarragon
½ teaspoon oregano
Juice of 1 orange
¼ teaspoon orange rind, grated
  or finely chopped
2 onions, chopped
½ cup raisins, soaked in cold
  water
½ cup ketchup or chili sauce

Melt butter in a 10-inch frying pan; add olive oil, water, salt and black pepper. Bring to a boil; add beef; break up with a fork. Cover and simmer slowly for 5 minutes, stirring occasionally. Add the red pepper, tarragon, oregano and orange juice. Simmer for 5 minutes more. Stir meat to separate into small pieces. Add the orange rind, onions, raisins and ketchup. Simmer for 20 minutes, stirring occasionally, and adding water if mixture becomes too dry. Yield: 4–6 servings.

Carne Frita

SPICY FRIED MEAT

1½ pounds lean beef or pork
Water
½ cup shortening
2 medium onions, chopped
3 eggs, beaten

1 teaspoon salt
1 tablespoon finely chopped
  hot red pepper
3 cups cooked rice

Boil beef or pork in a large pot with a generous amount of water until the meat fibers separate easily, about 2 hours. Cool meat in broth; drain; separate meat into fibers. Melt shortening in a large frying pan; add onions, and when they turn a light yellow, add eggs, salt and pepper. Stir. Add the meat and cook until well fried. Serve over hot rice. Yield: 6 servings.

YEMEN

Yemen, bordering the Red Sea to the south of Saudi Arabia, is primarily an agricultural country. Farming is done on terraced mountainsides and in irrigated fields in the central plateau. The tanning of hides and the working of leather are important crafts. Traditionally, trade is a vital activity. In ancient times, Yemen controlled the shipping route between India and the Mediterranean. Today the modern facilities of the port of Al Hudaydah still contribute importantly to the economy. Yemen became a member of the UN on September 30, 1947.

Malfoof Mahshie

STUFFED CABBAGE

1 large cabbage	¼ teaspoon black pepper
Water	1 clove garlic, halved
1 cup rice	2 cups canned tomatoes
1 pound ground lamb or beef	Juice of 1 lemon
1 teaspoon salt	

Wash cabbage; cut away outer leaves, stem and core and discard. Boil cabbage in large kettle of water until pliable, about 10 minutes. Separate each leaf with a fork; let leaves cool. Line the bottom of a 10″ x 15″ baking pan with larger leaves.

Cook rice according to package directions until almost tender; drain. Add meat, salt and pepper.

Remove center stem of inner cabbage leaves; cut each leaf into 2 pieces; rub with the cut end of the clove of garlic. Place about 2 tablespoons of rice and meat mixture on each piece of cabbage leaf; roll leaf firmly around the mixture as if rolling a frankfurter; tuck ends under and place edge side down on cabbage leaves in baking pan.

Combine tomatoes and lemon juice; pour over cabbage rolls. Cover with lid or foil. Bake in a preheated 350°F. oven for 1 hour. Yield: 20–24 appetizers.

YUGOSLAVIA

Yugoslavia is made up of six territories that were formerly kingdoms or provinces of the Austro-Hungarian empire: Serbia, Croatia, Slovenia, Bosnia-Herzegovina, Macedonia and Montenegro. The country was established in 1919 as a monarchy. It became a federal republic in November 1945. The beautiful Dalmatian coast attracts large numbers of tourists, and the cuisine is hearty and delicious in all parts of the country. Yugoslavia became a member of the UN on October 24, 1945.

Hrvatske Punjene Gljive

CROATIAN STUFFED MUSHROOMS

2 pounds large fresh mushrooms
3 tablespoons fat
½ pound finely ground veal
2 teaspoons minced garlic
½ cup chopped onion
1 tablespoon finely chopped parsley
1½ teaspoons salt

Sauce:

½ cup chopped onion
2 teaspoons minced garlic

⅓ cup fat
1 tablespoon flour
1 tablespoon finely chopped parsley
1½ tablespoons finely chopped pickle
1½ teaspoons salt
½ teaspoon black pepper
¼ teaspoon dry mustard
1½ tablespoons lemon juice
1 cup sour cream
½ cup white wine

Remove stems from mushrooms and chop. Melt fat in heavy skillet over medium heat. Add veal, garlic, onion, and chopped mushroom stems. Sauté until lightly browned, stirring occasionally. Add parsley and salt; mix well. Fill mushroom caps with mixture. Place in greased shallow baking pan. Bake in a preheated 375°F. oven for 20 to 25 minutes.

To make sauce: Sauté onion and garlic in melted fat until lightly browned. Add flour and stir until blended. Add remaining ingredients; mix well. Bring to boil. Serve hot with the stuffed mushrooms. Yield: 6 servings.

Podvarak

BAKED SAUERKRAUT

¼ cup diced onion	3 small hot peppers,
3 tablespoons butter	finely diced
¼ teaspoon black pepper	¼ cup water
	2 cups sauerkraut

Cook onion in butter until yellow. Add pepper and hot peppers. Simmer for 5 minutes, adding 1 or 2 tablespoons of water, if needed. Add sauerkraut and remaining water; cover and simmer for 20 minutes. Bake in a preheated 300°F. oven for 1 hour, add water, if needed. Yield: 4–6 servings.

Pikantne Šnicle

SAVORY VEAL CUTLETS

6 veal cutlets, about 2 pounds	1 teaspoon lemon juice
4 tablespoons oil	1 egg yolk, beaten
1 cup chopped onion	1 pint sour cream
Rind of 1 lemon, finely	1 tablespoon prepared mustard
chopped	½ teaspoon salt

Pound the veal until thin. Brown both sides of veal quickly in hot oil. Remove from oil and keep warm. Add onion to remaining oil and cook until transparent; add lemon rind and juice. Combine egg yolk, sour cream, mustard and salt with onion mixture. Place over low heat until mixture is hot but not boiling. Pour sauce over cutlets. Yield: 6 servings.

Slovenačka Pita od Šijiva
SLOVENIAN PLUM PIE

Pastry:
5 cups flour
2½ teaspoons salt
1½ cups butter
1 egg
1 cup ice water

Pie Filling:
3½ pounds ripe plums, pitted
2 cups sugar
1 pound nuts, ground
1 tablespoon cinnamon
Grated rind of 1 lemon
½ cup melted butter

1 egg, beaten

To make pastry: Sift together flour and salt. Cut in butter with a fork or pastry blender until texture resembles that of cornmeal. Beat egg slightly; add ice water. Pour all at once over flour mixture and mix with fork. The dough will be moist. Divide dough into thirds. Roll out each piece to ⅛-inch thickness to fit oblong baking dish 13" x 9" x 2".

To make filling: Cut plums in round slices about ¼ inch thick. Place in bowl and sprinkle with half the sugar. Combine nuts, remaining sugar, cinnamon and grated rind. Line baking dish with one piece of the dough. Arrange half the plums on top of dough. Cover with half the nut mixture. Sprinkle half the melted butter over nuts. Cover with second piece of dough. Arrange second layer of plums, nut mixture, and butter on top. Place third piece of dough over filling and trim ½ inch beyond rim of baking dish. Seal dough by folding top crust under bottom crust. Flute edge. Brush top of dough with egg. Bake in a preheated 375°F. oven for about 1 hour. Yield: 12 servings.

ZAMBIA

Zambia, formerly called Northern Rhodesia, was granted its independence by Britain on October 24, 1964, and joined the UN on December 1 of that year. The economy depends heavily on copper mining, most of which takes place in the north-central area. The hydroelectric energy necessary to smelt and refine the copper comes

*from the Kariba dam on the Zambesi River, where the
famous Victoria Falls are also to be seen. A large portion
of the population is engaged in farming. Corn, cassava,
millet, peanuts, tobacco and cotton are grown.*

Makunde na Tamba Akuteleka

VEGETABLE STEW

1 onion, diced
2 tablespoons oil
½ pound squash, peeled and
   sliced
½ pound cabbage, cut in quarters and sliced
½ pound cauliflower, cut in
   flowerets

½ pound potatoes, peeled
   and cut in sixths
1 cup peas, fresh or frozen
1 cup water
1 beef bouillon cube
½ teaspoon salt
½ teaspoon sage
¼ teaspoon black pepper

In a 12-inch saucepan, sauté the diced onion in oil until limp.
Add all the vegetables and sauté on low heat until oil is absorbed.
Add water, bouillon cube and seasonings. Stir until seasonings
are mixed thoroughly and cube is dissolved. Cover and simmer on
very low heat for about 1 hour. Vegetables should be tender but
not mushy.

Large-scale
buffet menus and recipes
to serve 50 persons

DIPLOMATIC RECEPTION

Funghi Ripieni (Stuffed Mushrooms)

ITALY

Kefta (Meatballs)

ALGERIA

Baklava (Turkish Pastry)

TURKEY

AFRICAN NIGHT

Market-Zeïtun (Braised Beef with Olives)

TUNISIA

Jollof Rice (Chicken and Meat with Rice)

LIBERIA

Yellow Peach Pickle

SOUTH AFRICA

Wonders Dessert

DAHOMEY

FAR EAST BUFFET

Rindang Udang (Shrimp with Green Pepper)
MALAYSIA

Asado de Carajay (Pork Paprika)
PHILIPPINES

Aba Curriya (Deviled Fish)
CEYLON

Inti-puff (Coconut Surprise)
MALAYSIA

LATIN AMERICAN FIESTA

Mousse de Aguacate (Avocado Mousse)
COSTA RICA

Arroz Jimeno (Veal and Pork with Rice)
PERU

Seviche (Pickled Fish)
ECUADOR

Almond-Chicken Arima
TRINIDAD AND TOBAGO

5 CONTINENTS DINNER

Involtini (Rolled Veal with Pâté)

ITALY

Bengali Kurma Mahi (Bengal Fish Curry)

INDIA

Kokt Lamm med Dill Sås (Boiled Lamb with Dill Sauce)

SWEDEN

Roast Turkey with Chestnut-Sausage Dressing

UNITED STATES

Shorbat Robe (Yogurt and Cucumber Salad)

SUDAN

Leche Asada (Custard with Cognac)

PERU

DIPLOMATIC RECEPTION

Italy

FUNGHI RIPIENI (STUFFED MUSHROOMS)

100 large fresh mushrooms
2 quarts bread crumbs
1 tablespoon salt
2 teaspoons black pepper
1 cup finely chopped parsley

8 cloves garlic, minced
1¼ quarts chicken bouillon
1 cup olive oil
1 quart white wine

Cut off and chop stems of mushrooms. Combine bread crumbs, chopped stems and seasonings. Add enough bouillon to moisten. Stuff mushroom caps with mixture; brush caps with oil. Place in flat ovenproof dishes. Pour wine in dishes; bake in a preheated 350°F. oven for about 30 minutes. Baste several times, using additional bouillon or wine if needed. Yield: 100 stuffed mushrooms.

Algeria

KEFTA (MEATBALLS)

8 slices dry bread
2 cups milk
4 pounds ground beef or lamb
2 cups finely chopped onion
2 teaspoons dried dill weed
2 cups fresh parsley or 1 cup
    dried parsley

2 teaspoons dried mint leaves
4 eggs, slightly beaten
1 tablespoon salt
1 teaspoon black pepper
Oil or fat for deep-fat frying

Soak bread in milk until soft; squeeze out excess milk. To the bread, add all ingredients listed, except fat for frying. Mix ingredients very thoroughly; if too thick to shape easily, add milk in which the bread was soaked. Form mixture into 1-inch balls. Fry in small batches in deep fat at 370°F. until balls are golden brown. Remove from fat, drain and keep hot till all are done. Yield: about 160 meatballs.

Turkey

BAKLAVA (TURKISH PASTRY)

Pastry: (See Note)

2½ quarts (2½ pounds) sifted flour

⅓ cup (5 ounces) salt

2½ cups (1 pound, 4 ounces) shortening

10 eggs, slightly beaten

⅔ cup water

(Use 4 8" x 8" pans)

Filling:

7½ cups (2 pounds) finely chopped walnuts or almonds

1 pound brown sugar

2 pounds butter, melted

Syrup:

3 pounds sugar

1 quart water

¼ cup lemon juice

Combine flour and salt. Cut shortening into flour until mixture is consistency of cornmeal. Blend eggs and water; add to dry ingredients and mix until thoroughly dampened. Turn onto wax paper; knead lightly 6 to 8 times; let rest ½ hour. Divide pastry into 20 portions; roll each portion paper-thin on a lightly floured pastry cloth into 8" x 8" squares. Place 1 square in bottom of each 8-inch-square pan.

To make filling: Mix all ingredients together and divide into 16 portions. Spread 1 portion of filling over pastry. Lace 2nd layer of pastry on top of filling. Spread with another portion of filling. Continue making layers until 4 portions of pastry and 4 portions of filling have been used in each pan. Place 5th portion of pastry on top of each. Cut *baklava* into diagonal sections across the pan; then cut to form diamonds.

To make syrup: Combine syrup ingredients and boil for 5 minutes. Pour ⅛ of the syrup over each *baklava*. Bake in a preheated 350°F. oven for 35 to 40 minutes. Serve remaining syrup, cooled, over warm *baklava.*

Note: Filo dough, thin sheets of prepared pastry, can be used in place of the pastry in this recipe; it can be bought at stores that sell Near Eastern or Greek foods.

AFRICAN NIGHT

Tunisia

MARKET-ZEÏTUN (BRAISED BEEF WITH OLIVES)

14 pounds round steak, cut in
  1-inch cubes
2 tablespoons salt
⅔ cup oil
3 cups water
5 28-ounce cans tomatoes

8 tablespoons minced parsley
8 cloves garlic, crushed
2 teaspoons black pepper
4 10-ounce jars pimiento-
  stuffed green olives

Brown salted beef cubes in oil in a 3-gallon pot; add water to loosen browned bits in pan. Combine tomatoes, parsley, garlic and pepper; add to meat and simmer for 1 hour. Add olives and continue to simmer for 30 minutes or until beef is tender. Sauce should be thick.

Liberia

JOLLOF RICE (CHICKEN AND MEAT WITH RICE)

18 pounds frying chicken,
  cut up
1½ cups oil
3 pounds smoked ham, cut in
  1-inch cubes
12 medium onions (3 pounds),
  sliced
3 tablespoons salt
1½ teaspoons black pepper

1 tablespoon ground allspice
2 No. 10 cans tomatoes
2¼ pints tomato paste
2¼ pints water
1½ pounds green beans, fresh
  or frozen
6 cups rice
6 quarts salted water

Cook chicken in hot oil in Dutch ovens or large frying pans until chicken is brown. Add ham, onions, salt, pepper and allspice. Cook until onions are tender, stirring occasionally. Add tomatoes, tomato paste and water; stir to mix ingredients. Place green beans on top of meat mixture; cover and simmer for 20 minutes or until vegetables are tender. Cook rice for 10 minutes in salted water; drain. Add rice to meat and vegetables and continue to simmer for 15 minutes or until rice is tender and blended with sauce. Additional water may be added.

South Africa

YELLOW PEACH PICKLE

4 29-ounce cans sliced peaches	2 teaspoons turmeric
2⅔ cups peach juice	4 teaspoons curry powder
1 quart vinegar	4 teaspoons cornstarch
4 teaspoons black peppercorns	2 cups chopped onion
4 teaspoons coriander seeds	4 tablespoons chopped chili
4 teaspoons whole allspice	pepper, or 2 tablespoons
2 teaspoons salt	crushed red pepper
1⅓ cups brown sugar	

Drain peaches and measure peach juice. Simmer peach juice and vinegar, with peppercorns, coriander and allspice tied loosely in a muslin bag, for 10 minutes.

Mix salt, sugar, turmeric, curry powder and cornstarch. Add 2 cups of pickle mixture; blend and return to pickle mixture. Cook until thickened, stirring constantly. Add onion, peaches and chopped chili pepper or crushed red pepper; cook for 10 minutes. Remove spice bag. Fill pint jars and seal, if not to be used soon. Serve as a relish with chicken, turkey, lamb, or fish. Yield: 8 pints.

Dahomey

WONDERS DESSERT

3½ quarts sifted flour	½ cup oil
8 teaspoons salt	Fat for frying
3 cups butter	4 cups sugar
2 cups water	4 teaspoons cinnamon or mace

Combine flour and salt in mixing bowl, cut in the butter until mixture resembles coarse meal. Stir in half the water; add the remainder and the oil; mix only until dough holds together when pressed. Place dough in manageable portions on floured board and knead gently 8 to 10 times. Roll dough, a portion at a time, into ¼-inch thicknesses, keeping remainder covered. Cut into strips of various widths and about 2 inches long or into triangles or circles. Fry in 1 inch of fat in heavy frying pans at 375°F., turning once, until delicately browned on both sides and cooked throughout, 8 to 10 minutes. Drain on absorbent paper. Dust with mixture of sugar and spice. Serve warm or cold as dessert or snacks.

LATIN AMERICAN FIESTA

Costa Rica

MOUSSE DE AGUACATE (AVOCADO MOUSSE)

8 large avocados, peeled, seeded, cut in small pieces
¼ cup grated onion
4 teaspoons salt
2 teaspoons Worcestershire sauce

3 envelopes unflavored gelatin
3 cups cold water
1 cup boiling water
2 cups whipped cream
2 cups mayonnaise

Blend the avocado, onion, salt and Worcestershire sauce until very smooth. Soften gelatin in 1 cup of the cold water. Add boiling water and stir until dissolved; stir in remaining 2 cups cold water and cool. When gelatin mixture is the consistency of egg white, gradually fold in whipped cream, mayonnaise and the avocado mixture. Pour into molds, rinsed with cold water; refrigerate until set, preferably 1 day in advance of serving. Serve on slices of tomato placed on lettuce leaves.

Peru

ARROZ JIMENO (VEAL AND PORK WITH RICE)

100 thin slices of veal
  (about 11 pounds)
50 thin slices of pork
  (about 14 pounds)
2½ tablespoons salt
2 teaspoons black pepper
2 cups flour
3 cups oil
1 quart sherry
1 quart water
½ cup cornstarch mixed with 2
  cups water

1 quart diced onion
1½ quarts diced green peppers
1 quart diced sweet red
  peppers
8 cloves garlic, minced
1 cup butter
5 quarts cooked rice
1 cup raisins
1 cup sliced almonds
16 hard-cooked eggs, chopped
4 cups cooked peas
½ cup minced parsley

Season veal and pork with salt and pepper; dust lightly with flour. Brown veal quickly in 2 cups of hot oil. When brown, add sherry; simmer for 5 minutes; remove veal. Add half of water to wine sauce; thicken with cornstarch paste. Simmer for 5 minutes. Return veal to sauce and keep warm.

Brown pork in remaining oil; add remaining water and simmer until water evaporates and pork is tender and well cooked. Add more water if necessary.

Cook onion, sweet green and red peppers, and garlic in butter slowly until tender, but not browned. Add rice, raisins, almonds and eggs. If necessary, cover and place in a preheated 250°F. oven, or over hot water, to keep warm.

Place rice mixture in a mound in center of serving platters; place meats around rice; pour sauce over meat. Garnish rice with green peas and the meat with chopped parsley.

Ecuador

SEVICHE (PICKLED FISH)

9 pounds thin fillets of bass or
  any delicate fish
4½ cups lemon juice
2 cups orange juice
¾ cup ketchup
6 medium onions, chopped

6 chili peppers, minced
6 sweet red peppers, chopped
6 sweet green peppers,
  chopped
1½ cups corn kernels
4½ teaspoons salt

Lay fish fillets on a platter side by side. Cover with 3 cups of the lemon juice. Cover and refrigerate overnight. Drain fillets and place on serving platters. Combine all other ingredients, including rest of lemon juice, into a sauce; spread over fillets and serve as an appetizer.

Trinidad and Tobago

ALMOND-CHICKEN ARIMA

1 quart chopped onion
1 quart chopped cucumber
1 quart thinly sliced carrots
3 pounds canned water
  chestnuts, washed, drained,
  thinly sliced
2 pounds canned, sliced
  mushrooms, drained
4 pounds canned, sliced
  bamboo shoots, drained

1 gallon boiling water
5 quarts diced raw chicken
1½ cups olive oil
1 tablespoon salt
1 tablespoon monosodium
  glutamate, optional
1 quart split almonds or
  walnuts

Combine the first 6 ingredients and pour the boiling water over them; cover and let stand 10 minutes. Uncover; drain. Cook chicken over low heat in 1 cup of the olive oil for 15 to 20 minutes; add vegetables, salt, and monosodium glutamate, if used. Combine chicken-vegetable mixture well and divide among 4 large roasting pans. Cook covered in a preheated 325°F. oven or ovens for 20 minutes, stirring occasionally. Meanwhile, cook almonds or walnuts in remaining oil until crisp and slightly brown. Serve topped with nuts.

FAR EAST BUFFET

Malaysia

RINDANG UDANG (SHRIMP WITH GREEN PEPPER)

8 medium onions (2½ pounds), finely chopped

24 green onions including tops, finely chopped

2 cups oil

8 green peppers, cut in thin strips

24 large tomatoes (11 pounds), peeled and chopped

4 cups blanched almonds, slivered

4 pounds fresh shrimp, shelled, cleaned and deveined

4 teaspoons basil

4 teaspoons thyme

8 teaspoons salt

2 teaspoons white pepper

1 cup flour

6 cups Coconut Milk (pages 23 and 40)

Using a 20-quart kettle, if available, sauté onion in oil for about 3 minutes. Add all of the ingredients except the flour and coconut milk; simmer for 3 minutes. Make a paste of the flour and ¼ cup of the coconut milk; add the remaining coconut milk, mix thoroughly, and add to mixture. Cook, stirring constantly, until it boils. Serve over rice.

Philippines

ASADO DE CARAJAY (PORK PAPRIKA)

14 pounds boneless pork shoulder butt, sliced in long slices

1 tablespoon black pepper

¼ cup salt

8 cloves garlic, crushed

½ cup oil

8 bay leaves

2 cups vinegar

½ cup paprika

1½ quarts water

32 medium-size onions, quartered

1 28-ounce can tomatoes

Brown pork with pepper, salt and garlic in oil, in a 3-gallon pot. Add bay leaf, vinegar and paprika. Continue browning for about

10 minutes; add water, onions and tomatoes. Cover; simmer mixture for 1 hour or until pork is done, checking occasionally and adding water if necessary.

Ceylon

ABA CURRIYA (DEVILED FISH)

10 large onions, chopped	⅓ cup sugar
¼ cup oil	2 quarts light cream or
½ cup dry mustard	Coconut Milk (pages 23
⅓ cup chili powder	and 40)
8 bay leaves	1 cup vinegar
3 tablespoons salt	14 pounds fresh or frozen fish
½ cup Worcestershire sauce	

Cook onions in oil until yellow. Add seasonings and blend; add cream or coconut milk and stir until sauce is smooth. Add vinegar slowly while stirring.

If fresh fish is used, boil for 5 minutes in salted water and drain; if frozen fillets are used, follow directions on package. Add fish in large pieces to sauce and heat.

Malaysia

INTI-PUFF (COCONUT SURPRISE)

1 cup plus 2 tablespoons dark brown sugar, packed	1 cup water, cold
1 cup plus 2 tablespoons granulated sugar	3 4-ounce cans flaked coconut
5½ tablespoons cornstarch	Plain pastry, 3 recipes
	3 eggs, beaten

Combine sugars, cornstarch, and water in saucepan. Bring to a boil while stirring; cook until thickened. Add coconut and stir until blended. Let mixture cool.

Roll pie dough on floured surface to ⅛-inch thickness. Cut out 50 4-inch circles, rerolling dough as necessary. Place 1 teaspoon of coconut mixture on half of each circle. Brush edges with egg; fold circle over and seal edges with fork. Place on cookie sheet;

prick tops with fork and brush tops with egg. Bake in a preheated
400°F. oven, 20 to 25 minutes or until golden brown. Cool on
wire racks. Yield: 72 Surprises.

5 CONTINENTS DINNER

Italy

INVOLTINI (ROLLED VEAL WITH PÂTÉ)

16 pounds veal cutlets,
  cut very thin
2 tablespoons ground rosemary
3 cups flour
1 pound grated Parmesan
  cheese
3 tablespoons salt
2 teaspoons black pepper

8 4-ounce cans *pâté de foie
  gras*
½ pound butter
½ cup chopped parsley
1 cup oil
2 quarts Marsala or dry white
  wine

Sprinkle each slice of veal with rosemary and pound steak with
meat mallet or edge of saucer. Dredge cutlets in mixture of flour,
cheese, salt and pepper; pound both sides of meat again.

Combine *pâté de foie gras,* butter and parsley; spread thinly on
1 side of each piece of veal. Roll each piece tightly (with *pâté* mixture inside) and secure with toothpicks. Sauté gently in oil for 5
to 10 minutes or until veal is brown. Add the wine and simmer for
5 minutes or until rolls are tender. Serve sliced, cold, as an appetizer or hot with rice.

India

BENGALI KURMA MAHI (BENGAL FISH CURRY)

16 dried chili peppers, finely crushed

3 tablespoons turmeric

3 tablespoons salt

16 pounds halibut steak, cut in 1-inch cubes

¼ cup oil

Curry Sauce:

2½ tablespoons coriander seeds

2½ tablespoons cardamom seeds

2 tablespoons cumin seeds

5 tablespoons mustard seeds

14 pounds onions

2½ tablespoons turmeric

1½ tablespoons cinnamon

2 teaspoons chili powder

2 tablespoons salt

25–30 cloves garlic

2 cups vegetable oil

8 pounds tomatoes, peeled and sliced

2 quarts yogurt

Mix chili peppers, turmeric and salt together. Sprinkle over halibut cubes and coat well. Heat oil in large frying pans and brown the fish on all sides. Remove fish from pans, drain and set aside.

To make curry sauce: Grind together coriander, cardamom, cumin, and mustard seeds, with half the onions. Add the turmeric, cinnamon, chili powder and salt to the ground onion-and-spice mixture. Slice remaining onions. Cook sliced onions and garlic in oil until brown. Add the ground onion-and-spice mixture and the tomatoes to the browned onions and garlic. Cook gently until tomatoes are tender, about 10 minutes. Add yogurt and cook over medium heat for 5 minutes more.

Add fried fish to curry sauce and simmer for 10 minutes. Remove garlic. Serve hot with tomato chutney.

Sweden

KOKT LAMM MED DILL SÅS
(BOILED LAMB WITH DILL SAUCE)

20 pounds breast or
   shoulder of lamb
1 tablespoon salt for each
   quart of water
2 teaspoons black pepper-
   corns
10 bay leaves
1 small bunch of dill
1 teaspoon ground black
   pepper

Dill Sauce:
½ pound butter
1¼ cups flour
5 quarts stock from cooking
   lamb
1 cup chopped dill
1 cup vinegar
½ cup sugar
Salt
10 egg yolks, beaten

Place meat in very large kettle or several kettles and cover with boiling salted water. Bring to boil, skim; add peppercorns, bay leaf, few sprigs of the dill, and pepper. Cover and simmer 1 to 1½ hours or until meat is tender. Cut in pieces, place on hot platter, and garnish with remaining dill sprigs. Serve the dill sauce separately.

To make the dill sauce: Melt butter, add flour, and stir until well blended. Add stock gradually while stirring; then cook slowly 10 minutes, stirring occasionally. Add dill, vinegar, sugar and salt. Remove from heat. Mix a little of the hot sauce with the egg yolks. Mix with remaining sauce.

United States

ROAST TURKEY WITH CHESTNUT-SAUSAGE DRESSING

4 10- to 12-pound turkeys
Salt

Dressing (for each turkey):
1 pound chestnuts
2 cups day-old bread, cubed

1½–2 cups milk
3 green onions, chopped
1 cup diced celery
2 tablespoons butter
1 pound bulk pork sausage
¼ pound butter, softened

Prepare each turkey for roasting. Sprinkle inside of each cleaned, dry turkey with salt. (Save giblets and necks to make a broth for the gravy.)

To make chestnut-sausage dressing: Peel the chestnuts by making a slit in each shell with a pointed knife. Bake the nuts in a preheated 400°F. oven for 15 minutes or boil for the same length of time in water to cover, then drain. When nuts are cool remove shells and inner skins. Cook chestnuts in water until tender. Put through food mill using fine blade or chop finely. Soak bread in milk. Cook onions and celery in butter until transparent but not brown. Add sausage meat to onion and celery mixture; combine well and cook over low heat until sausage is slightly browned. Combine bread, chestnuts and sausage mixture.

Stuff turkeys with this mixture. Use poultry pins or short skewers to keep opening closed, lacing the skewers with twine to make secure. Press thighs of each bird close to the body; tie with twine. Rub the outside of each bird with ⅓ of the butter; place, breast side up, on a rack in a shallow pan. Cover loosely with aluminum foil; roast, separately if necessary, at 350°F. for 4–5 hours, basting occasionally. Remove foil during last 30 minutes for bird to brown. Keep birds warm while making a pan gravy, using broth in which giblets and neck were simmered. Yield: 12–15 servings for each turkey.

Note: Dressing can be baked separately in covered casseroles and served with turkey.

Sudan

SHORBAT ROBE (YOGURT AND CUCUMBER SALAD)

10 large cucumbers, pared and chopped	1 tablespoon salt
	¾ teaspoon garlic powder
5 pints yogurt	¾ teaspoon black pepper

Peel and chop cucumbers; combine with yogurt, salt, garlic powder and pepper. Serve on lettuce.

Peru

LECHE ASADA (CUSTARD WITH COGNAC)

8 14½-ounce cans evaporated
  milk
2⅔ cups water
1 pint cognac

2 cups sugar
24 eggs, slightly beaten
1 teaspoon cinnamon
1 teaspoon nutmeg

Add water to evaporated milk; scald. Combine other ingredients. Add the hot milk. Pour into individual molds of oven glassware or earthenware. Set the molds in baking pans; pour in hot water nearly to the top of the molds. Bake in a preheated 350°F. oven for 45 minutes or until inserted knife comes out clean. Serve cold as dessert, plain or with cream or fruit sauce.

Acknowledgments

My deepest appreciation to Mildred Horton, the 1960–1965 American member of the Executive Committee of the International Federation of Home Economists, and the hundreds of generous friends of the UN throughout the world who tracked down and perfected the culinary specialties in this book.

Contributors of Recipes: Mrs. Paul Abernathy, Miss Charlotte Adams, Mme. Diop Alassane, Mrs. Ahmed Mouwahid Aly, Mrs. Rivka Angel, Mr. Nessim Arditi, Mrs. Simone Attwood, Mrs. Tillie Avrami, Mr. André O. Backar, Miss Norma Bandak, Bangor Overseas Women's Club, H. E. Mr. James Barrington, Miss Rosa Bejar, Mrs. Jean K. Benjamin, Mr. C. F. N. Bentley, H. E. M. Armand Bérard, M. Maurice Bertrand, Mrs. Judith Bingham, Mrs. Angela Bitsios, Mrs. Lee Blackwell, Mrs. Winifred Blatchford, Mr. Vadim Bogoslovsky, Mrs. Betty Boyd, Sra. Dora B. de Boyd, Mr. S. A. Bronnikov, Mrs. Alma Buffum, Sra. Corina de Caballero Tamayo, M. Caimerom Measketh; Hon. John A. Calhoun, Mrs. Carmen Carbonaro, Mrs. Dorothy Carpenter, Mr. Thomas A. Cassily, Sra. Graciela Ponce de Leon de Cattarossi, Mrs. Indira Chakravarty, Chef Maxime Chalmin, Miss Maria Osinena Charaley, Miss Grace Chen, Commander Harry Archer Clark, U. S. N. (Ret.), Mme. Odette Cohen, H. E. M. Sori Coulibaly, Miss Marie José Damas, Sra. Ana H. de Cuevas, Mme. Andrée de Molenaar, Mr. Robert de Vaughn, Patricia W. Dean, H. E. Dr. Francisco A. Delgado, Mme. John Dubé, Princess Dumbadze, Mrs. Mirtha Dunn, Mr. William L. Eagleton, Jr., Mrs. Dwight D. Eisenhower, Miss Selma Ekrem, Mrs. Nermin El Masri, H. E. Mr. Hassan Nur Elmi, Mrs. Marjorie P. Essien, Miss Joan Evanish, Mrs. Afaf Fahmy, Dr. A. G. Ravan Farhadi, Mr. August Fleischer, H. E. Mr. B. G. Fourie, Miss Sylvia Howard Fuhrman, H. E. Sr. Alfonso Garcia-Robles, H. E. Dr. Vasco Vieira Garin, Mme. Régine Gbedey, Miss Olga B. Gechas, Mr. Ignacij Golob, Miss Maureen Adikes Grenier; Mr. Alfonso Grez, H. E. M. Georges Hakim, Miss Grace Halsell, Mrs. J. G. H. Halstead, Mr. Kurt Hampe, Mr. Mario C. J. Harrington, Miss Rozina Hirji, Mrs. Dorothy Hart Hirshon, Mrs. Hans Hoffmann, Mr. Charles A. Hogan, Mme. Louis Ignacio-Pinto, Joan Jackling, M. Ernest M. Jean-Louis, Mr. Keith Johnson, Miss Charlotte Kahler, H. E. Mr. Philip M. Kaiser, Mr. Frank P. Karefa-Smart, Mr. Joseph Kazigo, Mrs. O. H. Kelfa-Caulker, H. E. Mr. Eamonn L. Kennedy, Mr. Tibor Keszthelyi, Dr. Flemmie P. Kittrell, Mrs. Sara Korle, Mrs. Vanda Kreacic, H. E. Mr. Karel Kurka; Mrs. Mon Ling Landegger, M. Jules Laventure, Mr. Patrick Laver, Mr. Alphonse Lema, H. E. Mr. Bohdan Lewandowski, Miss Mette

Lie, Mrs. Janice Liebowitz, Mrs. Teow-Chong Lim, Mr. Harry Lindquist, Dr. Chang S. Liu, Patricia Lubar, Berenice MacFarquhar, Mr. Henry Madoshi, Mrs. Gunapala Piyasena Malalasekera, Mrs. Anna Marich, H. E. M. Achkar Marof, H. E. Srta. Carmen Natalia Martinez Bonilla, Mrs. Betti Richard Matsch, H. E. Dr. Koto Matsudaira, Miss Marie Lee McBroom, Mr. W. McIlquham Schmidt, Mrs. Mildred Mehl, Mrs. Thomas P. Melady, H. E. Mr. Turgut Menemencioglu, Miss Anne Michaels, Mr. Waclaw Micuta, Miss Tonia Moffat, Mrs. Zulaikaha Moosa, Mr. Marcos A. Morinigo; Miss Magdalena W. Muya, Mr. Justin N'Garabaye, Mrs. Jacqueline Kennedy Onassis, Mr. E. U. Oton, Mrs. Julian V. Pace, M. Tiao Phouangsavath, Sra. Luz B. de Pinies, Sra. Clara de Ponce de Leon, Sr. Raúl Quijano, Mrs. Marta C. Raymond, Mrs. Beatrice Reachelson, Mr. M. Jusuf Ronodipuro, Mrs. Ellen Rosen, Mrs. Teresa Rossides, Mr. Federico Rufe, Miss Najwa Sarkis, Mr. Serafim Serafimov, Countess Manuela Serra, H. E. Mr. Rishikesh Shaha, Mrs. Basima Saeed Shammas, Mr. R. W. Sharp, Mrs. Jacq Siracusa, Mr. A. R. Sitnikov, Mrs. Emilia A. Sley, Miss Elizabeth Smith, Mrs. Sheilah Solomon; Mrs. Alkione Stathakos, H. E. Mr. Adlai E. Stevenson, Mrs. El Nur Ali Suleiman, Mrs. Marie Syrovy, Mrs. Najiba Tabibi, Mr. M. A. K. Taha, Mme. Jacqueline Tapsoba, Miss Elisabeth Taylor, Miss Mollie Thompson, Mrs. Thor Thors, Mrs. Elizabeth Ticknor, Mrs. Franca Tolbert, M. Robert Treboux, Hon. Marietta P. Tree, Sra. Marta Yolanda de Trigueros, Mrs. Bess W. Truman, H. E. Sr. Vincente Urcuyo Rodriguez, Mrs. Homa Vakil, Mrs. Jitinder Valhali, Mr. J. P. A. M. van den Bogaert, Mr. Carlos S. Vegega, Miss Constance Venable, Mrs. Fernando Volio, Miss Agatha Wangeci, Mrs. Earl Warren, Miss M. Watson, Mr. D. Weahplah Wilson, Mme. Junie Woulbroun-Bovesse, H. E. M. Pierre Wurth, Miss Ophelia Yuén, Mrs. Guri Lie Zeckendorf.

Home Economists: Mrs. Ruth Ackerman, Mrs. John P. Andrews, Mrs. John Bang, Mrs. Murray Black, Dr. A. June Bricker (Executive Director of the American Home Economics Association), Mrs. Gerald L. Brower, Mrs. Sybil Butleman, Miss Cassandra Campbell, Miss Janet Christensen, Mrs. Selma H. Cohen, Miss Zora Colburn, Miss Charlotte J. Colby, Miss Mary Collins, Mrs. Robert Conway, Mrs. Eula Bee Corban, Mrs. Robert Deal, Mrs. R. C. Diehl, Jr., Mrs. Ruth Dougherty, Miss Belle Dubin, Mrs. Alma C. DuMont, Mrs. Dean Dybing, Mrs. Barbara Erickson, Mrs. Ruth Ferguson, Mrs. Fred C. Francis, Mrs. A. H. Fricke, Jr., Mrs. Marjorie Fritzsche, Mrs. Elaine Gaines, Mrs. Shirley Heit, Mrs. John N. Herron, Miss Mary Lee Hicks, Miss Mildred Horton; Mrs. I. Reid Howland, Mrs. William Imershein, Mrs. Dorothy S. Jackson, Mrs. Charlotte V. Jacobson, Mrs. Dorothy L. Jefferson, Mrs. A. C. Jenkins, Mrs. Ruth Johnson, Mrs. Carolyn Jones, Mrs. T. Khan, Mrs. Martin Koenig, Mrs. Janet Koral, Mrs. Eileen Lambert, Mrs. Helene Landau, Mrs. Lillian Lester, Mrs. Selma Lieberman, Mrs. Anna Marich, Mrs. Emily E. Mattox, Mrs. Eric Mayhew, Miss Gladys

McCartney, Mrs. Ora M. McLeod, Mrs. E. A. Mueller, Mrs. Barbara Murphy, Mrs. Travis Nelson, Mrs. John L. O'Brien, Mrs. Edith Ordan, Mrs. J. Donald Osborne, Miss Ruth E. Ostrander, Mrs. Ann Ritterman;

Mrs. Charles J. Roesch, Mrs. Carol P. Romberg, Mrs. Barbara Romero, Mrs. Marjorie Schrier, Mrs. Helen K. Schwartz, Mrs. Earl Slade, Mrs. W. C. Sloan, Mrs. Robert Soost, Mrs. Elaine Truesdell, Mrs. Eleanor Werner, Mrs. Margaret E. Whitbeck, Mrs. S. H. White, Mrs. Mildred Winston, Mrs. Katherine Woodhouse, Mrs. Robert H. Young, Mrs. Millicent Zarr.

Test Kitchens: Home Economics Department of Queens College; Home Service Department of Best Foods, Division of Corn Products Co.; Kellogg Company; The Kraft Kitchens; The Lipton Kitchens; NABISCO; The Pillsbury Company; Sealtest Foods Consumer Service; Theodore R. Sills and Co.; and Standard Brands Incorporated.

INDEX

Aam ki chutney (tomato chutney), 108
Aba curriya (deviled fish), 46, 259
Abrak (stuffed grape leaves), 139
Afêlia (pork and potatoes), 61
Afghan pelau, 9
African spinach, 44
Aguacate picante (spiced avocado), 53
Ají de gallina (chicken in pepper sauce), 179
Akwadu (banana pudding), 88
Alcoholic beverages (see Liquor; Wine)
Almond cake, 83–84
Almond-chicken arima, 212–13, 257
Almond rice dessert with cherry sauce, 69
Almonds
    chicken and almonds with sherry, 199–200
    pastry with almonds, 13–14
    Turkish pastry, 216–17
Aluke chop (potato cakes), 160
Aluko achar (dressed boiled potatoes), 161
Anchovies, in Jansson's temptation, 205
Anticuchos (marinated broiled meat), 179–80
APPETIZERS (hors d'oeuvres, snacks)
    fish
        fish balls in sauce, 191–92
        marinated, 203–4
        pickled, 73, 257
        shrimp-avocado salad, 235
    fried, 105
    liver paste, 169–70
    marinated beef strips, 157–58
    marinated broiled meat, 179–80

meat ball, 14
    with tomato sauce, 215
meat pie
    individual, 29–30
    little, 70–71
mushroom
    with sour cream, 184
    stuffed, 120, 251
pâté
    Flemish liver pâté, 24–25
    rolled veal with pâté, 121–22, 260
pork
    little meat pies, 70–71
    Old Indians, 165
    pork in jelly, 79
Apple pie, 28
Apples
    baked apple dumpling, 231
    chicken-stuffed, 190
    in red cabbage, 205–6
Arroz con frijoles (Cuban rice with black beans), 58–59
Arroz con pollo (chicken with rice), 99
Arroz Jimeno (veal and pork with rice), 177–78, 256
Artichokes
    baked stuffed, 121
    in olive oil, 216
Asado de carajay (pork paprika), 182, 258–59
Ashaks (leek ravioli), 11–12
Aubergine orientale (Oriental eggplant), 153
Aubergines en peau (stuffed eggplant), 98
Avocados
    avocado mousse, 57, 255
    avocado salad
        guacamole, 91

Avocados (*cont'd*)
  shrimp-avocado, 235
  avocado whip, 32–33
  spiced, 53
Ayam panggang (barbecued chicken), 147

Baba cake, 84
Babka (Grandmother's delicious cake), 185
Bacalhau do céu (heavenly codfish), 186
Baigan awr dahí (eggplant in sour cream), 174
Baked apple dumpling, 231
Baked fillets of whiting, 18–19
Baked fish, 62
Baked fish, Moscow style, 223
Baked fish–Spetsai Island, 89
Baked hash with yogurt topping, 34
Baked lamb and wheat, 135
Baked rice dessert, 28
Baked rice with chicken livers, 226
Baked sauerkraut, 243
Baked stuffed artichokes, 121
Baklava (Turkish pastry), 216–17, 252
  filo dough for, *shopping for*, 217, 252
Banana akara, 193
Banana fritters, 193
Banana medley, 209
Banana pudding
  Ghanaian, 88
  Nepalese, 161
  West Indian, 24
  (*See also* Plantains)
Banana tart, 33
Barbecued chicken, 147
Bass
  pickled, 73, 257
  sea (*see* Sea bass)
Bean stew, 130–31
Beans
  soups (*see under* SOUPS, bean)
  fried, 37
    refried, 155
  rice and
    chicken, meat, and rice, 138, 253–54
    Cuban rice and black beans, 58
    Haitian, 96
  in stews
    bean stew, 130
    fish stew, 237–38

spinach stew, 87
Béchamel sauce, 186
BEEF
  beef casseroles (*see under* CASSEROLES)
  beef goulash, 94
  beef sauces (*see under* SAUCES, meat)
  beef soups
    with carrots and cabbage, 170
    cold Russian cream soup, 222
    lima bean, 53–54
    peanut butter, 201
    red bean soup, 145
    turnip soup with meatballs, 113–14
  beef stews (*see under* STEWS, beef)
  boiled
    in cold Russian cream soup, 222
    liver dumplings, 142
    parboiled, with coconut and rice, 167
    shrimp and beef in spinach sauce, 66–67
    with vegetables, 182
  braised
    beef and onions, 52
    with okra sauce, 47
    with olives, 214, 253
    in the style of Provence, 80–81
  broiled marinated, 179–80
  browned shredded, 144
  corned, in okra and cornmeal mush, 95
  curried, 45
  roast
    in hunter's stew, 183–84
    pickled, with sour cream, 63
    Portuguese pot roast, 187
  spicy fried, 240
  strips of
    fried, 147
    marinated, 157–58
  stuffed, 72
  sweet and sour, with fruit, 199
  (*See also* Beefsteaks; GROUND MEAT; VEAL)
Beef and onions, 52
Beef and shrimp in spinach sauce, 66
Beef balls in tomato sauce, 215
Beef-celery sauce, 111
Beef in the style of Provence, 80–81
Beef stew à la Rwanda, 188–89

Beef tamales, 92
Beef with carrots and cabbage, 170
Beefsteak pie, 239
Beefsteaks
  beef meat rolls, 16
  beef and onions, 52
  braised, with olives, 214, 253
  pocket steak, 19–20
  steak pie, 239
  steak stew with rice, 168–69
  strips of
    fried, 147
    marinated, 157–58
  stuffed, 72
Beet soups
  beets in vegetable-yogurt soup,
    184
  borsch, 219
Beignets (fritters), 191
Bel Paese cheese in corn pie, 175–76
Bengal fish curry (Bengali kurma
    mahi), 107, 261
Beverages
  iced chocolate, 32
  kvas, 222
  (See also Coconut milk; Liquor;
    Wine)
Bigos Mysliwski (hunter's stew),
    183–84
Bint assahn (pastry with honey), 198
Black beans with Cuban rice, 58–59
Black-eyed peas, seafood, and plan-
    tains, 167
Blueberry crisp pudding, 43
Bobotee (meat timbales), 195–96
Boeuf à la mode Provençale (beef in
    the style of Provence), 80–81
Boeuf et crevettes avec une sauce
    d'épinard (beef and shrimp
    in spinach sauce), 66
Bohobe ba poone a tala (mealie
    bread), 137
Boiled beef with vegetables, 182
Boiled lamb with dill sauce, 204, 262
Bondo gumbo (lamb stew), 166
Bo'neschlupp (green bean soup),
    141–42
Bonito in dashi sauce, 127
Borsch (spring beet soup), 219
Boshebo (cashew nut sauce), 31
Boulettes, 191–92
Boureka (meat squares), 118
Braised beef with olives, 214, 253
Braised chicken with olives, 158–59
Brandy, in fruit cake, 230

(See also Cognac)
Bread
  bread and cheese soup, 18
  bread pudding
    banana pudding, 24
    Christmas pudding, 229
    Mexican, 156
    queen of puddings, 164
  bread stuffings
    for artichokes, 121
    for chicken breast fillets, 38–39
    for meat rolls, 16
    for mushrooms, 120, 251
    sweet, 13
    for turkey, 233, 262–63
  Christmas braid, 65–66
  hush puppies, 234
  mealie, 137
  Paraguayan, 176–77
  rye, 204–5
  tasty Indian, 108–9
Bread and cheese soup, 18
Browned shredded beef, 144
Brownie pudding, 236
Brussels sprouts in bean stew, 130–31
Bulgur wheat (cracked wheat)
  Iraqi, 115
  lamb and
    baked lamb, 135
    stuffed leg of lamb, 152
  in Libyan couscous, 140
  shopping for, 115, 140
  wheat salad, 136
Butter tarts, 42–43
Butternut squash cream, 176

Cabbage
  in meat and vegetable rolls, 114–
    15
  peppers stuffed with, 136
  red
    Danish, 68
    Swedish, 205
  in soups
    beef with carrots and cabbage,
      170
    borsch, 219
    Haitian vegetable soup, 95–96
    Luxembourg vegetable soup,
      141
  stuffed
    Hungarian, 101
    Yemeni, 241
  (See also Sauerkraut)

Cacerola de pollo y elote (chicken and corn), 57–58
Cake royal, 172
Cakes
  almond
    cake royal, 172
    French, 83–84
  baba, 84
  cassava, 138–39
  chocolate cake squares
    Hungarian, 102
    Lamingstons, 20
  fruit, 230
  grandmother's delicious, 185
  King Haakon's, 171–72
  tipsy, 231–32
Canapés (see APPETIZERS)
Capirotada (bread pudding), 156
Caramel custard, 142–43, 157
Carbonada (sweet and sour beef with fruit), 199
Carciofi ripieni al forno (baked stuffed artichokes), 121
Carimanolas (stuffed sweet potato balls), 174–75
Carne assada à Portuguêsa (Portuguese pot roast), 187
Carne frita (spicy fried meat), 240
Carne mechada (stuffed meat), 72
Carrots, beef with cabbage and, 170
Cary au jus de coco (chicken in spicy coconut sauce), 40
Cashew nut sauce, 31
Cassava cake, 138–39
Casseroles
  beef
    beef and beer, 26–27
    golden beef-potato pie, 97
    Lancashire hot-pot, 228
    meat squares, 118
  cheese
    cheese in beefsteak pie, 239
    cheese in chicken and corn, 57–58
    cheese in golden beef-potato pie, 97
    ham, cheese, and endive, 26
  eggplant, 235
  lamb
    with saffron, 189–90
    vegetable and, 61
  lentil, 119
  pheasant, 224
  rice
    beans and rice, 96

fish and rice, 134
seafood
  codfish, 186
  fish and rice, 134
  haddock, 74–75
  Jansson's temptation, 205
  veal with tomato topping, 194–95
Catfish stew with vegetables, 237–38
Celery-beef sauce, 111
Chakchouka (mixed vegetables with eggs), 15
  pasha's, 214–15
Chawan mushi (chicken and shrimp mustard), 125
CHEESE
  artichokes stuffed with, 121
  baked fish with, 223
  cheese casseroles
    cheese in beefsteak pie, 239
    cheese in chicken and corn, 57–58
    cheese in golden beef-potato pie, 97
    ham, cheese, and endive, 26
  cheese dumplings
    cottage cheese, 220
    cottage cheese in fruit dumplings, 64
    potato and cheese, 220
  cheese noodles, 122–23
  cheese pies
    cheese in corn pie, 175–76
    cheese in macaroni dish, 151
    cheese tidbits, 30
    cheese sauce, potatoes with, 54
  in soups
    bread and cheese soup, 18
    chicken soup, 122
    yogurt, 135
Cheese steaks, 118–19
Cheese tidbits, 30
Chelo (golden rice), 112
  chicken with, 112–13
Chêng yü ju szŭ (steamed fish), 50–51
Cherry sauce, 69
  rice dessert with, 69
Chestnuts
  chestnut dressing, 155
  chestnut-sausage dressing, 233, 262–63
  commercial, 81
  lamb fillets over, 81–82
Chi tang (chicken soup), 50

Chick-peas, chicken or lamb with, 159–60
CHICKEN
  almond-chicken arima, 212–13, 257
  baked
    Afghan pelau, 9
    fillets à la minister, 221
    Kabuli pelau, 10
    with walnut sauce, 12
  barbecued, 147
  braised
    with chick-peas, 159
    with olives, 158–59
    in pepper sauce, 179
    seafood and chicken with noodles, 181
    with sherry and almonds, 199–200
    Tunisian couscous, 213–14
  chicken giblets
    baked rice and livers, 226
    in chestnut dressing, 155
    liver-stuffed chicken breasts, 38–39
    marinated broiled livers, 179–80
  chicken pies
    little meat pies, 70–71
    three meats pie, 42
  chicken soup (see under SOUP, chicken)
  chicken stew (see under STEWS, chicken)
  chicken-stuffed apples, 190
  corn and, 57–58
  curried
    Pakistani, 173–74
    Tanzanian, 208–9
  fresh vegetable-chicken salad, 133
  fried
    Congolese, with peanut butter sauce, 55
    Ivory Coast, with peanut butter sauce, 123–24
    Southern, 232
  pickled, 31
  with rice
    Afghan pelau, 9
    arroz con pollo, 99
    baked rice with chicken livers, 226
    chicken with chick-peas, 159–60
    chicken and meat, 138, 253
    chicken and vegetables, 128
    with coconut, 167

    fried rice, 193–94
    golden rice, 112
    Kabuli pelau, 10
    in vegetable soup, 95–96
  with seafood and dashi sauce, 127
    shrimp and chicken custard, 125
  stewed
    chicken-spinach medley, 168
    with dumplings, 101
    Guinean goulash, 94
    Honduran chicken, 99
    with hot sauce, 77
    with nuts, 85
    vegetables and chicken, 128
    with water chestnuts, 51–52
    in wine sauce, 75
  with stuffing
    chestnut dressing, 155
    chicken breast fillets, 38–39
    chicken mold, 48
    Pakistani, 173–74
    sweet stuffing for chicken, 13
Chicken à la Moambé, 55
Chicken à la N'Gatietro, 123–24
Chicken and shrimp custard, 125
Chicken and spinach medley, 168
Chicken and vegetables, 128
Chicken breast fillets, 38–39
Chicken fillets à la minister, 221
Chicken in pepper sauce, 179
Chicken in spicy coconut sauce, 40
Chicken in wine sauce, 75
Chicken mold, 48
Chicken or lamb with chick-peas, 159–60
Chicken paprika with dumplings, 101
Chicken soup, see under SOUP, chicken
Chicken stew, see under STEWS, chicken
Chicken-stuffed apples, 190
Chicken with chestnut dressing, 155
Chicken with golden rice, 112
Chicken with hot sauce, 77
Chicken with nuts, 85
Chicken with sherry and almonds, 199–200
Chicken with walnut sauce, 12
Chiffon pie, pumpkin, 236
Chiles rellenos (fried stuffed green peppers), 93
Chinese cabbage in yosenabe, 127
Chipá guazú (corn pie), 175–76

Chipá Paraguay (bread), 176–77
Chlodnik (cold vegetable and yogurt soup), 184
Chocolate, iced, 32
Chocolate brownie pudding, 236
Chocolate cake squares, 102
Chocolate date nut pie, 119–20
Chocolate frosted squares, 20
Chocolate frosting, 20
Chocolate gelado, 32
Chopped meat *(see* GROUND MEAT)
Chowder, spiced fish, 132–33
Christmas braid, 65–66
Christmas Eve salad, 156
Christmas pudding, 229
Chupin de pescado a la Uruguaya (Uruguayan fish soup), 238–39
Chutney
in meat timbales, 195–96
mint, 106
tomato, 108
Chzarenaya ryba po-Moskovski (baked fish, Moscow style), 223
Cinnamon fritters, 90
Clams
chicken and, in dashi sauce, 127
in fish soup, 238–39
sole with mushroom sauce and, 27
Coconut desserts
banana pudding, 88
cassava cake, 138–39
coconut in chocolate frosted squares, 20
coconut delight, 192
coconut surprise, 148, 259–60
custard, 46
macaroons in baked rice dessert, 28
Coconut milk, 40
fish, rice, and, 167
in puddings
fish, 146
pumpkin, 133
sweet potato, 124
in shrimp with green pepper, 146, 258
in soups
fish chowder, 132
mulligatawny, 44
Cod (codfish)
baked, 62
in fish balls, 191

in fish soufflé, 103
heavenly, 186
rice and fish casserole, 134
Coffee in iced chocolate, 32
Cognac
cognac sauce, lamb fillets with, 81–82
custard with, 180, 264
in lobster omelet, 82
Cold Russian cream soup, 222
Cold vegetable and yogurt soup, 184
Collard greens and fish, 56
Coo coo (okra and cornmeal mush), 95
"Cook up" (rice with meat), 87–88
Cooked tomatoes, 132
Cookies
macaroons in rice dessert, 28
shortbread, 227
Corn
chicken and, 57–58
corn pie, 175–76
corn stew, 234
in mealie pudding, 202
Cornmeal mush and okra, 95
Cottage cheese
in bread pudding, 156
dumplings, 219–20
cheese in fruit dumplings, 64
potato and cheese, 220
cheese tidbits, 30
Couscous
Libyan, 140
shopping for, 140
Tunisian, 213–14
Crab (crabmeat)
baked fish with, 223
in fish soup, 238
Crab sauce, 88
beef and, 211
Cracked wheat (bulgur wheat)
Iraqi, 115
lamb and
baked lamb, 135
stuffed leg of lamb, 152–53
in Libyan couscous, 140
shopping for, 115, 140
wheat salad, 136
Crayfish with coconut and rice, 167
Cream of wheat in potato dumplings, 63–64
Crème caramel, 142–43
Creme de abacate (avocado whip), 32–33
Crème vanille, 143

Cretons (pork in jelly), 79
Croatian stuffed mushrooms, 242–43
Csokoládé mignon (chocolate cake
    squares), 102
Cuban hash, 60
Cuban rice with black beans, 58–59
Cucumbers
    in salads
        health, 224
        herring, 78
        yogurt and cucumber salad
            Albanian, 13
            Sudanese, 202, 263
Curaimir (venison cutlets), 117
Curried shrimp
    Burmese, 36
    Indian, 106
Curry sauce, 107, 261
Custards
    with caramel sauce, 157
        crème caramel, 142–43
    chicken and shrimp (non-dessert),
        125
    coconut, 46
    with cognac, 180, 264
    floating island, 143

Daging goreng (fried beef strips),
    147
Dakooss (cooked tomatoes), 132
Dashi sauce
    chicken and seafood with, 127
        chicken and shrimp custard, 125
    commercial sauce mix, 127
    in seafood and vegetables, 126–27
Dates
    in butter tarts, 42
    chocolate date nut pie, 119–20
    leg of lamb stuffed with, 152
Delicious peas, 49
DESSERTS
    coconut delight, 192
    cookies
        macaroons in rice dessert, 28
        shortbread, 227
    fritters as
        banana fritters, 193
        beignets, 191
        cinnamon fritters, 90
        fruit beignets, 191
    fruit bars, 225
    with honey syrup
        cinnamon fritters, 90
        walnut and honey dessert, 90–91
    pastry

    with almonds, 13
    coconut surprise, 148, 259–60
    filo dough, shopping for, 217,
        252
    fried Czechoslovakian, 65
    fried Egyptian, 226–27
    with honey, 198
    Turkish, 216–17, 252
    wonders dessert, 67, 254–55
    plum fluff, 185
    rice
        baked, 28
        with cherry sauce, 69
        spicy, 130
    (See also Cakes; Custards; Pies;
        Puddings; Tarts)
Deviled fish, 46, 259
Deviled lobster, 200–1
Dill sauce, 204, 262
Dolmas (meat and vegetable rolls),
    114–15
Doro-weutt (chicken with hot
    sauce), 77
Dosa (pancakes), 109–10
Dressed boiled potatoes, 161
Dressings
    for boiled potatoes, 161
    for marinated salmon, 203–4
    (See also Salad dressings; Stuff-
        ings)
Drinks (see Beverages)
Dumplings
    cheese
        cottage cheese, 219–20
        cottage cheese in fruit dump-
            lings, 64
        potato and cheese, 220
    fruit
        baked apple, 231
        Czechoslovakian, 64
        Hungarian, 101
        liver, 142
        in pea soup, 68
    potato
        cheese and potato, 220
        sauerkraut with, 63–64
    whole wheat, 166

E matur (pastry with almonds), 13–
    14
Egg curry, 36
Eggah (Egyptian lamb omelet),
    225–26
Eggplant
    eggplant casserole, 235

Eggplant (*cont'd*)
  oriental, 153
  pickled, 188
  in sour cream, 174
  stuffed, 98
  veal with rice and, 207
EGGS
  egg drop soups
    chicken egg drop, 122
    sour egg drop meat ball, 129
  egg noodles, 122–23
  omelets
    the emperor's, 21
    lamb, 225–26
    lobster, 82
  (*See also* Soufflés)
Egyptian lamb omelet, 225–26
Empanadas de carne (individual meat pies), 29–30
Emperor's omelet, the, 21
Endive
  eggs and, 163
  ham, cheese, and, 26
Ensalada de guacamole (avocado salad), 91
Ensalada de Nochebuena (Christmas Eve salad), 156
Epinards à l'africaine (African spinach), 44
Erwtensoep (pea soup), 162
Escabeche de pollo (pickled chicken), 31
Ewa dodo (seafood, plantains, and black-eyed peas), 167

Fante kotokyim (crab sauce), 88
Fersk suppe og kjott (beef with carrots and cabbage), 170
Figs, leg of lamb stuffed with, 152
Filé, *shopping for,* 150
Filets de sole ostendaise (sole with seafood and mushroom sauce), 27
Fillings
  for baked lamb and wheat, 135
  cottage cheese
    for cheese dumplings, 220
    for cheese tidbits, 30
    for potato dumplings, 220
  dessert
    for butter tarts, 42
    for chocolate cake squares, 102
    cream, 171–72
    plum pie, 244
    for Turkish pastry, 216–17

  for meat pies
    individual pies, 29–30
    Salvadoran turnovers, 74
  for meat squares, 118
  for pancakes, 109–10
  for ravioli, 11
  (*See also* Stuffings)
Filo dough, *shopping for,* 217, 252
FISH
  baked
    fish and rice casserole, 134
    haddock, halibut, or cod fillets, 62
    heavenly codfish, 186
    Jansson's temptation, 205
    Moscow style, 223
    pudding, 146
    Spanish style, 74–75
    Spetsai Island, 89
    whiting fillets, 18–19
  baked stuffed
    fillet of sole, 116
    grilled, 116
  with coconut and rice, 167
  curried
    Bengal curry, 106, 251
    Maldive Islands curry, 149
  in dashi sauce, 127
  deviled, 46, 259
  fish soup, 238–39
  fish soy sauce, *shopping for,* 36
  fish stews
    with rice, 41
    spiced chowder, 132
    spinach stew, 87
    two-sauce stew, 150
    with vegetables, 237–38
  fried
    fish balls in sauce, 191–92
    fritters, 222–23
    seafood and vegetables, 126–27
  marinated, 203
  pickled, 73, 257
  with seafood and mushroom sauce, 27
  souffléd
    Belgian, 25
    Icelandic, 103
    Veracruz, 154
  (*See also* SHELLFISH)
Fish and collard greens, 56
Fish and rice casserole, 134
Fish balls in sauce, 191–92
Fish pudding, 146
Fish stew with rice, 41

Fish stew with vegetables, 237–38
Fish Veracruz, 154
Fish with coconut and rice, 167
Fiskibudingur (fish soufflé), 103
Flemish beef and beer casserole, 26
Flemish liver pâté, 24–25
Floating island, 143
Flounder
    fish pudding, 146
    in seafood and vegetables, 126–27
    steamed, 50–51
Fouja djedad (chicken stuffed apples), 190
Frankfurters in lentil casserole, 119
Fresh vegetable-chicken salad, 133
Fried appetizers, 105
Fried beans, 37
    refried, 155
Fried beef strips, 147
Fried chicken with peanut butter sauce
    Congolese, 55
    Ivory Coast, 123–24
Fried fish fritters, 222–23
Fried pastries, 65
Fried pastry, 226–27
Fried rice, 193–94
Fried stuffed green peppers, 93
Frijoles refritos (refried beans), 155
Fritters
    banana, 193
    beignets, 191
    cinnamon, 90
    fish, 222–23
    Senegalese, 191
Frostings
    chocolate, 20
    mocha, 102
FRUIT
    candied
        in Christmas pudding, 229
        in fruit cake, 230
    fruit compote, 227
    fruit fritters
        banana, 193
        Senegalese, 191
    fruit salads
        Christmas Eve, 156
        zesty orange, 190
    fruit tarts
        banana, 33
        butter tarts, 42–43
        raspberry, 22
    sweet and sour beef with, 199
    (See also specific fruits)

Fruit bars, 225
Fruit dumplings
    apple, 231
    Czechoslovakian, 64
Funghi ripieni (stuffed mushrooms), 120, 251
Fyrstekake (cake royal), 172

Gallina en chicha (chicken in wine sauce), 75
Gallina en escabeche (chicken mold), 48
Game
    Georgian pheasant, 224
    venison cutlets, 117
Gâteau pommes de terre (golden beef-potato pie), 97
Gâteau Wallon (apple pie), 28
Gâteau aux amandes (almond cake), 83–84
Gdra (chicken or lamb with chickpeas), 159
Gefüllter Kalbsbraten (veal rolls), 21
Gehaktnestjes (meat loaf nests), 162
Georgian pheasant, 224
Gnocchi leggeri (light cheese noodles), 122–23
Golden beef-potato pie, 97
Golden rice, 112
    chicken with, 112–13
Goulash
    Guinean, 94
    Hungarian, 100
Grabie (shortbread cookies), 227
Grandmother's delicious cake, 185
Grapes in Georgian pheasant, 224
Gravad lax (marinated salmon), 203
Gravy, giblet, 233, 263
Green bean soup, 141
Green pea soup, 68
Green peppers
    meat pies filled with, 29–30
    meat stuffed with, 72
    shrimp with, 146–47, 258
    stuffed
        fried, 93
        meat and vegetable rolls, 114–15
        pickled, 136
Grilled stuffed trout, 116
Grønaertesuppe (green pea soup), 68
GROUND MEAT (chopped meat)
    in casseroles

GROUND MEAT (cont'd)
 golden beef-potato pie, 97
 meat squares, 118
 in hash
  baked hash with yogurt topping, 34
  Cuban hash, 68
 meat balls
  appetizers, 14, 251
  Bulgarian meat ball soup, 33
  sour egg drop meat ball soup, 129
  in tomato sauce, 215
  turnip soup with meat balls, 113–14
 meat loaf nests, 162
 meat pies
  beefsteak pie, 239
  Maltese macaroni dish, 151–52
  three meats pie, 42
 meat sauces
  for ravioli, 11–12
  two-sauce stew, 150
 meat timbales, 195–96
 meat-tomato mixture, 206
 mushrooms stuffed with, 242–43
 rice with
  "cook up," 87–88
  Hungarian stuffed cabbage, 101
  lamb and rice-stuffed zucchini, 129
  stuffed green peppers, 93
  Yemeni stuffed cabbage, 241
 spicy meat dish, 240
 zucchini stuffed with, 207
  lamb and rice, 129
Gruyère cheese sauce, potatoes with, 54
Grzyby w smietanie (mushrooms with sour cream), 184
Guinean goulash, 94

Haddock
 baked, 62
 in fish balls, 191–92
 fish pudding, 146
 in soufflés
  Belgian, 25
  Icelandic, 103
  Spanish style, 74–75
  Veracruz, 154
Halibut
 baked, 62
 curried, 106, 251
 fish fritters, 222–23

 fish and rice casserole, 134
 in fish stew with rice, 41
HAM
 beef stuffed with, 72
 chicken with rice and, 138, 253–54
 ham casseroles
  endive, ham, and cheese, 26
  Flemish beef and beer, 26–27
 ham pies
  little meat pies, 70–71
  veal and, 19
 seafood and noodles with, 181
Hanaa kuri mas (fish curry), 149
Health salad, 224
Hearty bean soup, 71
Heavenly codfish, 186
Herring salad, 78
Honduran chicken, 99
Hors d'oeuvres (see APPETIZERS)
Hot and sour chicken soup, 210
Hot peppers (see Chili peppers)
Hrvatske punjene gljive (Croatian stuffed mushrooms), 242
Humita Mendocina (corn supreme), 17
Hunter's stew, 183
Huris hilib (veal with tomato topping), 194–95
Hush puppies, 234

Ibiharage (fried beans), 37
Icing (see Frostings)
Indian corn stew, 234
Indio viejo (Old Indians), 165
Individual meat pies, 29–30
Inti-puff (coconut surprise), 148, 259–60
Involtini (rolled veal with pâté), 121–22, 260
Itókó dya betatamu (shrimp and tomato stew), 76

Jambon et endive au gratin (ham and endive with cheese), 26
Jansson's temptation (Jansson's Frestelse), 205
Jollof rice, 138, 253–54

Kabuli pelau, 10
Kafta (kefta), 14, 251
Kaiserschmarren (the emperor's omelet), 21
Kansiyé (Guinean goulash), 94
Karedopeta (walnut and honey dessert), 90–91

Kebabs and skewer cooking (see
    Skewer cooking)
Kebat (priest stew), 35
Kefta (kafta), 14, 251
Kengphed (spiced fish chowder),
    132–33
Kera ko misthanana (banana pud-
    ding), 161
Kesäkeitto (summer vegetable soup),
    78
Kharoff (stuffed crown roast of
    lamb), 131
Khoreshe karafs (beef-celery sauce),
    111
Khoshaf shahira (dried fruit com-
    pote), 227
Kibbeh bissanieh (baked lamb and
    wheat), 135
Kidney beans
    bean soup, 71
    rice and, 96
King Haakon's cake, 171–72
Kirsebaersauce (cherry sauce), 69
Kiveve (squash cream), 176
Kokt lamm med dill sås (boiled lamb
    with dill sauce), 204, 262
Kong Haakon's kake (King Haakon's
    cake), 171–72
Kos me krastabec (yogurt and cu-
    cumber salad), 13
Kousa mahshi (lamb and rice-stuffed
    zucchini), 129
Kubba shalgum (turnip soup with
    meatballs), 113
Kufta soup (sour egg drop meatball
    soup), 129
Kuwe ikan (fish pudding), 146
Kvas, 222
Kyet-u-hin (egg curry), 36
Kyselé zelí s bramborovymí kned-
    líky (sauerkraut with potato
    dumplings), 63

LAMB
    boiled, with dill sauce, 204, 262
    braised
        with chick-peas, 159
        lamb oregano, 89–90
        Libyan couscous, 140
        with okra sauce, 47
        with olives, 158–59
        Tunisian couscous, 213–14
    in casseroles
        lamb with saffron, 189–90

    lamb and vegetables, 61
    curried, 45
    ground
        baked, wheat and, 135
        meatballs, 14, 251
        in meat and vegetable rolls, 114–
            15
        rice-stuffed zucchini and, 129
        in sour egg drop meatball soup,
            129
        in turnip soup with meatballs,
            114–15
    lamb fillets with cognac sauce over
        chestnut purée, 81–82
    lamb goulash, 94
    lamb omelet, 225–26
    lamb stew, 166
    rice and
        Afghan pelau, 9
        cabbage stuffed with, 241
        lamb with chick-peas, 159
        lamb and vegetables, 61
        rice-stuffed zucchini, 129
        stuffed crown roast, 131–32
    roast
        in hunter's stew, 183–84
        with mint sauce, 163–64
        stuffed crown roast, 131
        stuffed leg of lamb, 152–53
    spiced, 108
Lamb and vegetables, 61
Lamb fillets with cognac sauce over
    chestnut purée, 81–82
Lamb oregano, 89–90
Lamb stew, 166
Lamb with saffron, 189–90
Lamingstons (chocolate frosted
    squares), 20
Lancashire hot-pot, 228
Langosta diablo (deviled lobster),
    200
Le to (two-sauce stew), 150
Lebanie (yogurt cheese), 135
Leche asada (custard with cognac),
    180, 264
Leek ravioli, 11
Leftover meat (cooked meat)
    chicken-stuffed apples, 190
    in Old Indians, 165
    as omelet filling, 225–26
    rice with, 87
        fried rice, 193
    roast
        in hunter's stew, 183
        in vegetable-yogurt soup, 184

Leftover meat (cont'd)
    seafood and, with noodles, 181
    in tamales, 92
Leftover soufflé, 103
Lemon-soy sauce, 128
Lemonade, veal cutlets with, 97–98
Lentil casserole, 119
Leverpostei (liver paste), 169–70
Levivot gevina (cheese steaks), 118–
    19
Libyan couscous, 140
Lieverkniddelen (liver dumplings),
    142
Lima bean soup, 53
Linzer torte (raspberry tart), 22
Liquor
    cognac sauce, lamb fillets with, 81–
        82
    liquor desserts
        custard with cognac, 180, 264
        fruit cake, 230
        rum in baked rice dessert, 28
        rum pudding, 171
        rum sauce, 24
        rum syrup, 84
    in lobster omelet, 82
Little meat pies, 70–71
Liver
    chicken livers
        baked rice and, 226
        liver-stuffed chicken breasts, 38–
            39
        marinated broiled, 179–80
    liver dumplings, 142
    liver paste, 169–70
    liver pâté
        Flemish, 24–25
        in veal rolls, 121–22, 260
Lla-uchitas (cheese tidbits), 30
Lobster
    in baked fish, 223
    chicken and, in dashi sauce, 127
    deviled, 200
    lobster bisque for omelet, 82
    lobster omelet, 82
    lobster sauce, 88
Lofschotel (endive and eggs), 163
Lokmet elkadi (fried pastry), 226–
    27
Lomo de cerdo a la Peruana (sweet
    roast pork), 178
Loukoumades (cinnamon fritters),
    90

Ma ti chi k'uai (chicken with water

chestnuts), 51–52
Ma'alubi (veal with rice and egg-
    plant), 207
Maan nezim nzedo (fish stew with
    vegetables), 237
Macadamia nuts, chicken with, 85
Macaroni dish, Maltese, 151–52
Machanka (pork and sausage with
    sour cream), 38
Makbous flaifleh (pickled stuffed
    peppers), 136
Makunde na tamba akuteleka (veg-
    etable stew), 245
Malfoof mahshie (stuffed cabbage),
    241
Maltese macaroni dish, 151–52
Marinated beef strips, 157–58
Marinated broiled meat, 179–80
Marinated leg of veal, 80
Marinated salmon, 203
Market-zeïtun (braised beef with
    olives), 214, 253
Masala filling, 109–10
Mazurki (fruit bars), 225
Mbisi ye kalou na loso (fish and col-
    lard greens), 56
Mchuzi we kuku (chicken curry),
    208–9
Mealie bread, 137
Mealie pudding, 202
MEAT
    chicken and, with rice, 138, 253
    marinated broiled, 179–80
    meat pies
        beefsteak, 239
        individual, 29–30
        little, 70–71
    Maltese macaroni dish, 151–52
    Salvadoran turnovers, 74
    three meats pie, 42
    veal and ham, 19
    spicy fried, 240
    stuffed, 72
    (See also specific meats)
Meat and seafood with noodles, 181
Meat and vegetable mélange, 214–15
Meat and vegetable rolls, 114–15
Meat loaf nests, 162
Meat rolls, 16
    veal, 21
    vegetable and, 114–15
Meat squares, 118
Meat timbales, 195–96
Meat-tomato mixture, 206
Meat with okra sauce, 47

Meatballs
as appetizers, 14, 251
in tomato sauce, 215
meatball soups
Bulgarian, 33
sour egg drop, 129
turnip and, 114–15
Menazzeleh (meat-tomato mixture), 206
Meringue, 164
Michoui (stuffed leg of lamb), 152–53
Milosti (fried pastries), 65
Mint chutney, 106
Mint sauce, 163–64
Mixed vegetables with eggs, 15
Mizutaki (chicken and vegetables), 128
Mocha frosting, 102
Mokila n'gombe (oxtail stew), 55–56
Moo tang (spicy roast pork with pineapple), 210–11
Morg polo (chicken with golden rice), 112
Mousse de aguacate (avocado mousse), 57, 255
Mrs. Truman's Ozark pudding, 237
Muenster cheese in chicken and corn, 57
Mughle (spicy rice dessert), 130
Mulligatawny soup, 44–45
Munkaczina (zesty orange salad), 190
Murgh-i-mussalam (stuffed chicken), 173
Murgh qorma (chicken curry), 173–74
Mus curriya (veal curry), 45
Musaka (baked hash with yogurt topping), 34
Mushrooms
with sour cream, 184
stuffed
Croatian, 242
Italian, 120, 251
venison cutlets with, 117

Nasi goreng (fried rice), 193–94
Natilla (custard with caramel sauce), 157
Navy beans (white beans), fried, 37
Ndizi na nyama (banana medley), 209
Nezio adashim (lentil casserole), 119
Nfiang koss (fish stew with rice), 41

Nham salad (fresh vegetable-chicken salad), 133
Niños envueltos (meat rolls), 16
Noisettes d'agneau et purée de marrons (lamb fillets with cognac sauce over chestnut purée), 81–82
Noodle stew, 110
Noodles
Chinese (cellophane)
in chicken soup, 50
noodle stew, 110
shopping for, 50
light cheese, 122–23
meat and seafood with, 181
chicken and shrimp custard, 125
Nuts
chicken with, 85
chicken-nut arima, 212–13, 257
nut sauces
cashew, 31
walnut, 12
nut stuffings
chestnut, 152–53
chestnut-sausage, 233, 262–63
for lamb roast, 131–32
sweet stuffing, 13
zucchini stuffed with, 207–8
(*See also* Chestnuts)

Okra and cornmeal mush, 95
Okra sauce, meat with, 47
Okroshka soup (cold Russian cream soup), 222
Okuku-ngbolodi-ogede (chicken and spinach medley), 168
Old Indians, 165
Olives
braised beef with, 214, 253
meat stuffed with, 72
Omelets
Egyptian lamb, 225–26
the emperor's, 21
lobster, 82
Omelette cardinal, 82
Onions
Chinese beef and, 52
fruit with
banana medley, 209
pickled peaches, 254
Oriental eggplant, 153
Ovocné knedlíky (fruit dumplings), 64
Ovotchnoy salat (health salad), 224
Oxtail stew, 55–56

Oysters
  chicken and, in dashi sauce, 127
  in filets de sole ostendaise, 27
  in pocket steak, 19–20

Pakoras (fried appetizers), 105
Palaver stew, 87
Palm nuts, chicken with, 85
Pancakes
  Icelandic, 104
  Indian, 109–10
Pancit guisado (meat with seafood with noodles), 181
Papas chorriadas (potatoes with cheese sauce), 54
Paprikás csirke galuskaval (chicken paprika with dumplings), 101
Parsley, mushrooms stuffed with, 251
Pasha's chakchouka, 214–15
Pasta
  leek ravioli, 11
  macaroni dish, 151–52
  spaghetti in vegetable soup, 95–96
  vermicelli in chicken and seafood with dashi sauce, 127
  (*See also* Noodles)
Pastel de carne (beefsteak pie), 239
Pastelitos (little meat pies), 70–71
Pastelitos de picadillo (Salvadoran turnovers), 74
Pastry (pie dough)
  with almonds, 13–14
  for butter tarts, 42–43
  for coconut surprise, 148, 259–60
  fried
    Czechoslovakian, 65
    Egyptian, 226–27
  with honey, 198
  for meat pies
    individual pies, 29–30
    little pies, 70–71
  for plum pie, 244
  rough, 231
  Turkish, 216–17, 252
    filo dough, *shopping for,* 217
  wonders dessert, 67, 254–55
  (*See also* Pies; Tarts)
Pâté
  Flemish liver, 24–25
  rolled veal with, 121–22, 260
Pâté à la flamande (Flemish liver pâté), 24–25
Pa-zun hin (shrimp curry), 36
Pea soup

Dutch, 162
green pea, 68
Tyrolese, 22
Peaches
  pickled, 197, 254
  sweet and sour beef with, 199
Peanut butter
  in chicken stew, 86
  peanut butter soup, 201
Pears, sweet and sour beef with, 199
Peas
  delicious, 49
  meat rolls with, 16
  pea soups
    Dutch, 162
    green pea, 68
    Tyrolese, 22
  seafood, plantains, and, 167
Pepitoria de carne picada (spicy chopped meat dish), 240
Peppers (*see* Chili peppers; Green peppers; Red peppers)
Pescado a la Veracruzana (fish Veracruz), 154
Phazar ro-Gkuzinski (Georgian pheasant), 224
Pheasant, Georgian, 224
Picadillo Cubano (Cuban hash), 60
Pickled beef with sour cream, 63
Pickled chicken, 31
Pickled eggplant, 188
Pickled fish, 73, 257
Pickled stuffed peppers, 136
Pies
  cheese
    cheese in corn pie, 175–76
    cheese in macaroni dish, 151
    cheese tidbits, 30
  fruit
    apple, 28
    chocolate date nut, 119–20
    plum, 244
  meat
    beefsteak, 239
    individual, 29–30
    little, 70–71
    Maltese macaroni dish, 151
    Salvadoran turnovers, 74
    three meats pie, 42
    veal and ham, 19
  pumpkin chiffon, 236
  spinach, 83
Pig's knuckle in pork jelly, 79
Pikantne šnicle (savory veal cutlets), 243

Pine nuts, zucchini stuffed with, 207–8
Pineapple, spicy roast pork with, 210–11
Pinto beans
  bean soup, 71
  rice and, 96
Plaki (baked fish), 62
Plantains
  in chicken-spinach medley, 168
  described, 218
  seafood, black-eyed peas, and, 167
  shopping for, 188
  in stews
    beef, 188–89
    chicken, 218
Plat national (beans and rice), 96
Plums
  plum fluff, 185
  Slovenian plum pie, 244
  sweet and sour beef with, 199
Pocket steak, 19–20
Podvarak (baked sauerkraut), 243
Polish sausage in hunter's stew, 183–84
Pollo a la pepitoria (chicken with sherry and almonds), 199–200
Pollo Hondureño (Honduran chicken), 99
Pollo relleno con nueces (chicken with chestnut dressing), 155
Pönnukökur (pancakes), 104
Poori (tasty bread), 108
PORK
  braised
    pork paprika, 182, 258–59
    pork and potatoes, 61
    pork sausage with sour cream, 38
    seafood and pork with noodles, 181
    10-ingredient rice dish, 51
  curried, 45
  ground
    cabbage stuffed with, 101
    Cuban hash, 60
    leftover, in tamales, 92
    meat loaf nests, 162
    pork in Maltese macaroni dish, 151
    three meats pie, 42
  in jelly, 79
  in meat pies
    little, 70–71

Salvadoran turnovers, 74
    three meats pie, 42
    veal and ham, 19
  in Old Indians, 165
  pork liver
    Flemish liver pâté, 24–25
    liver paste, 169–70
  pork and sauerkraut stew, 100
  roast
    in hunter's stew, 183–84
    spicy, with pineapple, 210–11
    sweet, 178
  salt (fat)
    in bean soup, 71
    in peas and rice, 23
    in pheasant, 224
    pork liver paste, 169–70
    pork liver pâté, 24–25
    skewered lamb and, 196
  in soups
    chicken, 50
    pig's feet in pea soup, 162
    salt pork in bean soup, 71
  spicy fried, 240
  sweet potatoes stuffed with, 174–75
  with veal and rice, 177, 256
  (*See also* HAM; Sausage)
Pork and potatoes, 61
Pork and sauerkraut stew, 100
Pork and sausage with sour cream, 38
Pork paprika, 182, 258–59
Porotos exquisitos (delicious peas), 49
Portuguese pot roast, 187
Pot cheese steaks, 118–19
Pot roast, Portuguese, 187
Potage jardinière (vegetable soup), 141
Potato and cheese dumplings, 220
Potato cakes, 160
Potatoes
  boiled
    dressed, 161
    potato stuffing, 173
  browned in sugar, 104
  with cheese sauce, 54
  in Jansson's temptation, 205
  in meat dishes
    golden beef-potato pie, 97
    pork and potatoes, 61
  potato cakes, 160
  potato dumplings
    cheese and potato, 220
    sauerkraut with, 63–64
  potato-filled pancakes, 109–10

Potatoes *(cont'd)*
potato flour bread, 176–77
potato salads
potatoes in herring salad, 78
sweet potato, 47
potato starch in cake, 171
sweet
pudding, 124
salad, 47
Poulet au gnemboue (chicken with nuts), 85
Poultry
roast turkey, 233, 262–63
(*See also* CHICKEN)
Priest stew, 35
Psari fourno Spetsiotiko (baked fish —Spetsai Island), 89
Puddings
banana
Ghanaian, 88
Nepalese, 161
West Indian, 24
blueberry crisp, 43
bread
banana pudding, 24
Christmas pudding, 229
Mexican, 156
queen of puddings, 165
brownie, 236
Mrs. Truman's Ozark, 237
non-dessert
fish, 146
mealie, 202
pumpkin, 133
rum, 171
sweet potato, 124
(*See also* Custards)
Pudiina chutney (mint chutney), 106
Pule me drop (sweet stuffing for chicken), 13
Pule me harr (chicken with walnut sauce), 12
Pumpkin, corn supreme in, 17
Pumpkin chiffon pie, 236
Pumpkin pudding, 133
Pyrohy (potato and cheese dumplings), 220

Qchiou ganar (chicken stew), 86
Queen of puddings, 164

Raggedy beef stew, 59
Rågsiktbröd (Swedish rye bread), 204–5
Raisins

roast lamb stuffed with, 131–32
sweet and sour beef with, 199
Raspberry tart, 22
Ravigote sauce, 80
Ravioli, leek, 11
Rebra kuritsy (chicken breast fillets), 38–39
Red beans
bean soup, 145
refried, 155
Red cabbage
Danish, 68
Swedish, 205
Red peppers, meat pies filled with, 29–30
Red snapper
baked—Spetsai Island, 89
in fish soufflé, 103
Veracruz, 154
Refried beans, 155
Relishes
pickled peaches, 197, 254
pickled stuffed peppers, 136
(*See also* Chutney)
Rice
beans and
chicken, meat, and rice, 138, 253–54
Cuban rice and black beans, 58
Haitian, 96
beef and
boiled beef with vegetables, 182
spicy fried beef, 240
steak stew with rice, 168–69
chicken with (*see under* CHICKEN)
fried, 193–94
golden, 112
ground meat and
"cook up," 87–88
Hungarian stuffed cabbage, 101
lamb and rice-stuffed zucchini, 129
stuffed green peppers, 93
Yemeni stuffed cabbage, 241
lamb and
Afghan pelau, 9
lamb with chick-peas, 159
meat and vegetable rolls, 114–15
rice in lamb and vegetables, 61
rice-stuffed zucchini, 129
roast lamb, 131
in stuffed cabbage, 241
in pancakes, 109–10
peas and, 23

Rice (cont'd)
    veal, pork, and rice, 177, 256
    pork and
        fried rice, 193–94
        ham in Cuban beans and rice,
            58
        peas and rice, 23
        spicy fried pork, 240
        stuffed cabbage, 101
        10-ingredient rice dish, 51
        veal, pork, and rice, 177, 256
    rice desserts
        baked, 28
        with cherry sauce, 69
        spicy, 130
    seafood and
        fish with coconut and rice, 167
        fish and rice casserole, 134
        fish stew, 41
        fish stew with vegetables, 237–38
        veal with eggplant and, 207
Riganato (lamb oregano), 89–90
Rindang udang (shrimp with green
    pepper), 146–47, 258
Riz à l'amande (almond rice dessert
    with cherry sauce), 69
Roast lamb with mint sauce, 163–64
Roast turkey with chestnut-sausage
    dressing, 233, 262–63
Roasts
    beef
        in hunter's stew, 183–84
        pickled, with sour cream, 63
        Portuguese pot roast, 187
    lamb
        in hunter's stew, 183–84
        with mint sauce, 163–64
        stuffed crown roast, 131
        stuffed leg of lamb, 152–53
    leftover
        in hunter's stew, 183–84
        in vegetable-yogurt soup, 184
    pork
        in hunter's stew, 183–84
        spicy, with pineapple, 210–11
        sweet, 178
Robalo a la Española (haddock,
    Spanish-style), 74–75
Rodkaal (red cabbage), 68
Rödkål (Swedish rye bread), 204–5
Rolled veal with pâté, 121–22, 260
Rompudding (rum pudding), 171
Ropa vieja (raggedy beef stew), 59
Rum desserts
    pudding, 171

rum in baked rice dessert, 28
    sauce, 24
    syrup, 84
Rye bread, Swedish, 204–5

Salad dressings
    egg-yolk, 133
    for shrimp-avocado salad, 235
    sour cream, 78
Salade de patates douces (sweet po-
    tato salad), 47
SALADS
    avocado
        guacamole, 91
        shrimp-avocado, 235
    fruit
        Christmas Eve, 156
        zesty orange, 190
    green
        fresh vegetable-chicken, 133
        health salad, 224
        wheat salad, 136
    seafood
        herring, 78
        shrimp-avocado, 235
    sweet potato, 47
    yogurt and cucumber
        Albanian, 13
        Sudanese, 202, 263
Salçali köfte (beef balls in tomato
    sauce), 215
Salmon
    deviled, 46, 259
    marinated, 203
Salvadoran turnovers, 74
Sandwich spread, liver paste, 169–70
Sankhagha makoû (pumpkin pud-
    ding), 133
Sauce au poisson et boeuf (seafood
    and beef sauce), 211–12
SAUCES
    for beef soup, 170
    caramel
        Luxembourg, 142–43
        Mexican, 157
    cheese, potatoes with, 54
    cherry, 69
    coconut, 40
    dessert syrups
        for baklava, 216–17, 252
        for cinnamon fritters, 90
        for fried pastry, 226–27
        rum syrup, 84
        for walnut and honey dessert,
            90–91

SAUCES (cont'd)
  hot
    for marinated broiled meat,
      179–80
    for tamales, 92
  hot, chicken with
    Ethiopian, 77
    pepper sauce, 179
  for lamb
    apricot, 196
    cognac, 81–82
    dill, 204, 262
    mint, 163–64
    okra, 47
  meat
    beef-celery, 111
    beef and seafood, 211–12
    for leek ravioli, 11–12
    for Maltese macaroni dish, 151–
      52
    two-sauce stew, 150
  for meat pie, 42
  nut
    cashew, 31
    walnut, 12
  peanut butter, fried chicken with
    Congolese, 55
    Ivory Coast, 123–24
  for pheasant, 224
  ravigote, 80
  rum
    rum syrup, 84
    West Indian, 24
  seafood
    béchamel, 186
    béchamel, for Moscow style
      fish, 223
    beef and seafood, 211–12
    crab sauce, 88
    dashi, 127
    diablo, 200–1
    fish balls in, 191–92
    shrimp sauce, 27
    shrimp sauce, shopping for, 36
  sour cream
    pickled beef with, 63
    for stuffed mushrooms, 242–43
  soy
    in barbecue sauce, 147
    in beef marinade, 157–58
    in dashi sauce, 127
    fish, shopping for, 36
    lemon, 128
  spinach
    beef and shrimp in, 66–67

    spinach in beef and seafood
      sauce, 211–12
  tomato
    beef balls in, 215
    in fish stew, 237–38
    for meat rolls, 16
    tomatoes in crab sauce, 88
    tomatoes in seafood and beef
      sauce, 211–12
    in veal with rice and eggplant,
      207
  tortilla, in Old Indians, 165
  wine
    chicken in, 75
    sherry, 177–78, 256
    sherry and cream, 27
    sour cream and wine, 242–43
    white wine, 16
  yogurt
    Indian curry, 107, 261
    marinade, 173
    for stuffed zucchini, 207–8
  (See also Gravy; Salad dressings)
Sauerkraut
  baked, 243
  with potato dumplings, 63–64
  in stews
    hunter's, 183–84
    pork and sauerkraut, 100
  stuffed cabbage with, 101
Sausage
  chestnut-sausage dressing, 233,
    262–63
  frankfurters in lentil casserole, 119
  pork and, with sour cream, 38
Savarin au rhum (baba cake), 84
Savory veal cutlets, 243
Sayadiah (fish and rice casserole),
  134
Scallops in dashi sauce
  chicken and, 127
  vegetables and, 126–27
Schnicel (chicken fillets à la min-
  ister), 221
Sea bass
  fish soup, 238–39
  steamed, 50–51
Seafood (see FISH; SHELLFISH)
Seafood and beef sauce, 211–12
Seafood and vegetables, 126–27
Seafood, plantains, and black-eyed
  peas, 167
Semolina, shopping for, 140
Semolina dish, 209
Semur (noodle stew), 110

Seviche, 73, 257
Sheik el Mah'shi (stuffed zucchini),
    207
SHELLFISH
  avocado-shellfish salad, 235
  with coconut and rice, 167
  curried
    Burmese, 36
    Indian, 106
  in dashi sauce
    chicken and seafood, 127
    seafood and vegetables, 126-27
    shrimp and chicken custard, 125
  deviled, 200-1
  with green pepper, 146-47, 258
  meat and, with noodles, 181
  plantains, black-eyed peas, and,
    167
  pocket steak with, 19-20
  shellfish sauces
    beef and seafood, 211-12
    crab or lobster, 88
    shrimp, 27
    shrimp, shopping for, 36
  shellfish soups
    fish soup, 238-39
    lobster bisque in lobster ome-
      let, 82
    shrimp in chicken soup, 50
  shrimp fried rice, 193-94
  stuffed sole with, 116
  tomato-shellfish stew, 76
  (See also FISH)
Sherry
  sherried chicken
    with almonds, 199-200
    seafood and, 127
  sherry and cream sauce, 27
Shih chen chao fan (10-ingredient
    rice dish), 51
Shish kebab (see Skewer cooking)
Shorba (peanut butter soup), 201
Shorbat robe (yogurt and cucumber
    salad), 202, 263
Shortbread cookies, 227
Shrimp
  beef and
    sauce, 211-12
    in spinach sauce, 66-67
  with coconut and rice, 167
  curried
    Burmese, 36
    Indian, 106
  in dashi sauce
    chicken and seafood, 127

chicken and shrimp custard, 125
  seafood and vegetables, 126-27
  fillets of sole and
    shrimp sauce for sole, 27
    shrimp-stuffed sole, 116
  with green pepper, 146-47, 258
  meat and, with noodles, 181
  plantains, black-eyed peas, and,
    167
  shrimp-avocado salad, 235
  shrimp fried rice, 193-94
  shrimp sauce, shopping for, 37
  in soups
    chicken, 50
    fish, 238
    summer vegetable, 78-79
    vegetable-yogurt, 184
  tomato and shrimp stew, 76
Shrimp and tomato stew, 76
Shrimp-avocado salad, 235
Shrimp bhaji, 106
Sillisalaati (herring salad), 78
Sinigand na baka (boiled beef with
    vegetables), 182
Skewer cooking
  lamb with sauce, 196
  marinated broiled meat, 179-80
Sliwki w pianie (plum fluff), 185
Slovenian plum pie (Slovenačka pita
    od šijiva), 244
Sole, fillets of
  fish pudding, 146
  fish and rice casserole, 134
  with seafood and mushroom
    sauce, 27
  steamed, 50-51
  stuffed, 116
Sole atchen (stuffed fillet of sole
    supreme), 116
Sopa de frijoles (hearty bean soup),
    71
Sopa de habas (lima bean soup), 53
Sosaties (skewered lamb with sauce),
    196
Soufflé de poisson (fish soufflé), 25
Soupa sus topchetas (meatball soup),
    33
Soupe à la Malgache (vegetable
    soup), 144
Soupe au Giraumon (vegetable
    soup), 95-96
SOUPS
  bean
    beans in vegetable soup (Lux-
      embourg), 141

SOUPS (*cont'd*)
  beans in vegetable soup (Madagascar), 144
  green bean, 141–42
  hearty, 71
  lima bean, 53
  red bean, 145
  beef, with carrots and cabbage, 170
  bread and cheese, 18
  chicken
    Chinese, 50
    with egg drops, 122
    Haitian vegetable, 95–96
    hot and sour, 210
    mulligatawny, 44–45
  cold
    Russian cream soup, 222
    vegetable and yogurt, 184
  meatball
    Bulgarian, 33
    sour egg drop, 129
    turnip and, 113–14
  pea
    Dutch, 162
    green pea, 68
    Tyrolese, 22
  peanut butter, 201
  seafood
    lobster bisque in lobster omelet, 82
    shrimp in chicken soup, 50
    shrimp in vegetable-yogurt soup, 184
    spiced fish chowder, 132–33
    summer vegetable, 78–79
    Uruguayan fish soup, 238
  vegetable
    à la Malgache, 144
    cold vegetable and yogurt, 184
    Haitian, 95–96
    Luxembourg, 141
    summer vegetable, 78–79
  (*See also* STEWS)
Sour cream
  chicken paprika with, 101
  dumplings with, 219–20
  eggplant in, 174
  leek ravioli with, 11
  mushrooms with, 184
    sour cream sauce, 242–43
  pickled beef with, 63
  soup with
    borsch, 219
    cold cream soup, 222

  green bean soup, 141–42
  sour cream dressing, 78
  veal cutlets with, 243
Sour egg drop meatball soup, 129
Southern fried chicken, 232
Spiced avocado, 53
Spiced fish chowder, 132–33
Spiced lamb, 108
Spicy chopped meat dish, 240
Spicy fried meat, 240
Spicy rice dessert, 130
Spicy roast pork with pineapple, 210–11
Spinach
  African, 44
  beef and shrimp in spinach sauce, 66–67
  spinach pie, 83
  spinach stews, 76, 82
Split pea soup
  Dutch, 162
  Tyrolese, 22
Spring beet soup, 219
Squash cream, 176
Steak stew with rice, 168–69
Steaks
  beef (*see* Beefsteaks)
  cheese, 118–19
Steamed fish, 50–51
STEWS
  beef
    à la Rwanda, 188–89
    bean stew, 130
    corn stew, 234
    hunter's, 183–84
    noodle stew, 110
    oxtail, 55–56
    priest, 35
    raggedy, 59
    steak stew with rice, 168–69
    two-sauce, 150
    vegetable stew, 241
  chicken
    Gambian, 86
    noodle stew, 110
    plantains with, 218
    spinach stew, 87
    vegetable soup as, 95–96
  lamb
    hunter's, 183–84
    Niger, 166
  pork
    hunter's, 183–84
    sauerkraut and pork, 100
  seafood

STEWS (cont'd)
  fish stew with rice, 41
  fish stew with vegetables, 237–38
  shrimp and tomato, 76
  spiced fish chowder, 132–33
  spinach stew, 82
  two-sauce, 150
  spinach, 82
  spinach in shrimp-tomato stew,
    76
  vegetable, 241
  (See also Goulash; SOUPS)
Stracciatella (chicken soup with egg
  drops), 122
Stuffed cabbage
  Hungarian, 101
  Yemeni, 241
Stuffed chicken, 173–74
Stuffed crown roast of lamb, 131
Stuffed eggplant, 98
Stuffed fillet of sole supreme, 116
Stuffed grape leaves, 139
Stuffed leg of lamb, 152–53
Stuffed meat, 72
Stuffed mushrooms
  Croatian, 242
  Italian, 120, 251
Stuffed sweet potato balls, 174–75
Stuffed zucchini
  lamb and rice-stuffed, 129
  Syrian, 207–8
Stuffings (dressings)
  chestnut-sausage, 233, 262–63
  sweet stuffing for chicken, 13
  for fish
    sole, 116
    trout, 116
  for meat rolls, 16
  (See also Fillings)
Summer vegetable soup, 78–79
Supu wa nuemba zolfiira (red bean
  soup), 145
Svíčková pečeně (pickled beef with
  sour cream), 63
Swedish rye bread, 204–5
Sweet and sour beef with fruit, 199
Sweet potato pudding, 124
Sweet potato salad, 47
Sweet roast pork, 178
Swiss cheese
  Gruyère sauce, potatoes with, 54
  ham, endive, and, 26
Syrups, dessert
  for baklava, 216–17, 252

for fried pastry, 226–27
honey
  for cinnamon fritters, 90
  for walnut and honey dessert,
    90–91
  rum, 84
Szekely gulyás (pork and sauerkraut
  stew), 100

Tabbouli (wheat salad), 136
Tadjin ahmar (lamb with saffron),
  189–90
Tagin orz (baked rice with chicken
  livers), 226
Tagine (braised chicken with olives),
  158–59
Tamales de carne (beef tamales), 92
Tapioca cake, 138–39
Tarte liégeoise (baked rice dessert),
  28
Tarts
  banana, 33
  butter, 42–43
  raspberry, 22
  rice, 28
Tassau (veal cutlets), 97–98
Tasty bread, 108–9
Tavá (lamb and vegetables), 61
Tempura (seafood and vegetables),
  126–27
10-ingredient rice dish, 51
Three meats pie, 42
Timpana (Maltese macaroni dish),
  151
Tipsy cake, 231–32
Töltött kaposzta (stuffed cabbage),
  101
Tom yum gai (hot and sour chicken
  soup), 210
Tomatoes
  beef and, meat-tomato mixture,
    206
  cooked canned, 132
  tomato chutney, 108
  tomato sauce
    beef balls in, 215
    in fish stew, 237–38
    for meat rolls, 16
    tomatoes in crab sauce, 88
    tomatoes in seafood and beef
      sauce, 211–12
    in veal with rice and eggplant,
      207
  tomato topping, veal with, 194–95
  venison with, 117

Toppings
  cream, 171–72
  tomato, 194–95
  yogurt, 34
Torta de banana (banana tart), 33
Tortillas
  in Old Indians, 165
  shopping for, 165
  tortilla crisps, 155
  tortilla sauce in Old Indians, 165
Tourte aux épinards (spinach pie), 83
Tourtière de la Gaspesie (three meats pie), 42
Trout, grilled stuffed, 116
Tuna (tuna fish)
  deviled, 46
  plantains, black-eyed peas, and, 167
Tunisian couscous, 213–14
Turkey with chestnut-sausage dressing, 233, 262–63
Turkish pastry, 216–17, 252
  filo dough for, *shopping for*, 217, 252
Turnip soup with meatballs, 113–14
Two-sauce stew, 150
Tyrolese soup, 22

Ugali (semolina dish), 209
Ukheriin chanasan makh (marinated beef strips), 157–58
Uruguayan fish soup, 238
Vanocka (Christmas braid), 65–66
Varenga (browned shredded beef), 144
Varenyki (cottage cheese dumplings), 219–20
Vata cappan (coconut custard), 46
VEAL
  calf's heart, marinated broiled, 179–80
  calf's liver dumplings, 142
  curried, 45
  ground
    meat loaf nests, 162
    mushrooms stuffed with, 242
  leftover roast
    in hunter's stew, 183–84
    in vegetable-yogurt soup, 184
  marinated leg of, 80
  pork and
    ham and veal pie, 19
    with rice, 177, 256

tomato and
  tomato sauce in veal with rice and eggplant, 207
  tomato topping, 194–95
veal bones in vegetable soup, 144
veal cutlets, 97–98
  rolled, with pâté, 121–22, 260
  savory, 243
  veal rolls, 21
Veal and ham pie, 19
Veal curry, 45
Veal rolls, 21
Veau saumure Angoumois (marinated leg of veal), 80
Vegetable soup
  à la Malgache, 144
  cold vegetable and yogurt, 184
  Haitian, 95–96
  Luxembourg, 141
  summer, 78–79
Vegetable stew, 241
VEGETABLES
  eggs and
    mixed vegetables, 15
    10-ingredient rice dish, 51
  fresh vegetable-chicken salad, 133
  meat and vegetable mélange, 214–15
  meat and vegetable rolls, 114–15
  seafood and
    fish stew, 237–38
    tempura, 126–27
  (*See also* SALADS; *specific vegetables*)
Venison cutlets, 117
Viande à la sauce okra, (meat with okra sauce), 47
Vinete conservate în saramura (pickled eggplant), 188
Vlaams rundvlees en bier casserole (Flemish beef and beer casserole), 26

Walnut and honey dessert, 90–91
Walnut sauce, 12
Water chestnuts, chicken with, 51–52
West Indian banana pudding, 24
Wheat
  cracked (*see* Bulgur wheat)
  cream of, in potato dumplings, 63–64
  whole wheat balls, 166
  whole wheat bread, 209

Wheat salad, 136
White beans, fried, 37
Whiting, baked fillets of, 18–19
Wieners in lentil casserole, 119
Wine
  elderberry, venison cutlets with, 117
  muscat, pheasant with, 224
  red
    in hunter's stew, 183–84
    in plum fluff, 185
    in Portuguese pot roast, 187
    in priest stew, 35
    red cabbage with, 205
    in stuffed meat, 72
  sake, in chicken and vegetables, 128
  sherry (*see* Sherry)
  sweet, roast pork with, 178
  white
    in baked fish, 89
    beef marinade, 16
    in bread and cheese soup, 18
    chicken marinade, 155
    in chicken mold, 48–49
    in chicken with rice, 99
    sauce, 16
    sour cream and wine sauce, 242–43
    stuffed mushrooms with, 120, 251
  white or Marsala, in rolled veal with pâté, 121–22, 260
Wolof rice (steak stew with rice), 168–69

Wonders dessert, 67, 254–55

Yakhni (spiced lamb), 108
Yang ts'ung niu ju (beef and onions), 52
Yellow peach pickle, 197, 254
Yogurt
  cucumber and yogurt salad
    Albanian, 13
    Sudanese, 202, 263
  meatball soup with, 33–34
  spiced lamb with, 108
  vegetable and yogurt soup, 184
  yogurt cheese, 135
  yogurt sauces
    Indian curry, 107, 261
    marinade, 173
    for stuffed zucchini, 207–8
  yogurt topping, baked hash with, 34
Yosenabe (chicken and seafood with dashi sauce), 127

Zesty orange salad, 190
Zeytinyagli enginar (artichokes in olive oil), 216
Zharenya riba (fried fish fritters), 222–23
Zucchini
  in lamb with vegetables, 61
  stuffed
    lamb and rice-stuffed, 129
    Syrian, 207–8